Crossroads of Intervention

Crossroads of Intervention

Insurgency and Counterinsurgency
Lessons from Central America

Todd Greentree

Foreword by Robert W. Tucker

Naval Institute Press
Annapolis, Maryland

Naval Institute Press
291 Wood Road
Annapolis, MD 21402

First Naval Institute Press paperback edition published 2009.

Library of Congress Cataloging-in-Publication Data

Greentree, Todd R.
  Crossroads of intervention : insurgency and counterinsurgency lessons from Central America / Todd Greentree ; foreword by Robert W. Tucker.—1st Naval Institute Press pbk. ed.
      p. cm.
  Originally published: Westport, Conn. : Praeger Security International, 2008.
  Includes bibliographical references and index.
  ISBN 978-1-59114-343-7 (alk. paper)
  1. Counterinsurgency—Central America—History—20th century. 2. Insurgency—Central America—History—20th century. 3. Intervention (International law) 4. Central America—Politics and government—1979– 5. Central America—Relations—United States. 6. United States—Relations—Central America. I. Title.
  F1436.8.U6G74 2009
  355.02'180972809045—dc22
                              2009030017

Printed in the United States of America on acid-free paper

15 14 13 12 11 10 09   9 8 7 6 5 4 3 2
First printing

To Marjolaine, my wife.

Contents

A Photo Essay Follows Page 72

Foreword

Todd Greentree's analysis of U.S. involvement in the civil wars of El Salvador and Nicaragua, carried out in Vietnam's shadow as the Cold War reached its climax during the 1980s, offers us a valuable and original interpretation, not only of those particular conflicts, but of the timeless challenges of intervention and irregular warfare. It is worth remembering that the problems which preoccupied us then remain central issues in U.S. foreign policy today: How to sustain global power and legitimacy while avoiding the costs of bearing this position, especially when doing so results in a protracted investment of military force. If September 11, 2001, brought national attention to a new manifestation of international threat, the ill-considered invasion of Iraq and its disastrous aftermath brought to the fore the lesson that attempting to provide order to a fractious world cannot be taken lightly or for granted.

As far removed as it may seem, the United States encountered many thorny dilemmas in Central America that foreshadowed today's challenges. Examples abound. Carter, Reagan, and the first President Bush varied significantly in their tenor regarding the purposes of American power, but all three administrations grappled with the tension between large purposes and limited means while pursuing interventionist policies in Central America. Some pitfalls they managed to avoid. This was largely due to the prohibition against sending troops that inserted a critical guarantee against exaggerated interest and escalating costs. The Vietnam legacy infected partisan politics and erupted as a great divide over Central America policy. From polar extremes, ideological excess affected both parties equally. President Carter's immoderate optimism and his irresoluteness in dealing with the allied dictator Somoza who was losing his grip opened the door to the Sandinista revolution in Nicaragua and near-revolution in El Salvador. Ronald Reagan's Cold War exuberance made Central America a central stage in the Cold War, then led to misadventure and near disaster with the Contras, but his policies were essentially an extension of those that Carter put into place at the end his term. George H. W. Bush allowed pragmatism to prevail as the Soviet threat waned, but intervention in the civil wars of these small underdeveloped nations compelled all three administrations to contend with internal dynamics that were much more complex than the global struggle between communism and democracy.

The struggle that is currently upon us, while virulent enough, is more diffuse and less cataclysmic than the preceding contest, but hardly free from the guideposts of conflicts past much less disconnected from the nature of war itself. We found in Central America that predominant power was not an absolute, and that a quick and decisive intervention was not in the realm of possibility however desirable this might have been. Where protraction was the rule, perseverance was the only remedy for success, making militaristic solutions altogether unattractive. Like today, ideology had great power, both destructive and constructive. Democracy prevailed in the midst of terror and destruction, an antidote to failed autocracy and the false promise of radical revolution. That democracy defied the skeptic's conventional wisdom and prevailed in both El Salvador and Nicaragua is only a partial mystery. It should come as no surprise that democracy's advent was the product of determined multilateral endeavor, that its consolidation as well as the resolution of the conflicts themselves were not the result of U.S. unilateralism, but came about only through fundamental internal transformations and sustained realignment of regional and global forces.

The issue is not whether values have a part in America's pursuit of its interests—they are in fact inextricable—but how they should be balanced. Size and power have allowed the United States to absorb blunders and folly more easily than the less endowed nations who have been the subjects of its interventions. But this does not mean that it can isolate itself altogether from consequences. Perhaps with enough repetition, it is possible for a nation to learn from its experience and to incorporate lessons into collective institutional memory. Certainly this is a responsibility of leadership, and here Central America has much to teach. Todd Greentree's direct experience with many of the people and events from these conflicts gives this volume its evident depth and authenticity. His thesis that only the proximity of loss in Vietnam prevented the United States from sending combat troops to Central America is compelling, and he stands on some strong shoulders to derive new and original thinking about the character of irregular warfare that has contemporary application. This book is a valuable work for today and the future.

Robert W. Tucker

Preface

Central America was my first heart of darkness. Assigned as young Foreign Service Officer in early 1981 to report on El Salvador's darkest and bloodiest days, then sent to ride shotgun with the special envoy for Central America, the circumstances seemed at once predetermined and accidental, much like the wars themselves. Suddenly, these small backwater countries had become situations, crossroads of intervention at the intersection of revolution and superpower competition. They were stuck there, where they featured frequently on the evening news and in national debate, for over a decade. I was often uneasy with my role, and I believe I came to understand what Lawrence meant when he wrote in *Seven Pillars of Wisdom* about hitching the horses of evil to the chariot of good. Much of this book is a reflection on that understanding.

Having come of age during Vietnam, it was impossible not to question the certainties of the Cold Warriors who were our leaders, just as it was impossible not to perceive the brutally and then incompetently suppressed need for change that had driven Nicaragua and El Salvador into violence. But it was much more complicated than that. The revolutionaries who were supposed to be our adversaries tended to have more righteous and mystical identities, and often proved the better fighters. Although I did find honorable soldiers and men among our allies, there was much evil and nothing heroic about the death squads who sowed terror and hid their killing in the secrecy of night, or the Contras who spent much of their time alternatively blustering and sulking in their jungle camps, or Miami. No measure of idealism could have transformed them into real freedom fighters any more than Nicaragua under the Sandinistas could have become a people's paradise.

It seemed highly improbable at the time, but democracy did prove the way out. Compelled by wisdom, opportunism, the fear of defeat, and futility, adherents of both extremes found themselves relinquishing the power of violence for the legiti-macy of elections. These civil wars were long and ultimately dismal affairs plagued with great suffering and corrosion that reduced everyone associated with them to the level of their fortunes. While the United States achieved its aims, more or less, and Central America did evolve into democratic peace, intervention in the region had no tangible impact on the course of the Cold War, the greater purpose it was intended to serve. For this reason it is impossible to judge objectively and conclu-sively whether the costs were worth the effort.

It has been strange to look back and write about these nearly forgotten small wars while our current hostilities are such a preoccupation. The many connections of peo-ple, of policy, of politics, even of national mythology that make Central America a bridge between Vietnam and Iraq was a surprising realization. Despite the differen-ces in time and geography and culture, it became evident that these wars form a whole, in part by virtue of their natures, but more because they are contiguous chapters in the American story. Irregular warfare with its protraction and its dilem-mas has long been part of the American way of war, even if we serially forget because it does not fit with our preferred military or national self-image. Undoubtedly in the future, we will perceive threats on our periphery that will lead us to intervene, for better and for worse, especially as long as we remain a great power that aspires to world leadership.

More immediately, this book grew from a National Security Decision Making Seminar in December 2004. I made a presentation there about the U.S. experience in El Salvador as a lens for viewing the ongoing conflicts in Afghanistan and Iraq, jointly with Col. John Waghelstein (USA, ret.), former U.S. Military Group Com-mander in El Salvador, and one of our few authentic counterinsurgency professionals who long kept the flame alive. I thank Dr. Thomas Mahnken, former colleague at the Naval War College and currently of the Office of the Secretary of Defense, for extending the invitation and thereby creating the opportunity to pursue this work. I am extremely grateful to the Smith Richardson Foundation for its generous support and to the Philip Merrill Center for Strategic Studies at the Johns Hopkins Univer-sity School of Advanced International Studies for hosting this project.

As Robert Tucker says in his foreword, I was fortunate to stand on some very strong shoulders of all varieties of profession, experience, and conviction. I have tried faithfully to reflect many contributions, but it would be an enormous surprise if my treatment of such a controversial subject as U.S. intervention in Central America did not displease some, even at this remove. In any event, the views expressed in this book are entirely my own. Given the vast amounts of U.S. Government documents previously obtained through Freedom of Information Act releases, this work uses no classified information.

Among many Central American friends, associates, and former adversaries I would especially like to thank, from El Salvador, Ricardo and Maria Eugenia Casta-neda, Arnoldo and Cristina Villafuerte, Reynaldo Lopez Nuila, Eugenio Vides Casa-nova, Francisco Zamora, Hugo Barrera, Joaquín Villalobos, and Eduardo Sancho; and from Nicaragua, Arturo Cruz, Jr., Joaquín Cuadra, and Antonio Lacayo.

Colleagues from Central America days who were my models of Foreign Service integrity included Deane Hinton, Tom Pickering, Harry Shlaudeman, Mark Dion, Craig Johnstone, and Mike Senko. I am also honored to acknowledge Col. John McKay (USMC, ret.) who first showed me the way of the true warrior, and Lt. Cdr. Al Schaufelberger (USN) who made the ultimate sacrifice in El Salvador. Although the official community often displaces resentment over the way things are onto journalists, I have always admired their dedication and remain particularly indebted to Mark Danner, Julia Preston, and Ray Bonner, whose writings on Central America invariably searched for the truth, and to Susan Meiselas, whose photographs revealed a clearer window into that world.

Through long walks on Atalaya Mountain, Robert Tucker has been a most valued mentor and friend who generously shared the wisdom of his decades as a scholar of American foreign policy and national security. At SAIS, I greatly appreciated sharing Eliot Cohen's strategy and policy guidance and Frank Fukuyama's evolving views on state-building, while the success of the project owes much to the kind assistance of Philip Merrill Center Executive Director Tom Keaney and Program Administrator Courtney Mata. Former Under Secretary of Defense for Policy Fred Iklé was very openhanded with his time, and his crystal clear recollections of his days in the Reagan administration were indispensable. General Edward "Shy" Meyer, former Chief of Staff of the Army, and General Paul Gorman, former Commander of USSOUTHCOM, understood the nature of the conflict and the challenge that irregular warfare presented to the United States in Central America and elsewhere, and I thank them for sharing their experience and perspectives. I am also privileged to have renewed a long association with Luigi Einaudi, grand statesman of U.S. relations with Latin America, who was also the first person to interview me before I joined the State Department in 1980. Nadia Schadlow provided steady, gracious, and ever-understanding oversight of the book project at the Smith Richardson Foundation. Mark Peceny and Bill Stanley at the University of New Mexico offered well-considered advice both from their perspectives as political scientists and from their own work on U.S. policy and Central America. I would also like to thank UNM graduate students Knutt Peterson for his excellent work on the maps and Kent Blansett for his labors over the index; as well as Matt Kriteman, Katie Kalinowski, Gabriel Paul, Sarah Medina, Eric Witzke, and Megan Woodard, students in my Fall 2005 International Politics course, whose research projects made an important contribution to this book. The quality of this work owes much to the diligence and patience of copy editor Manohari Thayuman to whom I am most thankful. Finally, I express my gratitude to my editor at Praeger, Adam Kane, with whom I hope to share a continuing, rewarding, and fruitful association.

Todd Greentree
Santa Fe, New Mexico

1 ——————————————————

Introduction: The Strategy and Policy of Intervention in Central America

> Twenty years ago we had a similar situation. . . .
> —Vice President Richard Cheney, October 2004

THE INTERVENTION IMPERATIVE

Although no one knew it at the time, the wars of revolution and counterrevolution that occurred in Central America between 1977 and 1992 were also among the final superpower confrontations in the Third World at the end of the Cold War. Vietnam was a shadow that loomed over U.S. intervention in El Salvador and Nicaragua, and although those conflicts are already slipping over our horizon of remembrance, Central America is a bridge from Vietnam to Iraq and the other wars that began after the terrorist attacks of September 11, 2001. These were American wars even though American troops did not fight in them; they were battles in a larger war for the soul of the world, and they reveal much about our own nature as well as the timeless nature of irregular warfare and foreign intervention. If the American experience in Central America can be considered a qualified success, it was hardly a celebration of victory, and it also bears a cautionary tale about the limits of power and the terrible costs of war, even small wars. Today's interventions were unforeseen two decades ago when Central America provided our front page wars, and even though the characteristics, locations, and motives differ greatly, it is the American part of the story that binds them in comparison. By explaining why and how Central America happened in the way it did there is much to learn about the immutable challenges of policy and strategy in the wars of intervention that are certain to lie in our future.[1]

Surely it was no surprise to the audience at Case Western Reserve University in Cleveland, Ohio or to millions of television viewers when the election campaign

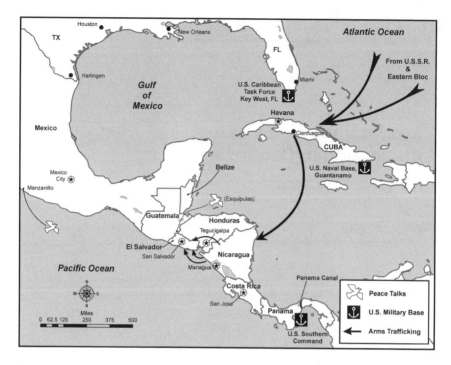

The Central American and Caribbean Theater. Map by Knutt Peterson.

debate on October 5, 2004, between Vice President Richard Cheney and Democratic Senator John Edwards turned to the subject of war. Over 130,000 U.S. troops were bogged down in a vicious counterinsurgency war in Iraq. Osama Bin Laden was still on the loose, and al Qaeda had become a hydra-headed threat. Asked what the Bush Administration would do about it in a second term, the vice president claimed enormous progress in Iraq, as well as in Afghanistan and the war on terror. Candidate Edwards countered by accusing Cheney of distorting the truth and charging the Administration with provoking disaster. But it was no doubt a surprise and a bit of a puzzle to most of the audience when in his rebuttal Vice President Cheney said:

> Twenty years ago we had a similar situation in El Salvador. We had—guerrilla insurgency controlled roughly a third of the country, 75,000 people dead, and we held free elections. I was there as an observer on behalf of the Congress. The human drive for freedom, the determination of these people to vote, was unbelievable. And the terrorists would come in and shoot up polling places; as soon as they left, the voters would come back and get in line and would not be denied the right to vote. And today El Salvador is a whale of a lot better because we held free elections. The power of that concept is enormous. And it will apply in Afghanistan, and it will apply in Iraq as well.[2]

The analogy was lost on most of his listeners, including candidate Edwards, who offered no further reaction, and the debate veered to other issues.

The Administration had consistently put before the public the U.S. occupations of Germany and Japan following World War II, where the United States did transform former enemies broken by the failure of aggression and years of total war. This was a dubious enough historical model. Yet what exactly was the point that Vice President Cheney was trying to make with the comparison to El Salvador? After all, Central American conflicts at the tail end of the Cold War and today's wars in the Muslim world seem to have little in common. Alleged success in Central America offered a precedent in fighting terrorists by bringing democracy to Afghanistan and Iraq through military intervention. The authorship of this grand approach lies with the Presidency of Ronald Reagan, and the line of descent from Reagan to the Administration of George W. Bush is direct, concrete, and personal. Perhaps the core token of this kinship is the 1997 Statement of Principles of the Project for the New American Century (PNAC). Five of the twenty-five signers—including the vice president—who are or were members of the second Bush Administration were also strong supporters and/or held positions in the Reagan Administration in which they dealt with Central America. Virtually all of them shared common overarching views, whether they cast themselves as traditional conservatives or adhered to the tenants of neoconservatism, that were fully exercised for the first time in Central America. The PNAC Statement of Principles professes that:

> We seem to have forgotten the essential elements of the Reagan Administration's success: a military that is strong and ready to meet both present and future challenges; a foreign policy that boldly and purposefully promotes American principles abroad; and national leadership that accepts the United States' global responsibilities.[3]

It is this common strategic vision between the Bush Administration and its ideological predecessor, with its emphasis on national security, assertion of military power, and support for democracy, that bridges today's interventions and yesterday's in Central America.

The subject deserves further examination: How well does the vice president's analogy hold? Just what kind of a model is El Salvador? What was the United States trying to accomplish in Central America? What was Central America all about anyway?

In two broad and important ways the vice president can claim that U.S. policy in Central America was successful. First, the United States achieved its strategic aim of defending against Soviet- and Cuban-sponsored communism following the "loss" of Nicaragua to Marxist–Leninist revolutionaries in 1979, by supporting counter-insurgency to contain it in El Salvador and sponsoring an insurgency to roll it back next door in Nicaragua. Second, in tune with the expansion of democracy that accompanied the end of the Cold War, guerrilla and government antagonists leapt the violent divide from arms to politics as democratic transformations capped termination of the wars in both El Salvador and Nicaragua.

However, the serious and bloody warfare that plagued Nicaragua and El Salvador should give pause before rushing to claim them as models for intervention. As the Prussian military theorist Carl Von Clausewitz noted, "It is legitimate to judge an event by its outcome for this is its soundest criterion. But a judgment based on the result alone must not be passed of as evidence of human wisdom."[4] Many of those who caught Vice President Cheney's comparison of El Salvador to Afghanistan and Iraq would have recalled much darker images than the one he intended. Their most powerful recollections of Central America would not have been of America's beneficent support for the advent of democracy, but of the Iran–Contra scandal that tainted President Ronald Reagan's second term, or of El Salvador's "dirty war" and the Death Squads. As bodies, blindfolded, with their hands bound behind their backs began to turn up around Baghdad, journalists, including some who had begun their careers covering Central America, began to write articles speculating on the "Salvadorization" of Iraq.[5]

For 50-odd years, containment was a galvanizing U.S. national security goal with universal application, but its essential purpose in Central America as in the rest of the Third World was strategically negative—to prevent the spread of Soviet communism. To counterbalance this negative aim with a positive aim, the United States promoted democracy, in the words of Joseph Nye, as the "default option."[6] Pairing intervention and democracy has the profound appeal of appearing to bring U.S. interests and principles in line. The notion that spreading democracy helps protect the nation because democracies tend not to fight one another offered a strong national security justification, but democracy could not in and of itself win a war, nor was it a sufficient cause for the American people to support going to war.

To take up the historical record, surely the vice president did not intend to evoke the flawed legacy of U.S. support for democracy at the point of bayonets that begins, not with the Reagan Administration, but with an intervention habit picked up in the Spanish–American War at the turn of the twentieth century and applied haphazardly in Cuba and especially the Philippines. A few years later, in Mexico, Haiti, the Dominican Republic, and Nicaragua, Woodrow Wilson's efforts to teach Latin Americans "to elect good men" gave full expression to America's liberal but contradictory vision of freedom compelled by force. The principal instrument was the U.S. Marines. The "Devil Dogs" as they came to call themselves in Nicaragua, spent most of the years between until 1912–1933 there conducting counterinsurgency operations against the rebel leader Augusto Sandino, but also supervising elections and nation-building. The Marine Corps *Small Wars Manual* of 1940 distills their experience from the Nicaragua, the Philippines, the Caribbean, and an encyclopedia of campaigns from "the French conquest of Indo-China to the Battle of Little Bighorn" into pragmatic lessons with ample contemporary application.[7] Most prominent among them concern the primacy of politics and the limitations of force in irregular warfare. The *Small Wars Manual* observed that, "The military strategy of small wars is more directly associated with the political strategy of the campaign than is the case in major operations.... The political objective indicates the general character of the campaign which the military leader will undertake."[8] This wisdom, hard won by the Marines, never did quite take in Washington, and in Nicaragua the outcome never did quite match intentions. Fatigue with the trials of intervention set in, and the Hoover Administration determined on a course of nonintervention in 1933.

The United States did not make Anastasio Somoza President, but remained politically complacent when he subsequently seized power, fragile Nicaraguan democracy gave way. The constabulary force that the Marines had established, the National Guard, became the power base of the Somoza dynasty that ruled—and purchased stability for the United States—from 1933 to 1979.

World War II completely overshadowed these early small wars, and the lessons have never stuck in the institutional memory of the U.S. Government, except perhaps in certain corners of the CIA and the Army Special Forces. Through several rough cycles they have been forgotten, relearned, and revalidated in Vietnam, El Salvador, and even today. Instead, the enduring tendency that evolved during the early American interventions remains present: Successive leaders embarked on interventions optimistically if not enthusiastically, justifying them as necessary to meet a perceived challenge to the United States, usually from a foreign power, only to discover frustration as an accumulating set of dilemmas and problems brought results that ended somewhere south of expectations. The response has been almost predictable, as changing administrations and definitions of national interests gave rise to relative neglect and distaste for the idea of intervention, with these prohibitions then relieved in the following cycle.[9] In predicting comparable successes to El Salvador in Iraq and Afghanistan, the vice president proposed a transcendent policy, one that disregards fundamental differences in time, geography, culture, and geopolitics between our Middle Eastern interventions and those in Central America. However, Ronald Reagan's interventions bear a critical distinction from George W. Bush's. Regardless of how warlike both leaders may have sounded at times or how vital the interests they may have proclaimed were at stake, the desire to avoid a disaster like Vietnam meant that there was no way that U.S. troops would be sent into combat in Central America.

In suggesting El Salvador as a democratic model for Iraq and Afghanistan, the vice president surely was not thinking about the outcome of the first elections in 1982. True it was heartwarming to witness as hundreds of thousands of Salvadorans turned out to vote, but they gave a majority in the assembly to an ultrarightist party that had promised to end the war with a bloodbath, and it was only blatant U.S. intervention that prevented their fanatic leader of questionable democratic conviction from assuming power. Nor would he have been thinking about the civil war that continued there for another 10 years. These were protracted and bloody civil wars, struggles of life and death to the people who were directly involved in them, no matter how ultimately insignificant El Salvador and Nicaragua may have been geopolitically. Given the costs and the distance between objectives and reality, perhaps it is with caution rather than pride that El Salvador and Nicaragua should stand as examples of American accomplishment.

Neither was Central America's final moment as a Cold War proxy war cost-free for the United States. Surely the vice president would not consider the political controversy over Central America that raged on the domestic front in the United States for most of this period a welcome ideal. It is hard to recall today how bruising partisan conflict over Central America unsettled the country during the Carter and Reagan Administrations.[10] This was more than a dispute over human rights. Vietnam still cast a deep and disquieting shadow among Congress and the public, provoking strong convictions that U.S. association with atrocities in El Salvador and paramilitary efforts to overthrow the Sandinista Government in Nicaragua amounted to complicity in unjust wars with unacceptable moral costs. Further, the breakdown of bipartisan consensus on Cold War foreign policy that followed Vietnam divided Congress as the deeply skeptical Democratic opposition asserted its power to confront the President, although not to the point where they would risk responsibility for "losing Central America to the Soviets."[11]

The Reagan Administration itself was split on Central America, with hardliners pitted against pragmatists to such an extent that Secretary of State George Shultz dedicated a significant portion of his memoirs to detailing how, "the process of managing foreign policy has gone completely off track [leaving] me at the end of my rope."[12] Thucydides, the celebrated historian of the Peloponnesian War, called this the problem of faction. It plagued democratic Athens in the Fifth century BC, just as it did the United States over Central America.

Cheney was entirely familiar with the factional aspect of American involvement in Central America, as well as the more idealistic project of promoting democracy. After serving as Gerald Ford's Chief of Staff, he was an outspoken hardline supporter of Ronald Reagan's Central American policies as Wyoming's Congressman in the 1980s. Serving as the ranking Republican member of the committee that investigated the secret diversion of funds from U.S. arms sales to Iran to fund the Contras, his minority report argued that:

> Judgments about the Iran–Contra Affair ultimately must rest upon one's views about the proper roles of Congress and the President in foreign policy. . . . [T]hroughout the nation's history, Congress has accepted substantial exercises of Presidential power—in the conduct of diplomacy, the use of force and covert action—which had no basis in statute and only a general basis in the Constitution itself. . . . [M]uch of what President Reagan did in his actions toward Nicaragua and Iran were constitutionally protected exercises of inherent Presidential powers. . . . [T]he power of the purse . . . is not and never was intended to be a license fore Congress to usurp Presidential powers and functions.[13]

The contentious political philosophy that rejects Congressional checks on executive power in conducting foreign affairs as represented in the Iran–Contra minority report is the same approach to government that Richard Cheney has pursued aggressively as George W. Bush's vice president.[14] The approach proved costly for interventions in irregular wars in America's backyard, and its wider application to today's conflicts has proven to have even greater consequences.

ISTHMUS WITHOUT JOY

The setting and events that form the case study of this book begin with geography that has destined Central America to lie within the U.S. sphere of influence, even though in other respects it is of limited strategic value. The region was experiencing rapid growth and pressure to modernize when it became a cockpit of Cold War confrontation in the late-1970s, but traditional agrarian economic and authoritarian political structures had persisted and underlay the revolutionary crisis that exploded in El Salvador and Nicaragua. The timeframe of open conflict and intervention begins during 1977 in Nicaragua when armed insurrection led by the Sandinista National Liberation Front (FSLN) began gathering strength. After overthrowing the former U.S. ally and dictator Anastasio Somoza in July 1979, the resulting revolutionary government quickly identified itself with Cuba and the Soviet Union. Nearly simultaneously in neighboring El Salvador, the Farabundo Martí National Liberation Front (FMLN) attempted to repeat the Sandinista's success. However, when their January 1981 Final Offensive failed to spark a national insurrection against the U.S.-supported Government of El Salvador, the FMLN transformed itself into a formidable guerrilla force that, with Nicaraguan, Cuban, and to a lesser extent Soviet assistance, fought the government to a stalemate that endured for another decade. In Nicaragua, after an ultimately unsuccessful effort at accommodation, the United States confronted the Sandinistas with the CIA-backed insurgency, the "Contras," compelling the revolutionary regime to wage a costly and sustained counterinsurgency with the support of its Cuban and Soviet allies. Convergent with the end of the Cold War, the conflict in Nicaragua ended in 1990 and in El Salvador in 1992. Both ended through negotiations and democratic transformations, not military victory.[15]

These were proxy wars, and the direct costs to the major external antagonists—the Soviets and the Americans—were relatively low. One of their most unusual and important features, however, was the domestic political controversy that dogged virtually every aspect of U.S. policy toward Central America and remained largely unresolved throughout this period. To keep things in perspective, these wars were tragedies for the nations and people who were directly involved in them. Were they civil wars? The answer is definitively yes, if we strip out ideological and revolutionary dimensions and use the definition: "Armed conflicts between the government of a sovereign state and domestic political groups mounting effective resistance in relatively continuous fighting that causes high numbers of deaths."[16] The casualties were enormous proportional to the populations: 50,000 dead out of 2.5 million in Nicaragua and 75,000 dead out of 5.5 million in El Salvador, the majority of them civilian. These are the most frequently cited general estimates; the exact truth will never be known. Everyone died: In Nicaragua, the National Guard executed the founder of the Sandinistas; the Sandinistas assassinated deposed President Anastasio Somoza in Paraguay. In El Salvador, FMLN guerrillas assassinated the foreign minister and attorney general and hundreds of small town mayors and officials; a right wing assassin shot the Archbishop while he was saying mass. Death Squads murdered thousands of suspected communists in every conceivable manner. The majority of the tens of thousands who lost their lives in the Central American violence were poor and nameless peasants killed by other peasants: Salvadoran soldiers and FMLN guerrillas, Sandinista soldiers and Contras, and civilians in large and indiscriminate numbers, families, clans, entire villages, the victims of torture, of bombardment, of massacre, of crossfire. Given the magnitude of this violence and its duration, the most remarkable aspect of these wars is how completely they ended and how free of revenge they have remained. How this end came about is also worthy of explanation, especially the changes that Marxist–Leninist revolutionaries and their conservative adversaries had to go through to make this enduring resolution possible.

There are other important questions: Why did political disputes in Nicaragua and El Salvador become civil wars in the first place? Why did these wars take the particular form they did? What were these wars about, really? And since the problems of intervention in irregular wars for the United States is the particular focus of this book: How and why did the United States intervene in them? Why do these ostensibly localized and controllable "small wars" become such big problems for the United States? As William LeoGrande, author of the most comprehensive account of U.S. involvement in Central America asks: "How could the United States have become so alarmed about such a small place?"[17]

CENTRAL AMERICA AND UNDERSTANDING IRREGULAR WARFARE

As occurs with most wars, the library shelves quickly filled with volumes that tell the Central American story in great detail from multiple perspectives. These accounts draw on journalistic and official records that are exceptionally large due to the intense political interest and the number of investigations these wars generated in the United States. This book does not attempt another historical narrative; any numbers of comprehensive ones already exist.[18] Rather it presents a strategy and policy analysis that holds Central America up as a case study of the dynamics, dilemmas, problems, and patterns of intervention and irregular warfare. If there is a central theme, it is how the intensity of interaction between political and military dimensions most distinguishes the nature of irregular warfare from conventional warfare. Related topics, such as the role of the media, economic factors, ethical issues especially those of human rights, and domestic politics in the United States, receive attention in relation to their impact on the primary dynamics between war and politics. There is a general perception that we face a brave new world of wars today. But it is important not to let the new obscure what is fundamental, even ancient. Here Carl Von Clausewitz's *On War* and Thucydides' Fifth BC *History of the Peloponnesian War* offer illustration and points of reference. It is intriguing enough to observe the many parallels between distant wars and our presumably much different present, but the additional purpose of turning so far back is to deepen our comprehension and our ability to conceive more clearly.

On casual observation, these small Central American wars appear unworthy of additional consideration. Certainly they did not much affect the greater march of history. But these conflicts were eminently complex, and each layer of interpretation, each perspective, reveals another level of understanding. This is true of the internal conflicts themselves, but it is also worth keeping in mind that Central America was a major preoccupation of the United States for over a decade, and had a major impact on relations between Congress and the executive. U.S. intervention in

Central America contains significant and enduring lessons regarding how political conditions determine strategy and how possession of predominant military power is no guarantee of success before the challenges and dilemmas of irregular warfare. *Crossroads of Intervention* aims in this way to offer an interpretation of value to policymakers and strategists, whether civilian or military, as well as to citizens who possess an interest in the application of past experience to the future.

Interest in irregular warfare comes and goes according to the circumstances in which it reenters the American experience. In the late-1970s, one cohort of journalists, politicians, and officers in the military, Foreign Service, and CIA made the jump from Vietnam to Central America. Another came of age in Central America and made the jump to Iraq. Despite the extensive and controversial history of U.S. involvement, attention tends to be case specific and no cumulative body of doctrine has evolved, perhaps because insurgency and counterinsurgency are not "real" war. America's long record of intervention in Central America should naturally have its place among the forgotten lessons of irregular wars with the new generation that is suddenly and urgently learning them again today. In the absence of anything comparably pragmatic and perceptive, the 1940 Marine Corps *Small Wars Manual*, with its origins in early U.S. interventions, and particularly in Nicaragua, found its way into the backpacks of many soldiers as they first deployed to Iraq and Afghanistan. Most of the new writing and thinking about irregular warfare concerns tactics and operations. The new *Army/Marine Corps Counterinsurgency Field Manual*,[19] forged in the heat of Iraq, skips over Central America, covers only half of the irregular warfare spectrum, and deals primarily at the operational and tactical levels. Ample room remains for deliberation on strategy and policy.

Crossroads of Intervention does not include a checklist of rules or do's and don'ts for conducting successful counterinsurgency operations, but it does build on two general operational principles for its central argument about strategy. Recently rediscovered gurus such as Bernard Fall, David Galula, Sir Robert Thompson, T. E. Lawrence, and Edward Lansdale form a long line who place political measures alongside military as equally important elements of counterinsurgency strategy.[20] El Salvador was the U.S. counterinsurgency war that followed Vietnam. There the United States found itself faced in the early 1980s with an extremely volatile situation in which an unstable government was attempting to implement reforms at the same time that official repression was inflaming insurrection. There is no doubt that military force was necessary to halt the advance of a radical revolutionary movement, but neither was it sufficient nor was direct intervention an option. For practitioners such as former Army Special Forces Col. John Waghelstein, head of the U.S. Military Group in El Salvador from 1981 to 1983, the central lesson of both El Salvador and Vietnam is the importance of assisting foreign militaries without turning the fights into a U.S. job. The central challenge became how to balance "reform and repression." The resulting counterinsurgency strategy combined security assistance with support to build a democratic center opposed to extremes on both the right and the left. This was a high-risk venture without recent precedent in the American experience. For several years, it was uncertain whether the Armed Forces had the wherewithal to survive against the proficient and determined guerrillas of the FMLN, and the extreme right was a powerful and obdurate force that threatened the political process until moderation began to set in after several election cycles. If El Salvador is hardly an ideal model, the perseverant combination of U.S. security assistance and political reform with a partner that was reasonably up to the challenge did result in relative success, and is certainly worth consideration as an alternative to direct intervention.

With the remote exception of the American Revolution, a striking feature of U.S. support for insurgency is its emphasis on military over political aims. This modern pedigree is derived from Allied support for partisan and resistance forces during World War II; their role was adjunct to conventional strategy against the Axis, in which their political orientations were largely irrelevant. In their Cold War versions, U.S.-sponsored insurgencies were, like other covert action methods, tools of *realpolitik.* Revolutionary or independent political intent mattered little as long as the chosen groups served anti-Communist objectives. The United States has also demonstrated an unfortunate tendency to abandon its clients once they no longer served national interests or otherwise became liabilities. This was certainly true for the major CIA-supported "Reagan Doctrine" insurgencies that fought the Soviets and their allies in Angola, Afghanistan, and Nicaragua during the 1980s. The Nicaraguan Contra insurgency was an authentic anti-Communist peasant army, but they were bereft of serious political leadership, with political and military arms that were disjointed. It was impossible to disguise their complete dependence on U.S. support, and the "Freedom Fighter" label grafted on in Washington did not necessarily reflect the motives and ideals of the insurgents themselves. Just the same, although the Contras fell short as a political insurgency and nearly sank in a swamp of controversy, this should not obscure their military efficacy as part of the U.S. anti-Sandinista strategy in Central America.[21]

The themes, concepts, and terminology that are common to irregular wars and intervention apply well to Central America. There should be little confusion regarding the term intervention, which is employed here in its dictionary sense:

> The interference of a country in the affairs of another country for the purpose of compelling it to do or forbear doing certain acts or of maintaining or altering the actual condition of its domestic affairs irrespective of its will.[22]

Interventions come in a range of sizes, forms, duration, and intent. Each has its own unique qualities and evolution, but they occur through two basic courses of action: overt aggression against another state or involvement in internal conflict. Interventions may consist of diplomatic, economic, covert, and military measures. They may be multilateral or unilateral, and will be subject to widely varying perceptions of international legitimacy. The immediate background and history, geography, international situation, and public opinion form the environment in which intervention takes place. Interventions are nearly always complex and controversial affairs subject to multiple uncertainties of danger, context, and consequences. Implicit and explicit judgments about interests, cost and risk, and the probability of success are inherent to intervention, with the decision to introduce military forces into combat a critical distinction in the level of commitment.[23]

This general characterization applies well to foreign intervention in Central America during the Cold War by the United States on one side and the Soviet Union and Cuba on the other. The conflicts in El Salvador and Nicaragua between 1977 and 1992 were in and of themselves not significant military challenges to the United States. However, Central America presented serious problems of policy and strategy for three successive presidents and their administrations. Presidents Carter, Reagan, and George H. W. Bush each had distinct concepts of the purposes of American power, which in turn influenced how they conceived of and reacted to those conflicts. Ultimately, however, all three U.S. Administrations portrayed Soviet and Cuban support for revolutionary forces as a serious enough risk to national security in its traditional sphere of influence to sustain militant courses of action. These Cold War concerns drove the United States to intervene unilaterally for over a decade in El Salvador and Nicaragua, without prospect of resort to a formal alliance, regional security commitment, or other multilateral arrangement. Diplomacy was not absent, but it substantially took second place until the termination phase of the conflicts. Unprecedented disagreement among the Latin American countries over U.S. policy forestalled action through the Organization of American States and the regional collective security agreement known as the Rio Treaty. Instead, two ad hoc arrangements, the Contadora Group that associated Mexico, Venezuela, and other regional states, and a separate Central American initiative, promoted diplomatic formulas for resolving the conflicts. NATO allies left the United States to do its bidding in Central America, although socialist governments, particularly in France and Germany, attempted to insert themselves in favor of the left from time-to-time. Public and Congressional opposition ensured that the military dimension of U.S. intervention was circumscribed. Even the Great Communicator Ronald Reagan was unable to raise American public opinion in favor of U.S. policies in Central America out of the low-20 percent range, despite going to extraordinary lengths. These constraints stemmed neither from limited aims nor fear of escalation, but primarily from the shadow of the Vietnam War which had concluded less than 10 years before.[24] It is not frivolous to consider that, had it not been for Vietnam, the United States almost certainly would have invaded Nicaragua, probably in 1979 to prevent the Sandinistas from coming to power.

The terminology is trickier when it comes to characterizing the type of war that was taking place. In its most generic form, irregular or unconventional war consists of organized, armed conflict between a nonstate group and a state, respectively identified as insurgents and counterinsurgents. In its many variants, an irregular war may be classified as a civil war, an internal war, a revolutionary war, a small war, a people's war, rebellion, a brushfire war, nontraditional war, unrestricted war, even collage or mosaic war. There are four elemental features that generally distinguish irregular wars from conventional wars:

- Interaction between political and military dimensions of irregular warfare is usually more integrated and immediate at all levels than in conventional war.
- Insurgent forces are weaker than the armed forces of their state adversary, at least initially.
- Both sides generally must follow indirect rather than direct strategies in confronting each other.
- Irregular warfare does *not* include conventional operations between the armed forces of states, although external states and other actors frequently are direct or indirect participants.

The forms or methods of irregular warfare can vary widely. Insurgents commonly operate as guerrillas, relying on surprise attack and avoiding open battle to offset their disadvantage in strength. They may engage in sabotage or intentionally conduct violence against civilians, although terrorism may not be their primary method. They frequently organize associated political action, such as mass demonstrations, labor strikes, and protest movements. A central feature of insurgencies is that political and military dimensions exist in dynamic relation to each other, and the primary effect of armed insurgent action is often intended to be political rather than military. Insurgent strategies vary greatly, but out of necessity must derive strength from weakness. They may, for example, include popular insurrection, prolonged warfare, rural or urban guerrilla warfare; irregular warfare may also be conducted in association with conventional operations. In the broadest sense insurgents can be understood as challenging the legitimacy and authority of the state by both military and political means, rather than challenging the armed force of the state directly. In Nicaragua, the FSLN achieved final success after a period of inconclusive rural guerrilla war by inciting a popular insurrection in the cities that led to the collapse of the Somoza regime. The FMLN experienced a converse strategic dynamic in El Salvador, first attempting an urban-based insurrection, and when that failed, beginning a prolonged people's war primarily as rural guerrillas that ultimately did not succeed.

At the strategic level, insurgents are generally the offensive force, irrespective of their relative inferiority and the particular aim they may be pursuing. Insurgents may seek overthrow of a government and imposition of a radical social, political, and economic revolution, or they may have more limited goals such as securing a measure of political autonomy or serving a warlord's personal ambition. The relative importance of religion, ethnicity, and ideology is critical to understanding the aims and nature of any particular irregular war.[25] In Central America, Catholicism and predominately peasant societies gave the struggle its particular dynamics and character, while the competing ideologies of the Cold War formed its political and international context. There was a major difference in motivation among insurgent groups. The FMLN was a radical Marxist–Leninist revolutionary movement bent on seizing power in order to transform Salvadoran Government and society, while the anticommunist Contras in Nicaragua were concerned primarily with confronting the Sandinista Government militarily in league with their U.S. sponsors.

The strategic purpose of counterinsurgency is defense of the state. Anthony James Joes says "The goal of counterinsurgency is to bring peace, or to establish a pattern of stability...."[26] The tools available to even a weak government facing an insurgency are generally formidable. Counterinsurgency strategy tends to rely first and foremost on the state security apparatus in some combination of police, intelligence, and military functions. Major domestic advantages accrue in the form of infrastructure, organization, and resources to maintain the armed forces, as well as control of the national communications system and intelligence assets. Governments may also use civil defense or other methods of popular mobilization, engage in irregular tactics against insurgents, and, at the hard end of "Dirty War," use state terrorism, punitive measures, and violent methods that approach total war. Authoritarian methods of sociopolitical control such as restriction of civil liberties, declared or de facto states of emergency, physical controls and displacement of the population, and political repression generally accompany exceptional law enforcement and military powers. Cooption, compromise, reform, or "winning hearts and minds" may also feature in counterinsurgency, depending on the nature of the regime and political competence of the country's leaders. Whether through soft or hard methods, the objective of counterinsurgency strategy is frequently understood as separating the population from the insurgents. In the broadest terms, the government's aim is to uphold its legitimacy and authority by defeating or otherwise neutralizing the insurgent's armed challenge.

The contrast between ineffective counterinsurgency strategy in Nicaragua, under both Somoza and the Sandinistas, and effective counterinsurgency in El Salvador offers an illuminating albeit highly relative object lesson. In Nicaragua, Somoza's exclusive reliance on National Guard repression against a burgeoning popular insurrection, with only cosmetic appeals to political change led directly to the collapse of his regime in July 1979. Once they were in power, the Sandinistas, with Soviet, Cuban, and other Eastern Bloc support, responded to the growing Contra insurgency by militarizing the country and hastening implementation of a police state. The burdens of counterinsurgency thus contributed directly to the circumstances in which the Sandinistas gambled on holding elections in 1990, and lost. In El Salvador, an analogous insurrection movement, inspired by success in Nicaragua, came to verge of seizing power in 1979. Instead, a coup brought a civil–military junta to power that introduced political and economic reforms, while a brutal campaign of repression, including Death Squads, continued in parallel. This combination of reform and repression—with U.S. backing—halted the insurrection and set the stage for relative government stability, but the insurgency ground on through another 10 years of stalemated civil war.

As was the case in Central America, irregular wars tend to be prolonged affairs, and, depending on the resilience of the contenders, frequently take a decade or more to reach resolution. The overarching strategic dynamic of an irregular war, consistent with identifying the insurgent side as the offense and the counterinsurgent side as the defense, is that the war ends only when the insurgents are defeated, win, or otherwise decide to stop fighting. According to Mao's theory of revolutionary war a final phase is achieved when insurgent forces grow strong enough to confront government forces in conventional battle, however, decisive military engagements only occasionally produce an outcome. Defeat in detail or attrition are often important factors, but irregular wars terminate more frequently through political means than they do through military victory. Insurrectional victories such as the Sandinista triumph are unusual, but the regime collapsed in the face of mass uprising and loss of international legitimacy, not because Somoza's National Guard was defeated. The El Salvador conflict remained a stalemate throughout the 1980s, with the FMLN unable to bring down the government of El Salvador either militarily or through insurrection, and the Salvadoran armed forces unable to defeat the guerrillas, until international negotiations brought it to termination in 1992. No different than the case with conventional war, a key issue is whether resolution by military or political means resolves the underlying causes of the conflict. There is no question that the processes that ended the Salvadoran and Nicaraguan conflicts in the early 1990s, combined of course with the fortuitous end of the Cold War, brought durable peace to both countries.

Some argue that technological and social developments have so transformed the nature of unconventional challenges since the end of the twentieth century that a newly evolved form of "Fourth Generation Warfare" renders understanding and lessons from even recent conflicts marginal.[27] On the contrary, this book takes as its core premise that warfare of all types has always been subject to adaptation and transformational change, but the elementary and fundamental principles of war, including irregular war, have enduring logic and historical continuity. In this respect, the previous U.S.-centered attempt to launch a new label with the unfortunate designation Low Intensity Conflict was not terribly enlightening. Both insurgents and counterinsurgents will inevitably call on new technologies to help them "shape the battlespace" and to increase the precision and lethality of weapons; they will use the global information and communications revolutions to shape the social and political environment of war. In Central America, shoulder-mounted Stinger surface-to-air missiles, and the CNN effect were new and influential instruments of war. However transforming both the end of the Cold War and the September 11, 2001 terrorist attacks on the United States were, they were not all-significant dividing points for the practice of irregular warfare. The discovery of new warfighting technologies and operational innovations by the United States as well as its adversaries should not obscure the application of basic principles in the ongoing deployments in Afghanistan and Iraq, the global "war" on terrorism, and whatever deployments may be in store for the future.[28]

Central America was in some important respects a proving ground for the political philosophy that has guided current interventions, and despite the major differences in geography, culture, and politics, there are many meaningful and durable parallels between Central America and current wars against radical Islamists and in Iraq. Insurgents aim to unbalance governments using whatever means they have available; their leaders inspire and mobilize; universal ideologies motivate them and link local causes to global movements; powerful allies assist them; they tend to organize themselves into networks with flattened hierarchies; they swim in the sea of their supporters. The United States tends to respond by conceiving of specific and even local challenges as part of a military crusade against a global adversary, a reaction with deep roots in American experience. More specifically, in Central America 25 years ago, as in the Middle East today, ideology competed with realism to drive policy. Common themes include a preference for unilateral action, maximalist aims, insisting on exclusive executive authority in time of war, preemption, regime change, and advocating military force to bring about democratic transformation. The long-term irregular aspects that dominated the conflicts were and are contrary to the basic structure and orientations of the civilian government and military with the exception of the Special Forces and Special Operations community. The major distinction today is that the United States has now shed its post-Vietnam reluctance to intervene directly, and so is shouldering much more of the burden of conflict.

It is the rare strategic analysis of conventional war that does not give at least passing notice to Clausewitz. However, it is more often assumed that little of his thought is relevant to irregular war. This may be partially true in that he did not write extensively about the specific operational problems of irregular warfare and is better known for his theories of conventional warfare among states. His masterwork *On War* does, however, contain a brief but insightful chapter on "A People in Arms," as well as multiple references to the role of irregulars in support of regular operations.[29] He apparently had little familiarity with American War of Independence or with the British-sponsored Iberian campaign, but his experience with the central strategic problem of the era was itself the product of the French revolution in which Napoleon marshaled the newly nationalistic population into a new form of military power that disrupted European stability and brought two decades of unprecedented war to the continent.

Clausewitz believed he was writing about the nature of war itself, and it is in fact no stretch to apply many of his insights to the situation in Central America 170 years later. The starting point is his most famous dictum that, "War is simply a continuation of political intercourse, with the addition of other means."[30] Modern revolutionary theory of People's War is attributed to Mao, but the line of succession is clear in the saying, 'Mao read Lenin, and Lenin read Clausewitz.' And with his dictum that 'Politics grows from the barrel of a gun,' Lenin is merely bending this first principle of Clausewitz to revolutionary purposes. The Salvadoran FMLN and Nicaraguan FSLN consciously pursued Leninist revolutionary strategies married to Marxist ideology without being aware initially of exactly what else then could or could not accomplish with force. As to whether we can learn anything by applying Clausewitz to the wars in Central America, Michael Handel writes:

> The actual circumstances of a war are of course the most important for understanding its unique nature. Yet whatever the characteristics of wars throughout history, they always contain a common element, namely the basic logic of war, or strategy. For example, the primacy of politics; the correlation of ends and means; the principle of concentration; and the role of friction will always be valid. The theory of war itself does not change, only its application, which varies in emphasis according to specific circumstances.[31]

The fundamental relationship between political ends and military means in irregular war is no different from conventional war. However, the dynamics between them is critically distinct. In Clausewitz's terms, the logic is the same, but the grammar is different. First, there is the problem of decisive force, the object of conventional military strategy, which neither side is capable of wielding against the other. Insurgents are too weak initially to challenge government forces directly, but neither is the government able to marshal its superior strength directly against insurgents, who will do their best under all but the most favorable circumstances to avoid battle. This basic asymmetry forces both sides to adopt indirect rather than direct strategies in which the political dimension often becomes a more immediate and intense aspect of the conflict than it usually is in conventional conflict. In conventional war the primary purpose of strategy is military in the sense that a chosen course of action is generally intended to contribute to victory over the armed forces of the opposing party, preferably as quickly and decisively as possible. But because unconventional war strategy cannot seek decisive military victory, at least in the first instance, a course of action is often intended to have a primary political effect, whatever its additional military effects may be, and to trade intensity for duration. As David Galula puts it in his classic *Counterinsurgency Warfare,* "So intricate is the interplay between the political and the military actions that they cannot be tidily separated; on the contrary, every military move has to be weighed with regard to its political effects and vice versa."[32] This is why it makes sense to think of strategic aims in irregular war in terms of political competence, as a contest for legitimacy and authority, not principally a conflict for military supremacy that are the traditional aims of conventional war.

Two contrasting examples from Central America are classic. In 1978, a small group of insurgent commandos seized the Nicaraguan Assembly while it was in session, held it for 3 days, then dispersed triumphantly to Venezuela, Panama, and Cuba, having secured their demands from the helpless government. The raid had no military impact on the National Guard, but as an act of propaganda, it was a key event in building the momentum of the insurrection and the legitimacy of the Sandinistas. Not only did it humiliate Somoza and heroize the Sandinistas, it dramatically showed students, shop keepers, and housewives who burned with resentment against Somoza's corrupt regime the possibility of revolutionary change and galvanized international opinion, especially in the United States. In El Salvador in November 1980, security forces surrounded a school where the Democratic Revolutionary Front (FDR), the coalition group of left-wing parties, was holding a public meeting. Hooded men, who later claimed to be members of the Maximiliano Hernández Martínez Death Squad, seized the six principal FDR leaders. The leaders turned up mutilated and dead a day later.[33] This raid had no military impact on the armed left, but it was an extremely effective—if double-edged—demonstration of the authority of state terrorism. The killings physically eliminated the last prominent leftist leaders who had not fled the country or gone into clandestinity, and the possibility of negotiations between the left and the government evaporated. Even as the Death Squads drove the opposition underground and deterred many from joining it out of fear, they radicalized others and further incited the growing insurgency.

The distinction between policy and politics is particularly crucial for war-making in democracies. For example, the principal aim of U.S. policy in Central America was to contain Soviet expansion. However, the expression of the policy was the product of American politics, particularly the contest between an assertive Congress and a strong Executive during the Reagan Administration. The difficulties of the Reagan Administration in applying its strategy in Central America can thus be understood as a failure to resolve policy through the political process. The result was unceasing political friction, comparable to Clausewitz's description of military friction in which, "Everything in war is simple, but the simplest thing is difficult."[34]

The Central American conflict provides abundant examples of another strategically useful concept, the crossroads, circumstances that elicit specific decisions, taken in the presence of alternatives, in which leaders choose particular a course of action (or inaction) that has a critical but often unanticipated effect on an outcome. For example, judging by outcomes, of all the challenges to state power in Latin America during the Cold War, the only two revolutions that were entirely successful—Cuba in 1959 and Nicaragua in 1979—occurred in countries where U.S. influence was ostensibly the greatest, at times when the administrations inadvertently contributed to them, either through complacency or policy. Extensive counterfactual analysis is not required to demonstrate that decisive political intervention by the U.S. at critical points prior to 1979 would have forestalled the development of a serious revolutionary challenge in Central America, making the subsequent military interventions in El Salvador and Nicaragua unnecessary.

The wars in Central America were at once revolutionary civil wars and an extended episode at the climax of the global Cold War that brought them from the periphery to the center. American intervention responded to a perceived threat to national security that stretched back to the Monroe Doctrine, but the tragedy that America had just experienced in Vietnam limited and determined its shape. At the same time, the structure and problems of these Central American wars had classic characteristics. The Peloponnesian War between Sparta and Athens in the Fifth century BC was often used as an archetype to give perspective to the struggle between the United States and the Soviet Union as well as many other conflicts before it.[35] The analogy is not merely striking, but carries with it a liberating power of timelessness. El Salvador and Nicaragua became theaters of the larger conflict, just as Athens and Sparta, locked in zero sum rivalry, encouraged, supported, and intervened in rebellions among the small island states of the Aegean. Athens was a mature and prosperous democracy, thoroughly militarized with a large navy and an alliance system. War was a feature of life to protect and extend its system, and the dilemmas the Athenians encountered, such as popular outrage over atrocities that violated Athenian principles of warfare or the ready habit of holding leaders publicly accountable for failure, would be familiar to the U.S. Administrations that were involved in Central America. Thucydides, author of the most famous account of the Peloponnesian War, was particularly concerned with the corrosive effect that civil war has on people and societies. His observation would not have been out of place in San Salvador or Managua during the 1980s:

> The sufferings which revolution entailed...were many and terrible, such as have occurred and will always occur as long as the nature of mankind remains the same. In peace and prosperity states and individuals have better sentiments, because they do not find themselves suddenly confronted with imperious necessities; but war takes away the easy supply of daily wants and so proves a rough master that brings most men's character to a level with their fortunes.[36]

Historical analogies illustrate; they offer pathways to insight, and at their best, they become tools for analysis and guides for application. If Thucydides and Clausewitz can help explain Central America, it is nevertheless unlikely that the exact circumstances that led the United States to intervene in those internal conflicts at the end of the Cold War will ever reoccur. However, in the larger historical picture, a general set of strategic dynamics becomes clear. Intervention is a complex affair. It inevitably complicates internal conflict, which has its own origins, causes, and dynamics that are often obscure to the external power. Clear and limited aims may increase the chances of success, and military force always has its effects, but force alone is rarely sufficient to produce victory in the traditional sense much less resolve underlying issues. If prolonged war may benefit the insurgent side, the longer an intervention goes on the more likely it is to generate dissent at home. Recent American experience fits entirely into this pattern, certainly in Central America, but comparably in Vietnam, Haiti, Kosovo, West Africa, Somalia, Afghanistan, and Iraq.

A first, critical step toward arriving at effective intervention policy and strategy is to make a serious effort to understand the nature of the conflict, distinguishing clearly between internal and external factors. Except perhaps in relatively simple and short-term instances, say the invasion of a small island nation, serious assessment of the interaction between political and military dimensions is essential. This leads back to the key questions concerning the effectiveness, or political competence, of the state: How well does the government meet its responsibilities toward society, particularly in providing security? Is there a lag between economic growth and the evolution of corresponding political structures? What pressures for modernization and political change challenge the government? Are there channels for peaceful expression of discontent? How effective is each adversary in its contest for legitimacy and authority? Answers to these general questions, tailored to take account of specific conditions such as ethnic and religious tensions, go beyond threat assessment to measure the underlying strengths and vulnerabilities of a state and its adversaries.[37]

In El Salvador and Nicaragua, external influences were critical, but it is far too simplistic to ascribe political instability to Soviet–Cuban subversion on the one hand or to American neo-imperialist exploitation on the other. Neither was socioeconomic inequity nor class alienation the direct cause of revolution. The regimes in these two poor countries had long staved off communist-inspired revolution with U.S. support, and any government that even seemed to look eastward risked American wrath.

The critical factor was state vulnerability and breakdown that resulted from dynamic interaction between internal and external forces, not external subversion as part of the global contest. These were ideological civil wars between the right and left, contests for power that also became struggles to modernize and restructure political systems.

As it was, sending U.S. troops to Central America was not feasible; therefore, intervention had to rely on other options, an integrated counterinsurgency approach in the case of El Salvador and an ostensibly covert insurgency program in Nicaragua. In the process, the United States became enmeshed simultaneously in political controversy at home and in the dilemmas of intervention in both countries. The American experience in Central America included both effective and ineffective intervention strategies in which the military and political dimensions should be evaluated as equally important. Although the vocabulary of today's conflicts has changed somewhat, the issues are entirely familiar: contention surrounding justifications for regime change and preemption as war aims, tension between unilateral action and international cooperation, the consequences of ignoring international law and norms, dispute over vital interests and the nature of threats to national security, exaggerated assumptions about the ability of U.S. power to effect change in weak and failing states, and the wisdom of promoting democracy, even at the point of bayonets.[38] Whether it is because the situation confronts or larger ambition compels, attempts to change the nature of even a small war and the nature of a country, even a small country, are unlikely to be exactly what we aim for. Ultimately, the threat of our adversaries may be the lesser danger in these small wars compared to the consequences of the choices we make. As always, a first best choice is to remember what we have learned about irregular warfare an intervention instead of having to rediscover it in the heat of crisis.

_____

What Was at Stake?

...we should consider any attempt on their part to extend their system to any portion of this hemisphere, as dangerous to our peace and safety....
—President James Monroe, December 2, 1823

THE INTERVENTION IMPERATIVE

Just what was at stake for the United States in Central America? The question is simple, but deceptive, and answering it anything but easy. Of course, national security interests drove U.S. intervention. The phrase conjures rational determination of those interests through straightforward and systematic assessment, identifying strategic priorities, calculating the military balance, and gauging threats, above all those from other great powers. The Soviet threat was the determining factor for the United States in Central America, as it was in the rest of the world during the Cold War. Certainly there were concrete strategic issues, but Central America seems a small and otherwise insignificant to have played as prominently as it did on the much larger field of superpower competition. The logic puts in mind LeoGrande's question about how the United States could have become so alarmed about such a small place.

Clausewitz understood perfectly that when it came to deciding what was at stake in any particular war, "the conclusions can be no more wholly objective than in any other war." Policy, he claimed, "...is representative of all interests of the community, and will be shaped by the qualities of mind and character of leaders, and more generally by the natures of states and societies according to the times and political conditions."[1] Purely rational choices never determined U.S. national interests in Central America. Rather, over a decade, three very different presidents and their administrations, along with changing congressional configurations and public moods, produced competing visions of what U.S. policy should be in Central

America within the larger debate over how the United States should treat its Soviet adversary. It was impossible to apply an objective set of national security criteria to determine how the United States should act in El Salvador and Nicaragua, because integral to such decisions were the highly subjective, complex, and mutable ways in which national interests are defined and threats to security are perceived. There were divisions among liberals and conservatives, realists and idealists, or to distinguish further, among neo-internationalists, neoconservatives, and neorealists. Each had their own theoretical and philosophical perspective of international reality which underpinned their widely varying foreign policy prescriptions. Translated into the political realm, the debate was often extreme, revolving not only around the question of how best to draw the line against the Soviets in Central America, but also whether that line even existed or mattered at all.

The Carter, Reagan, and Bush Administrations all expressed geostrategic and geopolitical concerns about Central America using terms that fit with the constructs of the Cold War and global containment. But their formulations had deep historical foundations in the Monroe Doctrine and the Roosevelt Corollary. The Monroe Doctrine, from President Monroe's December 2, 1823, annual message to Congress, considered it a general matter of United States "rights and interests" to prevent European monarchies from recolonizing Latin America, declaring that, "...we should consider any attempt on their part to extend their system to any portion of this hemisphere, as dangerous to our peace and safety." In 1906, as the United States was assuming its place as a great power, Theodore Roosevelt declared the Roosevelt Corollary to the Monroe Doctrine, to extend the principle of excluding foreign powers from the hemisphere by asserting the right of the United States to take action, "within any country washed by the Caribbean sea...." Roosevelt avowed, "We would interfere with them only in the last resort, and then only if it became evident that their inability or unwillingness to do justice at home and abroad had violated the rights of the United States or had invited foreign aggression to the detriment of the entire body of American nations."

Thus, tradition contributed directly to the contemporary assessment that communist revolutionaries in El Salvador and Nicaragua had "invited foreign aggression" and that Soviet efforts "to extend their system" were "dangerous to the peace and safety" of the United States. The corollary response was intervention. When the Sandinistas jumped loudly onto the Nicaraguan stage in the late 1970s, the United States was infected with a new episode of the "vortex" or "brushfire" syndrome. Perception that a foreign-inspired threat had suddenly erupted provoked intense attention; reaction combined militaristic treatments along with transformative economic and political measures intended to repair longer-term weaknesses; relative neglect toward the region resumed once the security preoccupation had waned. There is no need to recount here the well-documented history of U.S. interventions that roughly fit this pattern and date from the Spanish–American War. The global scale of Cold War superpower competition inspired increasingly ambitious interventions. Counterrevolutionary covert action was the prescribed instrument in response to the 1959 Cuban revolution that produced the Bay of Pigs debacle. The Kennedy Administration reacted to the 1962 Cuban missile crisis attempting to insulate all of

Latin America from Communist penetration by sponsoring a regional security architecture through the Organization of American States and launching the Alliance for Progress to promote economic development. In short order, security assistance to anticommunist dictatorships that proved relatively successful at suppressing subversion displaced funding for economic programs and distorted the grand vision of the Alliance, leading to its demise.

The brushfire syndrome returned at the end of the 1970s when the internal security formula began to fail in Central America. After an experimental phase in which the Carter Administration attempted to downplay the military dimension, geostrategic imperatives reasserted themselves. As a National Security Council review made unequivocally clear, the United States was in essence:

> ...committed to defeating the Marxist–Leninists in Central America. We believe that should we fail to do so on the current battlefields of El Salvador and Nicaragua, we shall have to face them in Mexico and on the canal where the stakes will be much higher.[2]

The dominos still stood in Central America, but they were threatened, and their stability was precarious at best. By 1984, the Bipartisan Commission on Central America, better known as the Kissinger Commission, had fully elaborated a national security rationale that underpinned a proposal for a major long-term U.S. political and economic commitment to the region. As the Commission report stated:

> The ability of the United States to sustain a tolerable balance of power on the global scene at a manageable cost depends on the inherent security of its land borders. It offsets an otherwise serious liability: our distance from Europe, the Middle East, and East Asia, which are also of strategic concern to the United States.... To the extent that a further Marxist–Leninist advance in Central America leading to progressive deterioration and a further projection of Soviet and Cuban power in the region required us to defend against security threats on our borders, we would face a difficult choice between unpalatable alternatives. We would either have to assume a permanently increased defense burden, or see our capacity to defend distant trouble spots reduced, and as a result have to reduce important commitments elsewhere in the world. From the standpoint of the Soviet Union, it would be a major strategic coup to impose on the United States the burden of defending our southern approaches....[3]

This geographic proximity was the most important factor which determined that the United States had to protect its national security on the battlefields of Central America between 1977 and 1992. From a strategic perspective, the United States was on the defensive in its traditional sphere of influence there during the Cold War. The 1980 Report by the Committee of Santa Fe, a small group of traditional conservatives close to Jeanne Kirkpatrick and headed by former Chairman of the Inter-American Defense Board Lieutenant General Gordon Sumner, used alarmist language to draw attention to the threat that Latin America posed to the United States as a platform for Soviet-backed subversion. Several of the Committee's members received early appointments in the Reagan Administration, where they helped set the tone of the Reagan Administration's approach to the region.[4] When Ronald Reagan called on Congress to hear his plea for support to Central America in an April 27, 1983 joint session, he used geographic argument:

> Too many have thought of Central America as just that place way down below Mexico that can't possibly constitute a threat to our well-being....Central America's problems do directly affect the security and well-being or our own people. And Central America is much closer to the United States than many of the world troublespots that concern us....El Salvador is nearer to Texas than Texas is to Massachusetts. Nicaragua is just as close to Miami, San Antonio, San Diego, and Tucson as those cities are to Washington....

To reinforce the President's message directly with the American people, dozens of Administration representatives fanned out across the country in a major public relations campaign. They customarily carried two props with them to help make the case. One was a chart that listed Soviet and Cuban arms transfers to Nicaragua and the Salvadoran guerrillas. The other was a map enlargement that showed how the Gulf Coast town of Harlingen, Texas is closer to Managua (1223 miles) than to Washington, DC (1935 miles). The Sandinistas could drive their Soviet tanks to the U.S. border in 2 or 3 days, so the stock punch line went.

DEFINING VITAL INTERESTS?

Of course, the argument did not stop with simple geography. Referring to the Caribbean Basin as "our fourth border" and noting that two-thirds of U.S. foreign trade and petroleum pass through the Panama Canal and Caribbean, the President elaborated in his joint session address that, "Nearness on the map doesn't even begin to tell the strategic importance of Central America...." He recalled that in early 1942, Hitler's submarines sank more tonnage there than in all of the Atlantic Ocean, and asked, "If the Nazis during World War II and the Soviets today could recognize the Caribbean and Central America as vital to our interests, shouldn't we, also?" Here the explicit rationale for intervention was historical as well as geographical, based on a definition of vital interests—meaning survival of the nation was at stake—that linked the importance of the region during the prior struggle against Nazi aggression to the current struggle against global Soviet aggression. A land invasion across the Southern U.S. border was ludicrous on the face of it, but the image was intended to demonstrate how seemingly remote threats in the proximate Third World were a threat to the homeland. The proximity of Soviet-backed Cuba and Nicaragua to critical sea lines of communication (SLOCs), recalling the precedent of the German submarine threat during the Battle of the Atlantic, transcended debate about whether or not the periphery could matter in the global balance of power. More idealistic notions of national credibility and defending freedoms were thus grounded in concrete security interests.

This distinction between geostrategic and less tangible geopolitical threats is significant. In *When the Third World Matters,* international relations scholar Michael

Desch presents the thesis that it is really only the former category that truly matters.[5] He divides the strategic interests of the United States, and other great powers generally, in any particular territory into two types: intrinsic and extrinsic. Any territories that do not possess these qualities are strictly residual. In addition to national territory, intrinsically strategic areas are those external to the homeland that contribute directly to the strength of the great power and determine the global balance of power. For the United States, these areas include not only Western Europe and Japan, but also the Persian Gulf due to reliance on petroleum imports. Extrinsic areas lack intrinsic value, but have strategic value because they are geographically proximate either to the homeland, other intrinsically valuable areas, or lines of communication between them. The instruments of war and associated technological advances to ships, aircraft, weapons systems, and so on, make it possible to use extrinsic areas to project power or conversely for an adversary to present a threat. It is interdependence between intrinsic and extrinsic areas that links otherwise peripheral states to a great power. In terms of policy and strategy, "The strategic mandate for the great power toward these areas is to either control them, have access to them, or be able to deny them to an adversary."[6] A realist and advocate for observing economy of force, Desch explicitly cautions against great power intervention to influence political structures in peripheral states, rather than limiting efforts to denying other powers access, as impractical and a waste of resources. Accordingly, a sound national grand strategy depends on carefully distinguishing between intrinsic and extrinsic interests to ensure coherent distribution of finite military resources among competing priorities. Desch uses Latin America as his central case to enjoin against over-investment in peripheral areas, but he also argues that recognizing the interdependent strategic value of extrinsic areas can affect the balance of power positively, while failure to do so can affect security adversely. From this perspective, for example, Jimmy Carter miscalculated by assuming that Central America was a cost-free area to downplay Cold War competition and impose human rights policy, an approach that helped to unleash revolutionary forces, usher Soviet and Cuban sympathizers into power in Nicaragua, and placed the United States in a reactive posture that led to costly and distracting interventions.

Applying this framework leads to the straightforward conclusion that Central America and the Caribbean had little intrinsic, but significant extrinsic value to the United States during the Cold War.[7] Under the assumption that the United States was on the strategic defensive in its sphere of influence against Soviet-backed aggression, there were three conceivable, if unrealistic threats that had currency at the time: internal subversion, a significant attack, and invasion. The United States was and is highly impervious to externally supported subversion, and Central America would hardly have provided a practical platform. Efforts by the Soviet intelligence service, the KGB, to station Nicaraguan guerrillas to reconnoiter targets and infiltrate them with migrant laborers along the United States–Mexico border during the 1960s achieved little more than to provide fuel for flare-ups of communist phobia.[8] Although isolated acts of sabotage and terrorism may have been feasible, no state or combination of states in the region had sufficient capability to carry out or support a significant attack by air, sea, or land, and U.S. defense capabilities would have overwhelmed such an attack in any case. Despite the Harlingen, Texas scenario, an invasion would have been even more futile. With a maximum speed of 45 mph and a range of about 300 miles, it would have taken Soviet bloc T-55 tanks of the Sandinista Peoples Army (EPS) over a week just to reach the border—that is if they had clear roads, plenty of fuel, and friendly countries along the way. Of course, Central America is filled with jungles and mountains, and there are no long-distance superhighways. Nicaragua barely had fuel for its domestic needs, and even in the improbable event that Honduras and Guatemala had fallen as communist dominoes, it is unlikely that Mexico would have thought using its territory to stage an invasion of its powerful and vindictive neighbor to the north was a very good idea. This begs the question further of what the Sandinistas might actually have done to harm the United States once they reached the border. As Desch sums it up, "There was never any major threat to the territorial integrity or internal security of the continental United States."[9] Indeed, however much they may have appreciated the attentions of the Reagan Administration, the citizens of Harlingen had little to fear.

But were there other circumstances under which it would have been realistic to characterize threats from Central America and the Caribbean as "vital" to U.S. national security? Although Ronald Reagan did not summon nuclear fears to portray the dangers from communist advances in the region, the 1962 Cuban missile crisis remained deeply ingrained as the most shocking and surprising reversal of security the United States had ever experienced.[10] The reintroduction by the Soviets of medium-range or submarine-launched ballistic missiles using bases in Cuba or Nicaragua certainly would have constituted a major threat, and would have violated the 1962 understanding by which the Soviet Union agreed to withdraw their missiles from Cuba and not to introduce nuclear weapons to the hemisphere again. With resolution, the Soviet leadership concluded that Khrushchev had rashly risked too much, regardless of whether his objective was to improve the strategic balance or to protect the Cuban revolution from the United States. The Cuban missile crisis led both the United States and the Soviet Union to realize very concretely the seriousness of exercising self-restraint. Nevertheless, the Soviets greatly increased their air and naval presence during the 1970s, with the Soviet Navy conducting twenty-six task force deployments, most of them nuclear capable, between their first entry in 1969 and 1986.[11] Concerned that this activity represented a threat comparable to the emplacement of land-based missiles in Cuba, U.S. administrations from Nixon to Bush I laid down clear warnings in private, particularly over the construction of a submarine base at Cienfuegos, Cuba, but none chose to turn it into a crisis.[12] The Soviet deployments tested U.S. resolve, but always stopped short of attempting permanent basing or otherwise provoking direct confrontation. The strategic benefits of doing either would have been limited, in light of the fact that the Soviet Union and the United States had achieved rough strategic parity by the 1980s and reached an agreement on intermediate nuclear forces in Europe. It is also worth noting that, Soviet introduction of ballistic missile or attack submarines to the Caribbean under circumstances of war or peace would not have needed absolutely to rely on land bases, however helpful those bases might have been.

The more realistic security threat to the United States did not involve another Soviet adventure in seeking a regional nuclear advantage, but rather the potential for wartime interdiction of shipping in the Caribbean Sea, which has thirteen sea-lanes including four major choke points between Gulf Coast ports and the Atlantic Ocean. In the 1980s, the White House characterized the revived specter of a menace to Caribbean SLOCs noting that:

> The major shipping lanes crisscrossing the region make it one of our major lifelines to the outside world, and, as a result, an area of crucial importance to the continued prosperity and security of the United States. The defense of the Caribbean, however, is complicated by hostile forces in Cuba and Nicaragua within easy range of these shipping lanes.[13]

The scenario harkens back explicitly to German submarine predations during World War II when for the first 6 months of 1942, the United States lost sea control of its inshore waters along the East Coast and Caribbean. For example, in May 1942 alone, U-boats sank a total of 108 ships totaling 491,000 tons in the Caribbean, primarily ore ships from the Gulf and tankers from Venezuela. These submarines, of which there were never more than a dozen in the area, were operating without the benefit of port access and attacking unprotected cargo ships; loss rates declined significantly throughout the Atlantic once the United States closed the vulnerability by organizing defensive convoys.[14]

Historical precedent provided the lesson, but a renewed threat to Caribbean SLOCs was also an inescapable assumption that helped determined global U.S. defense posture during the Cold War. The principal and enduring contingency that preoccupied defense planners was a Soviet invasion of Central Europe in which rapid U.S. power projection during initial mobilization would have been critical to the NATO response. In the absence of adequate prepositioning, the only possible way to sustain a NATO counter to the Soviet thrust and achieve full mobilization would have been by sea. There would have been a great premium on speed, with plans calling for the United States to complete initial sea reinforcement within 10 days of the NATO decision to mobilize. Failure to achieve this goal could mean that, "NATO might not have been able to prevent a quick and decisive Warsaw Pact victory without escalating to the first use of nuclear weapons."[15] An even greater proportion of U.S. supplies of petroleum, oil, and lubricants (POL) and materiel would have come from Gulf ports than had been the case in World War II; 55 percent of Army heavy lift and 90 percent of POL according to one authoritative estimate.[16] There would have been a significant threat to sea commerce transiting the region, particularly oil imports to the United States from the Persian Gulf, Western Africa, and Venezuela, but U.S. military shipping in the Gulf would have presented a critical vulnerability. (The Panama Canal, although still significant for commercial trade, had lost its strategic importance by this time, even though the notion of swinging fleets from the Pacific to the Atlantic remained in

U.S. defense plans throughout the 1980s, and the United States certainly would have responded to a Soviet attempt to access the Canal.[17])

In the critical opening phase of a conflict in Europe, available sealift would have been limited, and a relatively high number of U.S. naval and air force assets would have been required to protect convoys, even in purely defensive mode. There was no doubt the United States would have neutralized the threat, but the possibility of even small losses plus the diversion of resources from the European theater would have carried a high cost. In the worst case, losses and distraction in the Gulf of Mexico could have prevented NATO forces from achieving the initiative in responding to a Soviet attack, and ultimately proved critical to the outcome in Europe.[18]

How realistic in terms of Soviet capabilities and intent was this threat? As Robert Leiken noted in 1981, "Soviet military writers recognize publicly that U.S. strategic freedom in other parts of the globe depends on stability in the Caribbean."[19] In other words, they understood the extrinsic value of America's backyard and the corresponding strategic value of nominally peripheral (to them) Cuba. Even if, in strategist Colin Gray's phrase, Cuba was ultimately "hostage to U.S. sea power," the Soviets were prepared to challenge U.S. sea command in the Caribbean Basin as a means of offsetting superior United States and NATO advantages on land and at sea.[20] Cuba had acquired through Soviet largesse significant offensive capability to disrupt U.S. shipping, whether or not they operated in combination with Soviet forces, and their air defenses would have allowed them to sustain operations in the face of U.S. countermeasures, at least for a time. During the 1980s, Cuba had one of the largest militaries in Latin America, with over fifty advanced aircraft and eighty to ninety naval vessels capable of attacking ships. In addition to the expansion of naval deployments and port facilities in Cienfuegos, the Soviets operated reconnaissance aircraft out of Cuban airfields, and the signals intelligence facility at Lourdes was the largest outside of the Soviet Union. These assets greatly extended Soviet capabilities, not only in the Caribbean, but also across the Central Atlantic and into the Northern Atlantic as well.

In a more speculative vein, the Sandinista Navy's half-dozen patrol boats would have had virtually no ability to interdict shipping, and Nicaragua had very limited naval facilities to offer to the Soviets. However, it is conceivable that eventually Nicaragua, and a revolutionary El Salvador should it have followed in the Sandinista's path, could have provided the Soviet Union with facilities on the Pacific Coast. Unprecedented Soviet naval access to ports in the Eastern Pacific would have been especially valuable for extending ballistic missile on-station time and extending the operational range of hunter–killer submarines.

MEASURING VITAL INTERESTS

Just how plausible from the U.S. point of view was this threat? The answer is, it depends. In the first place, the danger of SLOC interdiction in the Gulf was a high-risk but low-probability contingency of a war that was itself of very low probability. It would have mattered little if the war had been short, dependent entirely on

NATO forces already on the ground in Europe, and restrained by mutual strategic arsenals. This was precisely the planning scenario that the Carter Administration relied on to justify switching from a maritime to a continental strategy, downsizing the navy, and relying on détente.[21] It would have mattered not at all if nuclear deterrence had failed. The danger would have materialized only in the event of large-scale and prolonged conventional conflict with the Soviet Union, in other words, only if a version of the World War II Battle of the Atlantic had repeated itself. The Reagan Administration favored this scenario, because American sea control in the Caribbean (and Atlantic and Pacific), in which the navy would sweep the ocean of enemy submarines while providing sealift for reinforcements and materiel, fit the vision of global strategic options that justified the revival of American military strength.

U.S. and Soviet competition in the Caribbean Basin was not a matter of static balance; the global strategic contest was highly dynamic within the region. The Eastern Caribbean island of Grenada, had the United States not invaded in 1983, almost certainly would have become a useful strategic base for long-range air operations, including reconnaissance and airlift to support activities within and outside of the region. Soviet air and sea-lift of Cuban troops to Angola and Ethiopia was already significant. At the same time, they were increasing their naval presence in the Caribbean—a status that, incidentally, did not vary significantly between the Carter and Reagan Administrations—Moscow was adopting a broader and more sophisticated approach to the rest of Latin America that included expansion of political and trade relations with larger South American countries, notably Brazil and Argentina. In pursuing these broader objectives, the Soviets exploited opportunities, but remained cautious, steering shy of direct military expansion that might provoke the United States. They were certainly unable and therefore unwilling to afford the cost of another Cuba. From this perspective, it is clear that Central America was a mixed picture for the Soviet Union; if they were not exactly prisoners of geographic fatalism, they certainly had no grand plan for advancing there geostrategically. No matter how ideologically committed the Sandinistas may have been, Nicaragua's strategic advantage could only have been marginally additive, at the greater risk of provoking a direct U.S. response. Grenada may have been a relatively minor military operation, but it was a serious object lesson in resolve. When the United States warned against it, the Soviets declined to deliver MIGs to the Sandinista Air Force as promised, and they ignored Castro's pleas to send a fleet to counter U.S. naval presence when it exercised off Nicaragua's Eastern coast.[22]

According to the minimalist national security argument, it should have been entirely sufficient to guard U.S. national security in the region without the distraction of intervening in Central America. The only consideration the United States needed to worry about in the Caribbean Basin was the SLOCs, because this was the only threat that could have affected the global balance of power in the event of war with the Soviet Union. Desch asserts that a combination of limited resource diversion to defend convoys combined with nuclear deterrence to prevent states from supporting Soviet objectives would have been entirely sufficient to guard U.S. strategic interests in the region.[23] The approach is attractive as an application of strategic parsimony and as a means of distinguishing among intrinsic, extrinsic, and peripheral priorities. However, such a strict formulation does not fulfill claims of objectivity or exclusivity, and in the final analysis does not offer sufficient basis for assessing the broad range of considerations that established what was at stake for the United States in Central America during the Cold War.

The central issue returns to the question of vital interest, that most valuable object for which presumably a nation or a people will go to war. The Caribbean SLOCs represented a tangible threat to national security, but using this threat as justification for declaring Soviet penetration into Central America a vital interest to the United States was an act of policy. As Bernard Brodie observes, "Vital interests are not fixed by nature, nor identifiable by any generally accepted standard of objective criteria. They are instead the products of fallible human judgment, on matters concerning which agreement within the nation is generally less than universal."[24] Vital interests are, in other words, highly subjective and variable, under the influence of tradition, politically determined, and defined in large measure by the prevailing administration, above all the President. Brodie continues, "Looking back, it does not appear that all the wars that we or other nations have fought concerned issues of gravest importance. The obverse is also true. Some international issues or conflicts of real importance are churned over and either resolved or left unresolved without anyone's thinking of resorting to arms over them."[25] This insight evokes the many small but often vicious proxy wars in the Third World that consumed so much of the zero-sum contest between the United States and the Soviet Union, even as the two superpowers did their utmost to avoid direct conflict. Central America certainly stands out among those wars, and returns still not entirely satisfied to that question of how the United States could have become so alarmed about such a small place.

The obvious truth in this case is that the three U.S. leaders—Carter, Reagan, and Bush—all perceived there to be something more than a specific military threat to national security at stake in Central America. Like the fear of dominoes toppling from Panama to Mexico, the notion of Sandinista tanks in Harlingen was not only distant, it was not realistic. Further, the Soviet/Cuban threat to Caribbean SLOCs (even the threat of nuclear missiles in the theater) may have been realistic and plausible, but it is not apparent how U.S. intervention in Nicaragua and El Salvador added up to an effective counterstrategy. This was a serious disconnect.

VITAL INTERESTS, REALLY

The real threshold for how U.S. Administrations conceived of Central America as being of vital interest lay elsewhere, in the more open-ended and abstract realm of the ideology and geopolitics of the Cold War and containment. As pioneering national security scholar Robert Osgood observed, "No state can escape the psychology that invests an intrinsically small conflict with great significance if it is part of an overarching contest for stakes approaching survival."[26] Where Carter's vision of interests initially aspired to a global shrinking of U.S. power, Ronald Reagan's vision was its bold opposite. When it came to strategic challenge, tradition offered a compelling draw. The Monroe Doctrine declared any foreign attempt to extend its system to the Western Hemisphere as dangerous to the United States, and the Roosevelt Corollary was a general justification of intervention to prevent it. In the aftermath of World War II, the lesson of the costs of failing to halt Nazi aggression were fresh in the minds of policymakers and the public. By 1947, the Communist specter haunted much of Eastern Europe and, U.S. officials believed, seemed poised to continue its determined spread to other nations if left unchecked. That year, President Truman declared the Truman Doctrine, committing U.S. economic and military support for Greece and Turkey to prevent their falling into the Soviet sphere, and thus putting into practice the policy of containment. Truman's rhetoric, combined later with the introduction of the Marshall Plan, and the expansion of covert action and other activities directed by the newly formed CIA, laid the foundation for the actions that Monroe or Teddy Roosevelt could only dream of when they spoke of defending Latin America. Truman had provided the formula and the tools that were applied in the 1970s and 1980s to the strategic problem in Central America, which simply stated was Soviet and Cuban sponsorship of revolution. Politics were generally more determining than concrete threat assessments—on both sides of the bipolar political order—and produced very different prescriptions. Jimmy Carter unilaterally—and somewhat prematurely—declared the Cold War more or less over in the Third World and sought a form of intervention in Central America that would put United States on the "right" side of history, only to think better of it when the Sandinista revolution took the Cuban path. Ronald Reagan and his people, on the other hand, entered office with an extreme perception of global Soviet designs reminiscent of a bygone era, and immediately discovered Central America in the crosshairs. According to Reagan's first Secretary of State, Al Haig:

> The strategic considerations were clear. Wars of liberation had not been confined to targets of opportunity. They had taken place in the most strategic areas of the world—in Southeast Asia, with possible control of the Straits of Malacca added to the other consequences of a North Vietnamese victory; along both littorals of Africa, threatening the lifelines of Western commerce; in Ethiopia and the Yemens and (with the help of the Red Army) in Afghanistan to form a noose around the Persian Gulf. Central America was another strategic choke point.[27]

Jeanne Kirkpatrick, godmother of the neoconservatives, similarly but even more forcefully pinpointed the strategic threat posed by communism and the Soviet Union in a 1986 speech to the National Press Club. In it, she stated that:

> ...the emergence of guerrilla movements against governments that call themselves Marxist/Leninist, proclaim socialist solidarity, and have been incorporated into the Soviet system [Cambodia, Afghanistan, Mozambique, Angola, Ethiopia, Nicaragua]... It is worth nothing that the countries were sucked into the Soviet orbit after January 1975 and the fall of Saigon. They are recent acquisitions. They were rapidly incorporated during a period in which the Soviet Union relied heavily on a military bloc presence to tie new acquisitions into its system. Each of these countries is a strategically valuable asset,

which the Soviets have displayed determination to preserve. In each country, political control was secured and is maintained with direct Soviet or Soviet bloc military intervention. Each offers the Soviets basing rights. Each government is protected by its own praetorian guard from changing its mind or orientation.[28]

Thus, for both Haig and Kirkpatrick, the situation was clear. Despite 40 years of attempted containment, communism had expanded and by the mid-1980s the Soviet menace was more dangerous than ever. Implicit in their remarks was that the United States must act quickly to stem the tide, especially in Central America.

It was Ronald Reagan himself who determined that the United States would push back in Central America. For him, fear, honor, and interest coalesced there, and he gave this small region the highest value to demonstrate the revival of American strength in the struggle for the soul of the world. He announced this to the world in a joint session of Congress in 1983. Echoing the sentiments of Harry Truman when he spoke of the responsibility that the United States had to defend the free governments of Europe following World War II, Reagan stood before Congress and declared that:

The national security of all the Americas is at stake in Central America. If we cannot defend ourselves there, we cannot expect to prevail elsewhere. Our credibility would collapse, our alliances would crumble, and the safety of our homeland would be in jeopardy. We have a vital interest, a moral duty, and a solemn responsibility.[29]

Here is how LeoGrande catalogs the benefits of this resolve:

A victory in Central America would be Reagan's first foreign policy success and its ramifications would be global. By defeating the Soviet challenge in Central America, the United States would demonstrate to the Kremlin and its Cuban proxies that the new president would not tolerate Soviet adventurism in the Third World. Such firmness would reduce the likelihood of Soviet troublemaking elsewhere. It would also send a message to Western Europe that the United States was once again committed to global leadership. And most important, it would demonstrate to the American people that the United States could project power into the Third World without becoming entangled in another Vietnam.[30]

One of the more curious enigmas—and important aspects—of Ronald Reagan's leadership was his ability to summon images of shared patriotic culture to reinstill shattered American confidence after Vietnam to project national power, without actually risking war with the Soviets.

Central America was an inadvertent choice. The violent evils of the internal conflicts, along with official misdeeds and contradictions in policy, contrasted enormously with his portrayal of America's global aspirations in El Salvador and Nicaragua. As Michael Sherry, the perceptive author of *In the Shadow of War* observed, "Ronald Reagan...came to the White House inexperienced and uninterested in the difficult calculations that national leaders made about budgets, weapons, wars, alliances, and crises." What mattered about martial renewal was posture, "...military strength to bear witness to, rather than to act on, American superiority and moral resolve."[31] This disconnect between demonstration and effect was especially evident on one occasion in the mid-1980s when a Secretary of the Navy was flying over the region in the company of other U.S. officials. Descending to observe a carrier battle group on exercise off the coast of El Salvador where the insurgency was raging, he exclaimed to the effect, "Wow, look at that sight! Doesn't it make you feel good to see our boys down there?"[32]

Central America was, however, also a fortuitous place to discover vital interests at stake. Soviet and Cuban intervention in Central America was real enough, but, although few really sensed it at the time, the USSR was already a diminishing power and it was meddling far from home. Intrinsic interests were absent, and the extrinsic ones were distant or improbable enough to mean that the strategic challenge to the United States remained in fact largely intangible. Those wars certainly were nasty brushfires, but the United States could also afford to respond defensively when the region blew up in the late-1970s, rather than investing in a long-term policy.[33] All of that high purpose, notwithstanding, in Central America there was a great chasm between rhetoric and resources, and the problem on the ground was not clearing the bear from the back yard, but the classic one of just how a great power should best go about responding to what should be small, controllable political–military clashes in its sphere of interest. The answer for the United States in Central America was precisely an economy of force strategy, subject however to a sustained muddle of domestic political faction and limits on aims and means.

The Problem of Limits

Is El Salvador going to become another Vietnam?...
—Walter Cronkite Interview with President-elect Ronald Reagan,
December 3, 1980

NEVER AGAIN

"Is El Salvador going to become another Vietnam?" This was the first question that Walter Cronkite asked Ronald Reagan in the first television interview after his election in 1980. The question was repeated during his first press conference as President and on many other occasions for the next 3 years. In reply, Reagan consistently did his wholesome and benign best to reassure the American people that he had no intention of sending U.S. troops to fight in Central America. The immediacy of Vietnam created a compelling and overwhelming fear of repetition and the resulting restraint on U.S. intervention was apparent enough. Ronald Reagan was dedicated to restoring America's power by drawing the line against the Soviets in Central America, but he adamantly eschewed sending American troops into combat. There were other voices in his early Administration, notably Secretary of State Al Haig, who gave the impression that military escalation was the President's real desire. When it came to action, however, Ronald Reagan was sensitive to the public mood that said "no more Vietnams," and the even stronger voices of Nancy Reagan and White House Chief of Staff Jim Baker were not going to let the President be labeled a warmonger.

There is a deeper discussion here. As an immediate successor to Vietnam, Central America also fit within the greater legacy of limited war during the Cold War. Here all of the protagonists—internal and external alike—fought at the intersection of Clausewitz and Mao where internal conflicts were wars within the global war, and mutually reinforcing limits fundamentally defined their nature. The circumstances in Central America were in this sense comparable to those that Robert Osgood first analyzed regarding Korea:

> The generally accepted definition of limited war that emerged in the West in the 1950s limited both the means and the ends of war. Limits wars were to be fought for ends far short of the complete subordination of one state's will to another's, using means that involve far less than the total military resources of the belligerents and leave the civilian life and the armed forces of the belligerents largely intact." When it came to internal revolutionary war, however, "...limited war is not only a matter of degree but also a matter of national perspective—a local war that is limited from the standpoint of external participants might be total from the standpoint of the local belligerents...."[1]

In this sense, one nation's periphery is always someone else's center. In Central America, the two superpowers saddled themselves with numerous limits that interacted with each other in often contradictory ways. Above all, the United States and the Soviet Union sustained their investments in the Central American wars as part of their total global struggle, but diligently refrained from taking actions that might lead to direct confrontation. This restraint had the principal effect of preventing escalation, while at the same time superpower intervention intensified and prolonged the fury of the internal conflicts. Cuba's participation as Soviet surrogate and revolutionary sponsor complicated the dynamics.

The United States was the predominant regional power, and its reasons for limiting the use of force were the most complex and compelling. Level of interest, degree of commitment, perceived chances of success, and public support all had restraining effects. Declarations of vital interest notwithstanding, the Soviet challenge to the United States in its Central American sphere of influence did not represent a direct threat, nor could it immediately affect the global balance of power. The United States had no formal alliance or treaty commitments in Central America, and in fact the majority of Latin American countries would have opposed any attempt to invoke the Rio Treaty for Hemispheric defense. As for America's allies, the Salvadoran Government and Nicaraguan Contras often appeared short on competence, and there were plenty of doubts that any measures the United States took could succeed. On the home front, if Congress and the public were unwilling to abandon anticommunism and containment altogether in Central America, opposition to U.S. policy was strong and determined. Liberal Democrats insisted on keeping human rights and diplomacy on the agenda and were in any case unwilling to grant administrations a blank check to pursue their desires.

Most immediately and publicly, the American tragedy in Vietnam cemented a first order of self-limit in place. "Never again" was a powerful national sentiment, and the lesson was that "no conflict in the Third World was worth U.S. troops."[2] Even in the absence of objective vital interests, without the precedent of the Vietnam debacle, Marines would almost certainly have ended up in Central America. The justifications would have been at least as strong—and certainly closer to home—as they had been for sending combat troops into Vietnam. But a 1981 Gallup poll (and there were any number of comparable ones that varied little over the years) showed that two-thirds of informed Americans believed El Salvador was potentially another Vietnam and only 2 percent favored sending in troops.[3] The U.S. military itself had no appetite for being dragged into another enervating intervention in the Third World, and after Vietnam concentrated with determination on the main show in Europe. With the twin impacts of Vietnam and Watergate having decimated government credibility, no argument of fact, at least short of overt Cuban or Soviet aggression would have overcome this reluctance to using force in Central America.

The strategic constraints were evident. The premium for action was not on paying any price, but on insulating the country from the costs of war, with the casualty threshold set virtually at zero. As for policy, Jimmy Carter used his mandate to exercise moral self-restraint in Central America. His administration found itself struggling for a moderate course, trying haplessly to ease Somoza out through multilateral action, then agonizing over the split hair of whether to provide lethal or nonlethal aid to the Salvadoran military. Reagan strived for the opposite, to use Central America as a venue for renewing U.S. power, but he too recognized that the country had not healed enough from the corrosion of Vietnam to propose direct intervention, and a very assertive Congress would have erupted to block him, even if his sense of strategic priorities might have inclined him in the other direction.

Elsewhere, such constraints on direct intervention were not as compelling. The first Reagan Administration intervention in Lebanon in 1982, skirted disaster when Marines on an ill-defined internal peacekeeping mission suffered 282 casualties in a barracks truck bombing, and the Administration had the prudence to withdraw them quickly. Reagan got a win with the invasion of Grenada in 1983. There, defeating a small militia and a few Cuban construction troops on a Caribbean island was an ideal low cost, low risk, close-ended enterprise that demonstrated the ability and determination to use American force, thus making a key symbolic point without triggering public ire or the post–Vietnam War Powers Act.

SELF-IMPOSED RESTRAINT

Nicaragua and El Salvador remained much touchier and difficult matters, where two other vexing Vietnam lessons translated into restraint. The firepower and attrition of the conventional U.S. strategy in Vietnam had proven a poor course of action against the political–military challenge of revolutionary war. Real counterinsurgency, in the instances where the United States attempted it throughout the war, in the Marine Combined Action Platoons (CAP), the Civil Operations Rural Development Support (CORDS) program, Special Forces and CIA internal defense operations with the Montagnards and other tribes in the Central Highlands, and even the controversial Phoenix Program, never became part of the overall effort and tended to be too little too late. As far as counterinsurgency went, the U.S. withdrawal from Vietnam brought quick and willing oblivion to its lessons. "...when the Army came out of Vietnam...it nevertheless decided that studying all that unpleasantness was somehow not worth the effort, as if ignoring the experience of Vietnam would somehow inoculate it from having to get involved in such messy and complicated conflicts again."[4] And like Vietnam, there were serious questions about whether the U.S. ally in El Salvador was up to it, not too corrupt, bloody-minded, and politically incompetent to defeat themselves and drag the United States down again with them. For those in the USG who understood these lessons of Vietnam, "never again" did not mean staying out of Central America, but getting it right this time. For Military Group Commander Col. John Waghelstein, the critical lessons derived from his experience as a Special Forces officer in both El Salvador and Vietnam point in the same direction. When it comes to involvement in someone else's irregular war, limit the use of force and limit the American presence. As he summed up his attitude:

> Contrary to the U.S. Defense Department's usual way of doing things, smaller is better. The traditional American Way of War is rarely the right option in someone else's insurgency.... We probably cannot deliver victory from outside and if we can, it probably is transitory. This means that the U.S. personnel and equipment footprint needs to remain small.[5]

Rather than chafing at the entirely arbitrary fifty-five-man trainer limit in El Salvador, Waghelstein welcomed it because it prevented them from Americanizing the war.

The self-imposed restraints that ensured the United States would not risk another quagmire in Central America also fit with prior decades of Cold War experience. Each superpower confrontation, beyond its specific and contingent lessons, contributed to the evolution of limited war strategy whose purpose was to prevent escalation, because what was at stake was not worth the risk.[6] The Berlin Blockade had demonstrated the importance of discovering alternate means of protecting interests and showing resolve, while forestalling aggression and avoiding direct conflict with the Soviet Union. In Korea, the United States successfully resisted direct state–state aggression in a secondary area while respecting sanctuaries and restraining use of force. The Cuban missile crisis reinforced the absolute priority of avoiding escalation in the nuclear age in which the risks had become existential. To these limits, Vietnam added the ambiguities and dilemmas of direct intervention in internal conflict, the contrary effects of misapplying conventional force, and the doubts inherent in a failure of will.

In Central America, the United States limited both its aims and means in several critical ways. In the first place, there was a great contrast between the declared purpose of containing global Soviet aggression and actual involvement in the internal conflicts themselves. Concrete aims, however defined, remained within the bounds of insurgency and counterinsurgency proxy wars where the locals were responsible for (most of) the fighting. Any options that might escalate into direct conflict among the Central American states or otherwise regionalize the wars were carefully avoided. The possibility of more direct confrontation was kept even more remote. Certainly there would be no going to the source by blockading, much less invading Cuba. Beyond the unwritten prohibition on using U.S. troops in combat, there were numerous other formal limitations on level of force, commitment, and resources.

Congress was the source of most of these limitations, which formed part of the larger post–Vietnam struggle to constrain executive power. The intent of restrictions on U.S. involvement was to keep these wars "humane" and emphasize diplomacy, without Congress bearing responsibility for abandoning Central America altogether. The legislative provisions that conditioned U.S. goals, programs, and aid to Central America were part of, as Peter Rodman put it, the ". . .vast network of restrictions and inhibitions—'micromanagement' is the word that presidents like to use—that has transformed the way the nation's foreign policy business is conducted."[7] Once the restriction on lethal aid to El Salvador was lifted in 1981, Presidential certification requirements translated directly into pressure on the government to improve respect for human rights, which in effect meant restricting their often indiscriminate use of force. The purpose of arbitrarily limiting the number of trainers to fifty-five was precisely to prevent gradual direct escalation that had led the U.S. military to disaster in Vietnam. Budgets battles over aid to El Salvador shifted largely to the Nicaraguan contra program beginning in 1982 and continued throughout, but the "massive" U.S. assistance, both economic and military, provided to Central America was in fact relatively small. In Nicaragua, where Reagan Doctrine support for anti-communist insurgents took policy one step beyond containment toward roll back, the Boland amendment prohibited measures to overthrow the Sandinistas and cuts to the covert action program ensured fitful supply operations. U.S. exercises based in neighboring Honduras became semipermanent, but remained carefully away from the border with Nicaragua to avoid direct clashes with Nicaraguan troops and any Cubans that might be accompanying them.

There were two principal consequences of these limits. First, in keeping costs and ambitions in Central America low, the danger of making too small an investment remained roughly in balance with the risk of failure. In the event that U.S. support proved not enough to help the Salvadoran Government survive, the Americans were not going to take over, but the "loss" of El Salvador would not much affect the global balance of power. By extension, if the danger of escalation in terms of magnitude was kept at zero, the trade-off was extension in duration.[8] Thus, after 10 years of doing it themselves, the Salvadoran military proved capable of no better than stalemate in a country the size of Massachusetts against a force of no more than 8,000 guerrillas. Similarly in Nicaragua, the fitfulness of U.S. support effectively limited Contra capabilities to harassing the Sandinista Government, albeit with serious impact. Compared to capabilities, limits ensured that the United States wielded a very light weapon. Keeping the costs and risks low meant that, despite all of the controversy, U.S. means were proportionate to their purpose, but on the ground, the wars were long and bloody for the Central American participants.

ENEMY PARTNERS FIGHT LIMITED WARS

The mutual capacity of the superpowers to deter extinguished their capacity to compel, and made the Soviet Union and the United States "enemy partners."[9] One principal result was to shift direct competition from areas of central concern in Europe and Asia, to areas of lesser danger in the Third World. If the Soviets "strived ceaselessly and opportunistically to expand their influence and weaken all competitors,"[10] after opportunity came their way in Nicaragua in 1979, they, like the United States, nevertheless observed the lessons of limited war and did nothing that might have broken Cold War etiquette by provoking escalation. There was no greater ambition, even in the most assertive phase of the Brezhnev era, and certainly no concrete Soviet plan to reverse the balance of power in the Caribbean Basin by inciting revolution, although Castro was welcome to try his luck and enjoy their subsidy. Soviet aims in supporting revolution in Central America may have held potential for strategic accommodation or a grand bargain on regional conflicts, a "sphere of influence deal involving Afghanistan as well as tying the United States down to the degree possible."[11] In the end, however, a balance of superpower good will never emerged on Central America, and enmity prevailed over cooperation right through the Gorbachev era.

By the late-1970s, several factors circumscribed Soviet aims and means in Central America and the Caribbean Basin more broadly. Khrushchev's and the KGB's early enthusiasm for using Cuba as a bridgehead to spread revolution throughout Latin America had long faded, and with the exception of some limited KGB enterprises, the Soviets stuck for them most part with supporting orthodox communist parties. The KGB's early efforts to arm guerrilla movements after 1959, some organized with the new Cuban Dirreción General de Inteligencía (DGI) and others on their own, had come to nothing. Nicaragua had appeared to be a particularly ripe target because of the parallels between Somoza and Batista, but elaborate if frugal Soviet sponsorship of the original FSLN ended with most of the founders eliminated along the Honduran border in 1963, a misfortune they suffered again in 1967.[12] The constraints of the Soviet system had begun to have effect. The regime was becoming decrepit, and its broad ideological appeal had begun to wane. The structural limitations of the economic system made it increasingly difficult to accumulate clients that might demand perpetual foreign aid—except for military assistance, their one area of prowess. Their so-called strategic acquisitions around the world, with the possible exception of oil-rich Angola, all suffered from weaknesses and vulnerabilities. Features that had made Vietnam, Cambodia, Yemen, Ethiopia, and Nicaragua targets for revolution in the first place became liabilities once they came into the Soviet orbit. And it was not long after the 1979 invasion, that Afghanistan became a direct and painful military burden, making them nervous about further military commitments, but anxious to shore up reputation with success, thus ready to exploit the Sandinista revolution, but wary of the U.S. reaction.[13]

Moscow in effect remained ambivalent and relatively cautious about supporting Nicaragua, and even more so when it came to exporting revolution to El Salvador and the rest of Central America. Taking advantage of revolution in Central America was of some use to the Soviets for superpower rivalry, but protecting Cuba was a first priority and there was much to lose from risking a reversal there. In addition, subsidies to Cuba continued to tax the ailing Soviet economy; they were simply not in position to afford another. Nor were they enticed by the Sandinista project that Fidel

Castro championed of "...turning the FSLN in a Marxist–Leninist vanguard party which, in alliance with Cuba and the Soviet bloc, would lead the class struggle not merely in Nicaragua but across its borders in Central America."[14] Nevertheless, with Castro's enthusiastic pushing, they went ahead and began building the Ejercito del Sandinista (EPS) into the largest force in Central America and increased arms shipments to Cuba, much of which found its way to the FMLN in El Salvador. Annual Soviet economic aid to Nicaragua during the mid-1980s ranged from $150 to $400 million but was insufficient whether for reconstruction or to meet import needs, and was a fraction of what they supplied to Cuba in the form of trade credits alone. They did increase critical oil supplies after Mexico halted them in 1986, but only by adding to Nicaraguan debt. The Soviets also made sure that the Nicaraguans knew they were discontented with mismanagement of the economy and their aid. By 1987, with Gorbachev in power, the Soviets were still supplying the EPS, but debt had piled up to $1.1 billion and:

> Moscow told Managua that it was time to achieve a regional settlement of security problems. Though Soviet commentators continued to express 'unswerving solidarity' with the Nicaraguan people and 'resolute condemnation' of U.S. aggression towards them, they failed to include Nicaragua on their list of 'socialist-oriented states'—a label which would have implied more confidence in, and commitment to, the survival of the Sandinista revolution than Moscow was willing to give. Both Cuba and the Soviet Union made clear to Sandinista leaders that they would not defend them against American attack.[15]

And that was as far as it went. Strategically, the Soviets confined themselves to defense of the regime in Nicaragua and indirect support for the revolutionary movement in El Salvador. Cuba, Bulgaria, and East Germany helped to build Nicaragua's internal state security apparatus. The Sandinista Army depended on Soviet and Cuban support for counterinsurgency against the Contras. The unprecedented build up to a 150,000 person military—projected fancifully to grow to 600,000 in the 1980 bilateral agreement—and all of those Soviet tanks and artillery would have made invading Nicaragua a nasty business, but would have required extensive logistic support for any sustained operations, and were otherwise useless for regional aggression. The Soviet military commitment to the Sandinistas was in fact limited to defensive measures, however threatening it may have appeared in the regional context.

Revolutionary ambivalence and material constraints aside, it was daring for the Soviets to operate so far inside the U.S. sphere of influence. It was ultimately the United States that set the limits in the region, and the Soviets accepted those limits without much challenge. They protested, but did nothing further in response to the U.S. invasion of Grenada in 1983 that removed the possibility of a strategic airfield in the Southern Caribbean. At the same time, Soviet arms shipments went directly into Nicaragua or via Cuba largely unchallenged, until Gorbachev began to make promises to limit them as regional peace initiatives gathered momentum in the late-1980s. The Soviets honored the one explicit hard line and refrained from providing the Sandinistas with MIG 21s that had been promised to them, a move that would have introduced a new offensive weapon system and antagonized the region.

The United States did not lay down a similar marker when the Soviets substituted Hind and HIP helicopters for counterinsurgency operations against the Contras. In this sense, as Soviet Foreign Ministry official Yuri Pavlov observed, Central America and Afghanistan were mutually embarrassing weak spots for the United States and the Soviet Union, and both sides at least tacitly recognized a *quid pro quo* in their respective interference.[16] In Central America, Soviet geographic fatalism would ultimately prevail. They could exploit opportunities, but if the United States chose to invade so close to home, what were they going to do to prevent it? No advantage from revolutionary solidarity would lead them to risk escalation, much less approach the level that had almost produced disaster in 1962. The obvious target under those circumstances would be Cuba, the one place in the region where the Soviet defense commitment was supposedly firm and the strategic benefits were clear. In Central America, however, there was certainly no incentive and plenty of downsides to provoking a test with the United States.

THE GODFATHER OF REVOLUTION

From its contrary position under the belly of the United States, Cuba occupied a radical symbolic space beginning in 1959 and lasting through the end of the Cold War that was far larger than its geography would otherwise suggest. As a nationalist, global revolutionary, and bearer of the communist flame, Fidel Castro was the godfather of revolution in Latin America, a larger than life leader who defied normal limits of his Caribbean island just as he defied the great power to his north. Castro was not interested in limited war; his avowed game was overthrow and revolution. To that end, Castro's role in challenging the West provoked deep fear in the United States during the Cold War—and provided justification for decades of authoritarian rule throughout Latin America—but to the Soviet Union, Cuba was a liability as well as an asset.

Cuba's material and strategic dependence on the Soviet Union defined its critical limits, and those limits were determined by the overriding constraints of the Cold War itself. Like West Berlin, Cuba became a geopolitical irony that penetrated the adversary's sphere of interest, its security guaranteed by a crisis-born bargain between the two superpowers. If Kennedy had won the greater part of victory in the 1962 missile crisis by compelling Khrushchev to back down and remove the offensive missiles he had ordered secretly emplaced in Cuba, Khrushchev could claim that he had won Cuba's security by gaining Kennedy's pledge not to invade. Although the CIA continued its fitful attempts to assassinate Castro until prohibited to do so in 1976, the United States never tried to redeem the Bay of Pigs or otherwise intervene directly in Cuba again. Interestingly enough, not only did the missile crisis agreement grant U.S. consent to the Cuban thorn in its side, no administration ever made a showing over the condition, secret until 1992, that Cuba would commit "no aggressive acts against any of the nations of the Western Hemisphere." However, neither did the Cubans regard the Soviet Union as their altruistic savoir. Castro was pained and furious that Khrushchev had declined to risk war over the island and instead negotiated the agreement over his head. He reportedly cursed that

Khrushchev "had no balls" and wrote to Khrushchev that he had "brought tears to countless eyes of Cuban and Soviet men who were willing to die with supreme dignity." However strategically and politically beneficial Cuba was to the Soviet Union, it was after all geographically vulnerable and distant from the bastion of the motherland, and Khrushchev did not confuse survival with honor.[17]

The truth was that, beyond its symbolic power to disrupt and inspire, Cuba operated within very constrained margins, and as for concrete gains, there was relatively little to show for Fidel's irrepressible "small power adventurism." Cuba's international role stemmed from its revolutionary enthusiasm, but its record of success in actually spreading revolutions as opposed to inspiring them was very limited. The embargo, political isolation, and regional consensus that the United States forged in the wake of the missile crisis all constrained Castro's scope for action. In addition, despite the hopes of small, determined groups to defeat armies and overthrow governments, Ché Guevara's ceaseless efforts to export revolution to Africa and throughout Latin America came almost to nothing. Direct support to movements in Argentina and Venezuela died swift deaths, as did Ché himself in 1967 in Bolivia. Cuba's independent efforts were as often as not an embarrassment to the Soviets and taken without their knowledge, leading them to question Castro's political maturity and adventurism. From Khrushchev on, political friction limited collaboration between Castro and successive Soviet regimes with Soviets advocating go-slow and Castro trying to incite rebellion.[18]

Fidel had plenty of capacity for independent action that did not rely on and often went counter to Moscow's preferences. On their own, the Cubans could assist revolutionary movements in many ways, primarily through the American Department of the DGI. They could send advisors, intelligence officers, and special operations troops, as well as doctors and teachers. They could provide political advice, assist with planning, organize weapons shipments, train thousands of Nicaraguan and Salvadoran revolutionaries, and treat the seriously wounded at hospitals on the island. However, Cuba's strategic and material autonomy were too limited to support significant military operations. The only possible sustained source for foreign exchange, arms, and transportation was the Soviet Union, supplemented with aid from other Eastern Bloc countries. Soviet material support was not important for the run-up to Somoza's overthrow when Venezuela, Costa Rica, and Panama were the main arms suppliers. But once the Sandinista's purged the moderates and emerged as the Marxist–Leninist leaders of the Nicaraguan revolution, it was Soviet support that armed their Cuban model. Alternate sources of arms supply to the Sandinistas proved minor adjuncts, with token commitments in solidarity. Of course, U.S. opposition was a factor in closing off other sources. France never repeated its single 1981 $15.8 million arms sale after vigorous U.S. and NATO protests. U.S. vigilance blocked a clandestine Libyan arms shipment when it transited Brazil in 1982. Similarly, covert arms reached guerrillas in Honduras, Guatemala, and especially the FMLN in El Salvador via Cuba and Nicaragua, but Moscow was the principal source either directly or through offsets. Even if Cuba had been capable of providing greater independent support to its allies in Central America, their commitment of 25,000-plus troops to Angola and several thousand more to Ethiopia had already brought them to the edge of overextension.

The paramount constraint was perceptions of U.S. reaction. As enthusiastic as Castro might have been about the Sandinista victory and desirous to support the Salvadoran revolution, Cuban combat forces could not fight in Central America without fear of retaliation, as they did in Africa. U.S. resolve in the 1983 invasion of Grenada increased Cuban caution, leading them to reduce their military presence in Nicaragua and to advise the Salvadorans to begin seeking a political settlement, both for its own security and to prevent U.S. escalation that might defeat revolutionary forces altogether. Cubans involved in counterinsurgency with the EPS against the Contras also consistently used caution on the Honduran border to avoid the possibility of direct confrontation with U.S. forces on exercise there. Castro frequently sought greater Soviet commitment, for example, reviving efforts to get the Soviets to signal support by sending a Soviet naval task force to Nicaraguan waters in 1985.[19] For the most part, the Soviets preferred Cuba to be in the forefront of revolutionary support, but at the same time they worried that Castro might get carried away.[20] The symbiosis is clear: Castro would not commit unless he wanted to, but could not commit without Soviet support. Above all, perceptions of the U.S. reaction conditioned what they believed they could get away with.

The Fall of Somoza and the Triumph of the Sandinistas

War is more than a true chameleon....

—Carl Von Clausewitz, *On War*

THE CULT OF THE DEAD

When the Sandinistas rode into Managua on July 19, 1979, their long and obscure guerrilla struggle against the despised dictator Anastasio Somoza culminated in a rapid triumph. The contest was a civil war by any definition, and the popular insurrection that brought it to a climax was the irregular warfare equivalent of a quick decisive victory and a classic case of how the weak win. Their achievement—the first successful revolution in Latin America since Cuba over 20 years earlier—was the result of effective political and military strategies that took full advantage of extreme domestic discontent and favorable international conditions. Through a combination of determination, guile, and revolutionary élan, the small leadership cadre of the Frente Sandinista de Liberación Nacional (FSLN), captured the hearts and minds of the Nicaraguan people, wooed moderates both foreign and domestic who would normally have had no sympathy for radical revolutionaries, and managed an internationally supported insurgent offensive that compelled the collapse of the Nicaraguan National Guard and Somoza's regime.

The Sandinista victory is equally the story of political incompetence, in which Somoza, with the unwitting help of his powerful American patron, lost his legitimacy and authority, and consequently his control over Nicaraguan society. The denouement took place on July 17, 2 days before the new revolutionary government occupied the National Palace in Managua when Somoza fled ignominiously to Miami, ushered out by the American Ambassador. The popular uprising had spread

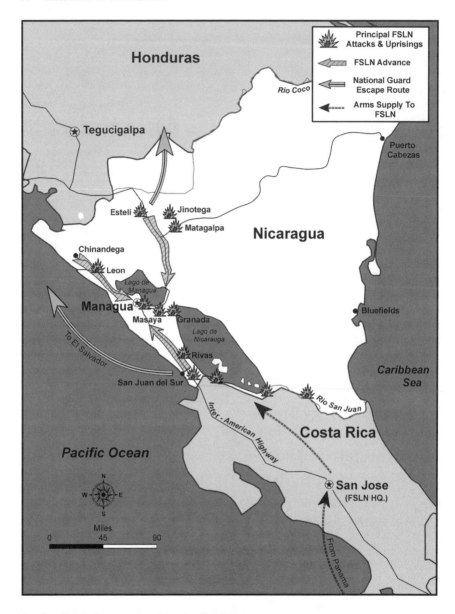

The Sandinista Insurrection. Map by Knutt Peterson.

like a brushfire, fueled by people of all classes and backgrounds, with tens of thousands of newly armed youths, the *Muchachos,* taking to the streets. The National Guard, beleaguered and nearly out of ammunition although not defeated militarily, stopped fighting and simply disintegrated. Last ditch American attempts to prevent the Sandinistas from coming to power by engineering a constitutional transition had failed abjectly. The surprise refusal of Somoza's hastily named interim president to hand power over to "communists" and keep the presidential sash for himself as insurgents overran Managua is memorable only because it was ludicrous.

The nine-member junta that led the Government of National Reconstruction was an unlikely collection of conservative businessmen and Marxist–Leninists. There was no question, though, that it was the Sandinistas who had finally brought Somoza down; except for appearance sake, they did not need to share their legitimacy with the traditional opposition members who had traveled with them...and they had the guns. The cabinet had only one Sandinista member, but it was FSLN representative and soon to be President Daniel Ortega who took the oath of office, and his brother Humberto who would soon head the army. By December, the nine-member National Directorate of the FSLN had replaced the junta and most of the cabinet to assume power directly and begin their project of transforming Nicaragua into a socialist country allied with the Soviet bloc. *New York Times* managing editor Abe Lowenthal dubbed new revolutionary Nicaragua, "Poland with palm trees."[1]

The Sandinista success was as decisive as any victory Clausewitz could have envisioned, and he would have recognized in it the critical importance of what he called "moral forces." Nicaragua's national mutiny against the Somoza dictatorship was not the result of a spontaneous popular uprising or a rural peasant revolt, although these were both aspects, but was achieved through a conscious and coordinated political–military strategy of armed insurrection, conceived and executed by a few dozen revolutionary leaders, most of whom had been hardened through years, and in some cases decades of clandestine struggle and futile guerrilla war in the countryside.[2] Prior to 1978, the FSLN had been more of an irritant to Somoza than a threat. Largely clandestine and organized into cells that committed bank robberies and kidnappings to gain funds, set bombs at government facilities, and occasionally came together to attack National Guard or Police outposts to gain attention and capture weapons. The security forces nearly always responded with immediate and devastating force to these incidents. A small and bickering kaleidoscope of opposition groups, sect-like enclaves of radicalism, had been active to various degrees since the mid-1950s. The early membership of the FSLN came from the orthodox Communist Party that followed the Moscow party line and eschewed violence, along with miscellaneous socialists and individuals with grudges against Somoza. These included several aged guerrillas who had fought with Sandino against the U.S. Marines and the National Guard in the 1920s and 1930s. For the tiny but dedicated armed factions who later grew into the Sandinista movement, it was truly a prolonged struggle where the fire of revolution burned fitfully but intensely. Their saga against an entrenched despot closely identified with a foreign power was, from their point of view, a war of national liberation. This globally unifying ideology that established their pedigree descended from the anticolonial struggles in the Third World against the European powers, as well as the more recent insurgencies in Algeria, Vietnam, the Congo, and elsewhere.

A desire to lend the Sandinistas the benefit of the doubt may have led to some confusion in the United States and elsewhere about their identity and aims, but there should be no doubt that the linkages between revolution in Nicaragua, Marxism–Leninism, and the Cold War were facts of life. The Sandinista's most powerful and immediate inspirations were the Cuban revolution and Fidel Castro. The Cubans enthusiastically believed that "...the destiny of Cuba was to inspire revolutions,"[3] and offered their island as the physical and ideological home away from home for Nicaraguans, along with other hopeful insurgents from throughout Latin America. Insurgent avatar Ché Guevara—the Osama Bin Laden of revolution—inspired these early efforts. He helped to fuse the original FSLN in the early 1960s, and was particularly close to it founding leader, young and austere Carlos Fonseca. Institutionally, export of revolution coalesced under the DGI where financial support, guerrilla training, and advice for Nicaraguans was one of their first and principal projects. Between Castro's overthrow of Batista in 1959 and the 1962 Cuban Missile Crisis, the Soviet Union also optimistically believed that Cuba was an ideal ally in its strategy of assisting national liberation movements as the bridgehead of revolution in Latin America. Nicaragua was a primary target, and during this period, the KGB recruited Fonseca along with several others, and provided direct funding and training for the new Sandinista organization.[4]

The goals of the FSLN changed not at all between its founding in the early 1960s to its triumph in 1979. According to a 1963 issue of the first official Sandinista publication, *Trinchera,* these were:

- free Nicaragua from the political and economic domination of the United States;
- overthrow the Somoza tyranny and destroy the National Guard;
- institute agrarian reform and industrialization;
- and establish a government of national unity under the direction of the FSLN.[5]

Augusto Sandino, who had fought the U.S. Marines and been betrayed and executed by the U.S. trained and equipped National Guard on the orders of Anastasio Somoza's father in 1934, was the perfect icon of the revolution. Thus united, the causes of fighting the Somoza dictatorship and Yankee imperialism provided a common nationalist basis for revolt, while conveniently obscuring the Leninist goals of its principal promoters.

As for revolutionary strategy, with the Cuban revolution as their model, the Nicaraguans fared no better than their compatriots that initially tried to follow the Cuban model in Guatemala, Peru, Venezuela, Argentina, and Bolivia throughout the 1960s and into the 1970s. The Sandinistas waged guerrilla war in relative obscurity, futilely following Ché Guevara's notion that a small band of dedicated guerrillas—a *foco*—operating from the remote countryside could spark a peasant revolt and then a national uprising. They modified this approach only slightly in the late 1960s by adopting Maoist People's War terminology and incorporating the inspiration of Vietnam. As with Ché's ignominious end in 1967 in the Bolivian jungle, the chief result was the death of Fonseca himself in 1976 in a National Guard ambush. The Guard periodically wiped out entire Sandinista bands, while other Sandinista members built tragic biographies of prison terms, torture, and exile. Within the intimate group of dedicated revolutionaries, the expectation of violent death was a sustaining and exalting feature of revolutionary conviction. Accordingly, Sandino was the first martyr in the pantheon and Carlos Fonseca the second. The appeal of martyrdom sprang not only from the modern revolutionary ideology, but also from deeper roots in Catholic and indigenous culture, thus adding to the Sandinista's popular sympathy. Sergio Ramírez, well-known Latin American writer and himself a secret FSLN member and subsequent vice president called it, "the cult of the dead."[6] FSLN fighters did not share an irrational death wish, nor did they seek military victory; armed action was their instrument of political legitimacy and through it their path to power. As former Sandinista (and Contra) Arturo Cruz observes, "Through its defeats the FSLN developed a reputation for bravery. It lost men but began to win the country's admiration."[7]

Typical of other insurgent organizations, the FSLN's primary obstacle to effectiveness was not National Guard vigilance and predation, but factionalism. There were three FSLN factions united on goals, but divided over strategy. The Prolonged Popular War (GPP) faction adhered to Fonseca's original *foco*-ist ideas. The Proletarian Tendency was urban oriented and focused on organizing the working classes. The third group, the Insurrectionary Faction or *Terceristas,* formed in the late-1970s, was new and bold. The *Terceristas* deviated from the orthodoxies of the other two factions by advocating two basic elements: creating the conditions for revolution by sustaining offensive, highly public insurrectional activity, and seeking tactical alliances with the noncommunist opposition. Led by the brothers Daniel and Humberto Ortega, the *Terceristas* assumed an uneasy dominance over the rest of FSLN, but their strategy became a formula for success.[8] Beginning in 1977, this Sandinista offensive seized the initiative by exploiting political opportunities and undertaking military actions for public effect. The voice of the revolution was Radio Sandino, which broadcast from Costa Rica, and the presence of international television and other media attracted by the unrest in Nicaragua heightened the instant "propaganda of the deed."

Fear of violent revolution led the moderate opposition to alternate between hostility and accommodation toward Somoza, while Somoza obdurately defended his regime with violence. Among a series of key events, at the end of 1977, a dozen prominent Nicaraguan academics, priests, businessmen, and professionals abandoned their ambivalence, forming the "Group of Twelve" and aligned themselves with the Sandinistas. The January 10, 1978, assassination of the opposition's most prominent leader, newspaper publisher Pedro Joaquín Chamorro, provoked outrage in Nicaragua and international scandal. "As soon as word spread of the shooting, businesses began to close throughout Managua, and tens of thousands of people followed Chamorro's body home from the hospital for the wake. It was the beginning of a mass outpouring of frustration and anti-Somoza rage."[9] The general presumption was that he had died at Somoza's bidding, and although no proof emerged and Somoza denied it, the assassination foreclosed any possibility of political reform through dialogue. Chamorro was hardly a Sandinista, but the FSLN made certain they figured prominently in his funeral and quickly elevated him into their growing pantheon of martyrs.

On August 22, 1978, a Sandinista team brazenly captured the National Palace and the entire Congress which was in session, then proceeded to negotiate with Somoza for 3 days, with Archbishop Obando y Bravo acting as intermediary. The hostage crisis and the negotiations became a national and international spectacle. To secure release of the Congress, Somoza released political prisoners, paid $500,000 in ransom, and paid for publication of an FSLN manifesto. Eden Pastora, "Comandante Zero," and his fellow Sandinista raiders flew to Panama and Venezuela in planes provided by the two nations' presidents and were received there as revolutionary celebrities. As much as the aura of the FSLN grew with the incident, Somoza's authority and legitimacy suffered serious blows. Encouraged and overoptimistic in the aftermath, the Sandinistas attempted to escalate in September by launching a series of guerrilla raids and calling for a nationwide "final offensive," only to be rebuffed by National Guard counterattacks and a tepid public response. This radicalism in turn scared some in the opposition to call for exclusion of the FSLN from any political arrangement. However, when Somoza attempted to halt what he called "the communist conspiracy" by arresting moderate politicians and bombing the barrios of Managua from the air, he succeeded in making himself more despised. It was a pattern that was to become ever more costly.

THE SULTAN

Like his father and brother before him, Anastasio Somoza Debayle ruled as a classic Latin American caudillo. The Somoza dynasty was based on a personalistic, unchecked, and violently exclusionary concentration of power, an extreme form dictatorship that Jeff Goodwin calls "sultanistic."[10] Somoza's principal tool for maintaining his regime was the National Guard. With the Guard as his center of gravity, Somoza appeared strong, but in the absence of other institutional linkages to society, this militarization of the state was also his vulnerability. Somoza's other sustaining asset was the United States. He expected that Washington would continue to support or at least tolerate him in the same manner it invariably had since 1936, when Somoza's father, Anastasio Somoza Garcia, assumed the presidency after consolidating his power as head of the National Guard. The Guard itself was a product of U.S. interventions between 1914 and 1934 and was intended to provide a nonpartisan foundation of stability and democracy. By the early-1930s, America had tired of it interventionist burdens in Central America and the Caribbean, and opted to become a noninterventionist "Good Neighbor" under the Coolidge and then the Roosevelt Administrations. Washington's acquiescence and indifference allowed the Somoza's to use Uncle Sam's legacy as their personal vehicle of power. There is an important lesson here.

When he put on the sash in 1967 after his brother Luis died in office, Anastasio "Tacho" Somoza quickly showed that he lacked the political acumen that his father and older sibling had used to keep the family in power through multiple conspiracies and coup plots, co-opting the politicians of the traditional Liberal and Conservative parties, and balancing them off against each other behind a façade of democracy. Tacho spoke American slang, was West Point educated, and had been head of the National Guard. He had a reputation for brutality that did not change once he took over the government. His politics were exclusionary, and following the 1972 earthquake that destroyed Managua and devastated much of the country, his diversion of recovery assistance into corruption and cronyism added many in the private sector to those among the opposition who had already learned to loathe the dictator. Thus alienated, the traditional elites, who should have been Somoza's principal supporters ultimately adhered to the one group that was armed and determined to overthrow him, the FSLN.

The 14,000-man National Guard was, like the ruler that they sustained, a classic Latin American military force, organized as a conventional army, but used primarily as instrument of internal control. Officers enjoyed complete impunity and answered only to the personal direction of the dictator. The Guard was U.S. trained, and their hand-me-down U.S. equipment included tanks, artillery, and a small air force, all for the purpose of defending Nicaragua against communism. Tacho Somoza's son, Tachito, was in line to succeed his father and meanwhile occupied himself by commanding an elite unit modeled on the U.S. Special Forces, the Escuela de Entrenamiento Basica de Infantería, or the Basic Infantry Training School. Whatever soldierly skills Nicaraguan troops may have possessed, the stock in trade of the National Guard was repression. A primitive anticommunist nationalism that Somoza had inherited from the United States and his father infused the Guard. According to their ethic, communism was the central threat to the state; any but the most loyal opposition could be labeled communist; communists do not value human life and are terrorists; therefore, any measure against them is justified. And, although Somoza believed himself to be the benign patron of his country, the National Guard was the stick that he used to control the population. His simplistic concept of counterinsurgency was based on a medical analogy. He wrote,

> [Revolutionary activity] was like a malignant cancer. You could stamp out the disease in one part of the body politic and it would suddenly appear in another part. Had I been a dictator, as was claimed by my political opponents and the international press, I could have eliminated the cancer entirely. This would have meant drastic action on my part and curtailment of the freedom I wanted the Nicaraguan people to have.[11]

Sure enough, at the Sandinista core were hardened adversaries, and Somoza deployed the Guard to confine the insurgents to remote rural areas and eliminate them wherever they could find them. But the therapy that he followed was drastically military and fatally devoid of any serious attempt at political reform beyond gestures designed to stall his opposition and keep them at bay. As the insurrection burgeoned, the National Guard, true to its nature, turned in suspicion on the population itself, bombing neighborhoods at will and making every young male subject to arrest, torture, and summary execution. Somoza and his American ghost writer completed his memoir during 1980, just before a Sandinista-contracted hit squad of Argentine revolutionaries assassinated him in Paraguay where he had fled. It was no coincidence that he called it *Nicaragua Betrayed,* the same title deposed Cuban dictator Fulgencio Batista chose for his memoir. Somoza blamed everyone for betraying him by design— Cuba, the Jesuits, the OAS, the international press, the State Department, and especially President Jimmy Carter—everyone but himself and his own paternalistic, vulnerable, and hopelessly inflexible mode of governing. It did not occur to him that he was Nicaragua's cancer.

CUBA AND OTHER FRIENDS

Somoza may have created the conditions for his own undoing, but the Sandinistas would never have succeeded in exploiting those conditions without the help of Cuba. The Nicaraguan insurrection was a virtual replay of Fidel Castro's overthrow of Batista's brutal dictatorship in 1959, complete with joyous crowds swarming over bearded guerrillas as they emerged from the hills and jungles and rode into the capital amazed at their own success. Images of Ché Guevara, patron saint of revolution, and of Nicaragua's own hero Augusto Sandino, appeared everywhere to symbolize the common destinies of Cuba and Nicaragua. The Sandinista triumph was an international celebration for Marxist–Leninist revolutionaries everywhere and for those who sympathized with their cause of social justice. Cuba in 1979 was sustaining a major military commitment in Angola and remained thoroughly dedicated to revolutionary expeditions, but Nicaragua was its first and only Latin American success.

Many insurgents and would-be insurgents dream of revolution, but few ever live to see success. The Sandinistas and the Cubans sustained the collaboration they began in the early 1960s, even if lack of success in exporting the revolution had caused the star of the DGI Department of the Americas headed now by Manuel Piñero to fall a bit. Directorate member Tomas Borge of the GPP faction was the lone surviving founder of the FSLN, and he remained close to the Cubans, but in early 1978 the *Terceristas,* led by the Ortega brothers Daniel and Humberto, had usurped him as the principal interlocutors of the revolution. Convinced that their bold insurrectional approach was opportunity knocking on Nicaragua's door, Fidel Castro became both personal and political godfather to the Nicaraguan revolution in this final phase, and even came to treat Daniel Ortega much as if he were a favored son. There was even a family parallel; like Fidel's brother Raul, Daniel's brother Humberto commanded the Sandinista Army. The extent to which the Sandinistas threw themselves into the Cubans' arms could be embarrassing. To have a meeting with Fidel was the height of honor for a Sandinista leader on pilgrimage to Havana, and to have Castro's personal tailor make your dress fatigues was to achieve the pinnacle of style. As Sergio Ramírez recounts in his evocative memoir of the Nicaraguan revolution, "It was not just the Cuban revolution that was a model, but Fidel as a figure. For some, to copy the gestures he made in speeches, his tone of voice, his turns, his reflexive silences while holding his hand in the air next to his beard, and even the way he supported himself on the podium, became a mimetic vice...."[12] Castro also played a more pragmatic role as broker and senior advisor. He admonished the three combative Sandinista factions to unify, hosted their often bitter deliberations, and in March of 1979, insisted on a nine-member FSLN Directorate with three representatives from each group as a condition for supplying arms in the final push against Somoza. He introduced the new Sandinista leaders to their indirect Soviet patrons, who, except for limited KGB support, had long since abandoned their enthusiasm for revolution in Latin America and had remained aloof during the insurrection. Castro's key political advice to the Sandinista's was to avoid Cuba's mistakes and embrace moderation by avoiding confrontation with the United States, the Catholic Church, or the private sector, at least before they had consolidated their power.[13] Cuban military support was also crucial to the Sandinista victory. FSLN guerrillas trained in Cuban military and intelligence centers and recovered from their wounds in Cuban hospitals. Millions of tons of small arms and ammunition flooded into the country from Cuba to fuel the Sandinista victory in 1979, and Cuban officials, headed by Julian Lopez who became Cuba's Ambassador to Managua, ran a small command center in Costa Rica to oversee weapons distribution and advise the FSLN.[14]

The Cubans were the principal inspiration and model for the Sandinista's, but they were hardly their only allies. Other Latin American governments played prominent roles both politically and militarily, as logistic bases and weapons suppliers. Where Cuba initially had to keep its support low key in order to minimize the risk of provoking a U.S. intervention, others did not feel so constrained, especially after it appeared that the United States actually wanted to dispose Somoza. Democratic Presidents Rodrigo Carazo of Costa Rica and Carlos Andres Perez of Venezuela, along with Panamanian strongman Omar Torrijos all had grudges against Somoza and his outmoded and thuggish brand of dictatorship. They began providing some arms to the FSLN in 1978, with Venezuela as the major source. When Perez's term ended in February 1979 and his pro-U.S. successor cut off the supply from Venezuela, he took the initiative to bring Castro into the arrangement, which resulted in a triangular—and not incidentally profitable—supply relationship between Cuba, Panama, and Costa Rica. Cuban arms flew via Panama, where Torrijos and his deputy Manuel Noriega played in both camps, to staging areas in Llano Grande, Guanacaste Province, Costa Rica for transshipment across the border into Nicaragua. In his account of the Sandinista victory, Humberto Ortega itemized arms received in forty flights from Cuba including FAL rifles, RPG-2 antitank grenade launchers, heavy machine guns, grenades, mortars, recoilless rifles, and even four-barrelled antiaircraft guns.[15]

Between February 1979, when the United States abandoned a mediation effort it had begun 6 months earlier, and July 1979, a virtual "Latin-wide assault on Somoza"[16] took shape. Other hemispheric nations eagerly joined Venezuela, Panama, and Costa Rica in boosting the Sandinistas politically precisely at the moment their military offensive gathered steam. In May, the Andean Pact declared the situation in Nicaragua to be a threat to hemispheric stability and urged Somoza to resign. On June 23, the OAS, in an embarrassingly lopsided 17-2 vote (with five abstentions), rejected a last ditch U.S. effort to organize a peacekeeping force and instead passed an unprecedented resolution calling for Somoza's replacement. Whereas in 1965, the United States unilaterally sent troops into the Dominican Republic and the next day the OAS sanctioned the action and sent troops to join, in 1979 hemispheric neighbors found it in their interest—and relished the chance—to take advantage of U.S. miscalculation and for once rebuff its presumption to dictate.[17] Mexican President Jose Lopez Portillo in particular took full advantage of the opportunity to antagonize the United States and pave the way for the Sandinistas. He grabbed center stage by breaking relations with Nicaragua, offering the Mexican Embassy in Managua as sanctuary, recognizing the Sandinista Government in exile, and providing them with financial support. As the new regime prepared to take over on July 19, Lopez Portillo sent the presidential plane to fly members of the cabinet from San Jose to Managua. So fulsome was Mexican support, at least initially, including shipments of free oil, that when a cabinet secretary asked how they should regard the Sandinista Government, Lopez Portillo responded, "As if they were a state of the republic."[18] Most of the Latin American leaders who so willingly championed the Sandinistas did not do so out of naiveté, but because they were focused on bringing Somoza down, and claimed that their efforts were aimed at helping Nicaragua make a moderate transition to democracy, or at least not leave it to Castro. For the most part lacking the Cold War fervor of the United States, they were still more willing to treat with Cuba, and certainly were beguiled by the Sandinistas strategy of deemphasizing their Marxism–Leninism. It was not long, however, before their Latin allies began to have second thoughts. Venezuela and Panama found to their surprise that the new EPS did not welcome their offers of military assistance, because they were receiving all they needed from Cuba and the Soviet Union. Costa Rica got cold feet too at the rapid military buildup across the border. The Sandinista charm did not survive their actual behavior once they had proclaimed their revolution socialist, made it apparent they had no intention of honoring the commitment to respect private enterprise and hold free elections they had made in a letter to the OAS, and allied themselves with the Eastern Bloc. Nevertheless, it was certainly enough to help ease their way into power.

INSURRECTION

The insurrectionary strategy of the *Terceristas* began to take hold in the second half of 1978. Although their first run at a final offensive was a false start, the intertwining of political and military dimensions proved increasingly effective. Small-scale fighting had been on the increase for several months, primarily guerrilla ambushes and attacks against government outposts in the countryside, but now the insurgency also became increasingly urban. The National Palace seizure on August 22 was a major jolt that for the first time demonstrated the efficacy of attacking Somoza through armed insurrection—with the FSLN in the lead. In response, uprisings broke out spontaneously in several locations, including the major town of Matagalpa. The FSLN had not planned to link the National Palace raid with broader military action, but in order to stay ahead of the building wave of popular opposition, they issued a call over Radio Sandino for a national insurrection and general strike on September 7. Thousands of Nicaraguan youths did join the FSLN in the streets where they succeeded in controlling several poor barrios in Managua and paralyzing towns both large and small throughout the country for nearly a week. However, they were not nearly well-enough armed or coordinated to prevent the National Guard from concentrating forces and seizing insurgent controlled areas back one-by-one. The FSLN was forced into a general withdrawal as thousands of Nicaraguans died in fierce aerial bombardments and summary executions. It was then that initiative passed to a period of United States-led international negotiations to prompt moderate regime change, a cause of some worry to the Sandinistas, but Somoza, having whipped the FSLN once again, yielded nothing. This outcome was deceptive and only temporary. The most important effect in the end was growing popular repudiation of National Guard brutality that increased sympathy for the Sandinistas. They garnered several thousand recruits and the seeds were planted for success the following year.

From the end of January to the first week of February 1979, Torrijos hosted *Tercerista* leaders, who were also consulting with their Cuban advisors, at the Rio Hato-Farallon military base in Panama.[19] They had two purposes, to reconcile serious differences of personality, ideology, and strategy enough to achieve unity of command and to draw up a plan for the coming final offensive. A major difficulty was Eden Pastora—as the CIA would discover when he later became a Contra—dashing hero of the National Palace raid and commander of insurgent forces in the critically important south. Pastora was highly idiosyncratic and was not a Marxist–Leninist, which meant that he remained outside the FSLN core leadership, much to his own chagrin. But he did despise Somoza and wanted to see him overthrown. This was the common aim that united the Nicaraguans. Once they had reached agreement in Panama, several senior *Tercerista* commanders flew to Cuba where they formed the nine-member Directorate incorporating the three FSLN factions. With unity of effort achieved, Fidel, after some reluctance given the Sandinista setback in September, signed on to the insurrection and authorized weapons shipments via the triangular Cuba–Panama–Costa Rica logistics arrangement.

With the arms flow turned on and their legitimacy rising, the FSLN commenced their "life or death" offensive phase in March of 1979. They assumed that this was their one big chance to seize power, and their plan called for a sustained nationwide offensive coordinated across time and space, without withdrawal or retreat. In overall command of FSLN forces from his headquarters, Palo Alto in San Jose, Humberto Ortega did not intend to challenge the numerous, well-armed, and still-resilient National Guard directly on the battlefield. Rather, the Sandinistas stuck with their insurrection strategy of guerrilla operations coordinated with national strikes and popular uprisings in provincial cities and the capital. The objectives of organized Sandinista forces included making the situation of the National Guard untenable throughout Nicaragua. They interrupted roads and otherwise disrupted communications; kept the Guard unbalanced, reactive and tied down with numerous small attacks; instigated uprisings in the cities and handed out arms to the population; and used larger units to seize cities and "liberate" territory. In the final stage, all forces converged on Managua. The offensive was intended to last 30–45 days, although it was to take more than twice that long.

In March when the offensive got underway the Sandinistas had about 2,000 guerrillas, about half of them veterans. By July they had grown to around 5,000 troops, freshly armed, with at least some training, and organized into columns ranging from a dozen to several hundred combatants. In command of these units were "Comandantes" who zealously guarded their factional identities. The *Terceristas,* who were in overall command and directed Cuban patronage, controlled three-quarters of the troops. The remainder were divided among the GPP and Proletariat tendencies, with arms carefully distributed proportionally. Supplementing them were local militia in rural areas and the *muchachos* who appeared on their neighborhood streets in numbers that grew daily and adhered spontaneously to FSLN units. Nicaragua also became a magnet for revolutionaries from throughout Latin America. Some 500-plus foreign fighters, eventually organized into three "International Brigades," arrived to support the FSLN from Panama, Colombia, Argentina, Uruguay, Chile, Mexico, Costa Rica, and the other Central American countries, along with a smattering from England, Germany, and Spain. According to Humberto Ortega, in addition to the Cuban liaison in Costa Rice, twelve Cuban special troops and intelligence officers also served with the FSLN.[20]

The Sandinistas organized their forces into three primary and four secondary "fronts" named after fallen comrades of varying size, preparation, and importance. The Southern Front, under the command of Eden Pastora, up against the Costa Rican border was the strongest and best-supplied, and proved the most serious distraction to the National Guard. But the northern front carried political weight; the capture of León, Nicaragua's second city, from the National Guard in early July was the turning point of the offensive, and it was from León that the government rode into Managua. The urban front in Managua kept the large Guard garrison tied down in the city and mobilized the citywide popular insurrection once the offensive had developed in the rest of the country. The other four fronts, of which the most important was the internal front that operated to the south of Managua and in the cities near the Pacific Coast, cut off highways, conducted ambushes, and helped keep the National Guard distracted enough to prevent it from reinforcing one area without abandoning another.

The Nicaraguan civil war may have been a small war, but both sides fought for their survival with great intensity. Between March and May 1979, the FSLN launched significant attacks in both the North and South, but the offensive appeared to be off to a slow start and was behind schedule. Pastora's forces seized the southern city of Rivas in a major assault, but were unable to hold it. The National Guard was defending and counterattacking well. Where communications were cut by land, it had air mobility to reinforce hot spots, and had prevailed over most FSLN attempts to take and hold cities. Most importantly, Guard forces concentrated effectively under the command of Colonel Pablo Emilio Salazar, "Comandante Bravo"—who would later escape with nearly 2,000 troops to Honduras where they would form the nucleus of the Contras—to prevent Pastora and his southern front units from breaking out of the area along the Costa Rican frontier. The U.S. Embassy in Managua, the intelligence community, and the White House concluded that the National Guard would withstand the assault. Somoza mocked the attacks as the "mimicry of an offensive," and some FSLN commanders from the PT and GPP factions who had harbored initial doubts, argued to postpone the insurrection.[21] However, sufficiently armed by now, confident that they were on the upswing, but also aware that this was their one big shot at victory, the Ortega brothers and the other *Terceristas* insisted on pressing forward. On June 4, the FSLN call to insurrection and a general strike came across Radio Sandino from Costa Rica. In this final 6-week phase, military and political action fused as combat progressed to full-fledged battles for control of the major provincial centers—Masaya, Matagalpa, Estelí, León—where the National Guard and police found themselves eventually besieged and forced to withdraw or surrender. Fighting on the Southern Front developed into almost conventional battles, and the capture of Masaya cut Comandante Bravo off by land from Managua and made it equally impossible for the Guard to reinforce its garrisons to the north. The FSLN had the National Guard off balance and outgunned.

Somoza, and those who fought on his side, tended to blame their defeat solely on lack of ammunition. There is some truth to this. By June, the Guard was already scraping bottom—virtually out of bombs, mortar, and artillery rounds, extremely low on small arms ammunition, and hard pressed to resupply or reinforce around the country. They had managed to get some ammunition transshipped through Guatemala, and received some from Spain, Brazil, and Argentina. Even though it became impossible to ignore the flood from Cuba, Panama, and Costa Rica that had arrived for the Sandinistas, the United States stuck to its one-sided embargo that denied arms to Somoza. An Israeli ship loaded with armaments that Somoza had managed to contract and considered a "lifesaving" last chance, turned back on June 14 as it approached Central America after strong U.S. pressure. By the end of June, the situation was irreversible.[22] But the assessment that firepower alone told the difference is misleading. Somoza's military problems were rooted in his political shortcomings. He claimed that he resisted advice from his National Guard commanders to arm the population, because he did not want to put civilians in jeopardy. In fact, as the fighting grew more furious, the dead surpassed 25,000 in a population of barely 2.5 million. Most of the victims were casualties of aerial bombardment, indiscriminate fire, and execution. It was the Sandinistas who were arming a population aroused and determined. The more violent National Guard counterattacks became, the more the violence worked against them as ever increasing numbers of Nicaraguans, wealthy and poor, students, and farmers, and shopkeepers joined in the fight against the despised Somoza. Arturo Cruz, at the time a Sandinista sympathizer, described the atmosphere:

> Managua was a city in revolt. The workers and peasants were not involved. The FSLN found its followers among the youth of the barrios and the universities. Many of them had no jobs, no future. The FSLN gave these kids the opportunity for a heroic death. They responded by taking up arms and fighting, committing wonderful acts of valor,

often dying as they did. The moral indignation of the country rose as the number of slaughtered young men and women rose. Every day the names of newly dead, many of them children in their teens, appalled and frightened the populace.[23]

Sandinista leaders recognized that the factors that had converged in their favor would not last. Attention within Nicaragua, but also internationally, had remained fixed on the offensive to get rid of Somoza. However, Cuba's role was increasingly obvious and had begun to provoke second thoughts among their Latin allies. They had received all of the arms they were going to get, and ammunition was a concern for them as well. Once the bulk of Sandinista forces had crossed into Nicaragua, Costa Rica deployed Civil Guard troops along the border to prevent spillover in the opposite direction. The one issue, though, above all that concerned the Sandinistas—and was to fixate them even more after they came to power—was the potential for foreign intervention, meaning from the United States. This they understood with perfect clarity was the one event that might derail their victory, and the FSLN leadership dedicated enormous energy to keeping the United States at bay.

UNCLE SAM STUMBLES

For their part, in June, the Carter Administration, which had let events take their course since February, awoke to the real implications of a Sandinista victory, and the with a growing measure of panic as the military situation reversed, began a reactive and at times contradictory damage control initiative aimed at preventing the FSLN from coming to power, or a least moderating the outcome. The Administration was simply not aware that the momentum of the military offensive within Nicaragua—not U.S. power—was driving events. The Sandinistas were equally unaware that President Carter himself had taken U.S. power in the form of military intervention definitively off the table.[24] In the complex political-diplomatic dance that ensued during June and July, the Sandinistas adeptly kept the lead and the United States bumbled behind with bad steps and bad timing. The FSLN had emerged as the heroic leader of the struggle to oust Somoza, but it intentionally appeared to take a political back seat by bringing prominent members of the moderate opposition into the cabinet and junta of the provisional government. One of them included Violeta Chamorro, the widow of martyred opposition leader Pedro Joaquín Chamorro. This gambit effectively precluded U.S. efforts to find any centrists who might have fabricated a third base of political power between Somoza and the Sandinistas. It was in this context that renewed U.S. attempts to prompt multilateral mediation failed. The Sandinistas' Latin American allies preferred to abet their victory to the ends of ousting Somoza and forestalling U.S. intervention, even though concerns about handing Nicaragua over to Castro were growing. Formal U.S. efforts culminated in humiliation at an OAS meeting on June 21 that rejected the notion of a peacekeeping force and agreed only on the need to oust the still-intransigent Somoza.

U.S. officials could not help but be aware that they were no longer the arbiters of Nicaraguan politics, but they still overrated their ability to influence the outcome.

The Special Coordinating Committee (SCC), the NSC-chaired interagency group that was the primary vehicle for setting U.S. policy, began to meet frequently in crisis mode, making tactical decisions intended to dictate how the transition of power would take place. In fact, it became increasingly ineffectual and out of touch. As Robert Pastor observed, "The Administration had no idea what alternatives were available, but threats made in desperation, are not generally inhibited by the absence of rational alternatives."[25] After the OAS failure, the United States struggled in series of last ditch efforts to control Somoza's departure by seeking to add more moderates to the provisional government and, especially as the situation grew direr, to preserve the National Guard. The FSLN derided the undertaking as trying to preserve "Somocismo without Somoza." The most critical issue was that the United States was not prepared to give the Guard the one thing they actually needed— ammunition—or to allow anyone else to supply them. President Carter involved himself directly at the beginning of July, calling on his one Latin American confidant, Omar Torrijos, who he had worked so hard with on the just-completed Panama Canal Treaty, to come to Washington. Torrijos, feeling "like a schoolboy called to the principal's office for a scolding,"[26] agreed to help get negotiations going with the FSLN, although in reality he joined other Latin Americans in attempting to balance concerns about handing Nicaragua over to Castro with ensuring that the United States did not intervene.

The interplay shifted to Costa Rica and the ranch of Costa Rican President Carazo in Puntarenas, where U.S. Special Envoy William Bowdler spent long hours deliberating with the Sandinistas and other Latin leaders. The Sandinistas were under enormous pressure to accommodate the worries of their Latin friends and to appease the United States, who they still feared might do something drastic to prevent victory. In the midst of their military offensive and preparations to install a revolutionary government, senior FSLN leaders dedicated long hours to dissembling in the negotiations. Nothing symbolized the confused tension better than the July 8 landing of a U.S. military C-130 in Guanacaste Province near the Nicaraguan border on a mission reported variously as "humanitarian" and "to protect American citizens." The Sandinistas, fearing this was a disguised prelude to intervention, convinced the Costa Rica congress to overturn President Carazo's reluctantly granted permission and the plane withdrew. Humberto Ortega observed that, "The art of negotiation is the art of knowing how to yield in order to obtain results,"[27] and the FSLN proved positively gymnastic on formation of the new government. They were prepared, after consulting with Castro, to add more moderates to the junta as the United States insisted, but ironically it was the two moderates who were already junta who demurred. Only one Sandinista was appointed to the cabinet, albeit this was hardliner Tomas Borge who went to the Interior Ministry where he would be in charge of internal security. Bernardino Larios, a former National Guard officer who had sided with the Sandinistas after Somoza had him jailed when a coup attempt failed, was named Minister of Defense. The Sandinistas also agreed to broad concessions in the stated goals of the revolution, formulated in a letter to the OAS. The one critical question of who would control the new Nicaraguan Army remained ambiguous, although the Sandinistas had no intention of yielding up this source of revolutionary power.

Meanwhile, U.S. Ambassador in Managua, Lawrence Pezullo, was calling on Somoza in his reinforced command center, The Bunker, where he had taken refuge and telling him outright that it was time to go. Somoza, in fact, had finally realized the game was up following the June 21 OAS resolution, had written his resignation letter, and claimed was waiting for the United States to tell him when to leave. In something of a final disconnect, Washington believed that by playing the "Somoza card"—controlling the timing of his departure—it could engineer the preservation of the National Guard and keep the government out of Sandinista hands. It was an illusion. Time, in fact, was on the side of the Sandinista offensive, and the longer Somoza held on, the more the focus remained on removing him rather than shifting attention to what came after. In the political end game, the United States scraped unsuccessfully for an acceptable National Guard officer who would remain in command, and finally the jerry-rigged formula for handing power off to an interim government ended in farce. Somoza made a last ditch flight to Guatemala where he pled for support from his fellow military regimes in the Central American Defense Council (CONDECA), but without a green light from the United States they proved unwilling. When he finally fled along with his high command on July 17, most of Nicaragua was effectively under FSLN control, with Managua in popular revolt and insurgent columns converging on the capital from the north and south. The National Guard was nearly out of ammunition, fuel, and hope. On July 18, when the Sandinistas brushed aside an offer to negotiate a cease fire and terms of a handover, the Guard surrendered unconditionally, then quickly collapsed and disintegrated. Several thousand officers and men fled, many of them by boat to El Salvador, and eventually found themselves in Honduras where they formed the nucleus of the Contras. On July 19, the Sandinistas took over, parading 90 miles by road from León to Managua and flying into the airport from San Jose, unopposed and in triumph. Humberto Ortega records the reversal: "That night...I moved to the Bunker, to sleep profoundly in the bed shortly before used by Anastasio Somoza Debayle."[28] After decades of weakness and futility, the Sandinistas, radical revolutionaries emerged in control after achieving unity, through masterfully effective coordination of political and military strategies, exploiting opportunities and errors of their adversaries, and perhaps, most importantly, by winning the hearts and minds of the Nicaraguan people and much of the world.

NO OTHER WAY OUT

The Sandinista victory seemed at the time inevitable and in retrospect may appear unremarkable. Somoza was after all a vulnerable and particularly vile dictator who had lost the support of his major international patron, and virtually the entire population had risen up against him. But in fact such complete reversals are unusual. The Somoza dynasty had lasted for over 60 years, Fidel Castro's overthrow of Batista had preceded the Sandinista success by 20 years, and the Shah of Iran's overthrow in

January 1979 was the only recently comparable event. The specific event needs some explaining; a thorough conceptualization leads to some valuable insights into the nature of irregular warfare that transcends the specifics of the ideological conflicts of the Cold War in Latin America and the Third World. In revolutionary warfare theorist Jeff Goodwin's analysis:

> The triumph of the popular insurrection of 1978–79 against the Somoza dictatorship was the result of several mutually reinforcing factors: the growing strength and popularity of the FSLN, growing elite and moderate opposition to Somoza; increasing international support for the Sandinistas and the concomitant geopolitical isolation of Somoza; the absence of a political opening from above; and the inability of Somoza's National Guard to contain, let alone halt, the rising tide of armed insurrection.[29]

This is a perfectly sufficient explanation of the conditions and drivers of the Nicaraguan civil war. The critical vulnerability was the nature of the Nicaraguan state under Somoza, his neopatrimonial and personalistic sultanism. Socioeconomic inequity or belief in the inevitability of revolutions were distinctly secondary considerations; there are too may poverty stricken nations with corrupt regimes among the ranks of today's weak and failing states that have not experienced overthrows, let alone revolutions.

It is a commonplace of guerrilla wars and revolutions that the political dimension is primary and "an active instrument of operation," as David Galula puts it.[30] The Nicaraguan war offers a great deal to be said about the intricate dynamics between politics and military force. Military action at all levels—tactical, operational, and strategic—was subject to political factors, and conversely all military actions had political effects. Perhaps this is obvious enough. Just because a war is small does not relieve its participants from the requirements of effective strategy. In this sense, irregular war is much like conventional war, with one critical difference: the intensity of interaction between political and military dimensions means that there should be no separation of the two, and the side that demonstrates the most effective coordination of the two elements at all levels is most likely to come out the winner. The central political feature that finally drove Nicaragua to insurrection was Somoza's rigid exclusivity that left no room for change, in Goodwin's phrase, "no other way out." Thus, as the various factors converged, the group that was best prepared to conceive, organize, and sustain an armed struggle—the FSLN—emerged after decades of futility to lead one. Although force was not the exclusive factor, military strategy was indispensable both to the Sandinista's success and the National Guard's misfortune.

If the wisdom of conventional war is that no side benefits from prolonged conflict, the wisdom of unconventional war is that insurgents can benefit from protraction. However, the conventional wisdom that if the insurgents are not losing they are winning is in fact circumstantial and contingent. Time can be conceptually on the insurgent's side, as long as a small and determined group can sustain faith in the justice and inevitable triumph of their cause. Correspondingly, insurgents, freed from the need to defend territory, gain the freedom to strike by surprise. Neither of these supposed advantages of time and space will help them much if they remain confined to remote base areas and the effects of attrition are relatively greater on them than on their opponents. On the contrary, the counterinsurgent state tends to have many advantages over an insurgent force. It generally possesses superiority of arms, personnel, and other resources such as an intelligence system and other features of an institutionalized security apparatus. Even in the absence of an effective strategy, counterinsurgents can often rely on these inherent advantages to prevent military defeat, as was the case with U.S. firepower in Vietnam. There is also the inherent strength of the defense, which lies in waiting and assuming lower risks compared to the attacking side. These central assumptions about the effectiveness of counterinsurgency in fact sustained the Nicaraguan National Guard—and the assessments of the U.S. Government—right up until its imminent collapse in July 1979. In truth, either side may take advantage of countervailing influences, such as a generous ally that tips the balance, but the strategic dynamics of strength and weakness for either side are contingent rather than fixed.

Galula's experience taught him that the insurgent side generally determines what he called the "strategic patterns" of irregular warfare.[31] Each of these strategic patterns—rural guerrilla warfare, urban terrorism, popular insurrection, and so on—calls forth a corresponding counterinsurgency strategy to combat it. To expand this concept, one overarching feature common to all patterns of irregular warfare is the general inability of either side to bring decisive force to bear on the other. This problem of decisive force, which the insurgent side also drives, determines the nature of military action for both the offense and the defense. The insurgent is too weak to mount a direct military challenge, and the counterinsurgent cannot do so because insurgent forces must avoid concentration to survive. As a result, counterinsurgency operations that mass forces in space and time and use tactics that depend on firepower are usually ineffective. The result is that both sides must take recourse in second-best strategies that are indirect and prolonged. The tendency for violence to extend outside of the military realm into societies as a whole, for example, in cases where counterinsurgents adopt a strategy of "total war" or insurgents turn to terrorism, can make irregular wars extremely costly, even if the conflict itself is relatively "low intensity." As is often observed, even though insurgents can be incredibly good at turning weakness to their advantage and counterinsurgents are frequently able to maintain the upper hand, such asymmetric strategies are the products of necessity not of choice. After all, what revolutionary or terrorist organization would not choose to defeat their adversaries rapidly and achieve their aims directly through the decisive exercise of force, if they had the means to do so? Because it is the more powerful side, counterinsurgents often can simply summon absolute superiority sufficient to suppress if not eliminate the insurgent threat, at least for a time. Such was the case with the Nicaraguan National Guard versus the FSLN from the early-1960s right up until 1978. However, even effective counterinsurgency generally devolves to playing cat-and-mouse or whack-a-mole, relying on police and intelligence work more than combat to defeat elusive insurgent elements in detail. What is least likely to occur, unless an insurgency reaches an advanced stage, is open fighting between the two sides to determine an outcome in the mode of conventional warfare. This did occur in the Nicaraguan case to some extent, but only in the final weeks of the 1979 offensive, primarily in the Southern Front, and then only when all of the other conditions that contributed to the insurrection had developed.

In the absence of decisive military force, the strategic dynamics of irregular wars frequently turns on the decisive political effects of armed action. Hostage-taking, for example, has a long if "dishonorable" heritage, the Peloponnesian War being full of examples. The honor that Somoza lost and the leverage that the Sandinistas gained there when they took his entire Congress hostage for 3 days in 1978 demonstrated that its asymmetric effectiveness has not declined over the ages. Once sufficiently armed, the FSLN expanded guerrilla operations to tie the National Guard down in multiple clashes and sieges around the country. Although they continued fighting hard until the end, the widely dispersed Guard was unable to defend territory, control the population and cities, maintain communications, or concentrate against FSLN attacks, and thus lost counterinsurgency effectiveness. But it was decisive exploitation of political conditions—Somoza's isolation and their assumption of the vanguard with broad domestic and international support—that allowed the FSLN to arrive at this final military stage and carry it through to victory. To put the strategic pattern of the Sandinista insurgency in terms of Mao's three phases of revolutionary warfare: The FSLN was stuck for many years alternating at low levels of action between phase one, incipient political organization, and phase two, use of guerrilla force. Then in a period of less than 2 years, the FSLN accelerated and short circuited the entire revolutionary process by leaping over the final phase of direct conventional military confrontation to overthrow of Somoza. The strategy of popular insurrection in effect achieved the irregular warfare equivalent of a quick decisive victory.

POLITICAL COMPETENCE

Nicaragua is an excellent case to explore the meaning of "decisive political action" in greater detail. The Nicaraguan civil war was an ideological contest for power between Marxist–Leninist revolutionaries who dedicated their total means to the unlimited aim of overthrowing Somoza and the anticommunist National Guard that was attempting to defend the survival of the state. As the war developed in the 1978–79 insurrectional phase, Sandinista attack sought military objectives—control over territory, provincial cities, and the capital. But this military dimension was intimately linked to the parallel war for Nicaragua's political center of gravity, which was a battle for state authority and the legitimacy on which power depends. The Sandinistas—the eminently weaker side—won their war first and foremost not on the battlefield, but by "winning hearts and minds," or to use another word, winning "legitimacy." Legitimacy is meant here in its most basic sense, the loyalty of the people, and in the case of Nicaragua popular acceptance of the Sandinistas as the rightful represent-atives of authority. From this perspective, the central strategic pattern of the Nicara-guan civil war was the process by which the FSLN acquired legitimacy and Somoza and the National Guard lost it. Because this was a revolutionary war in which the insurgents justified the use of arms to overthrow what they regarded as an illegitimate regime, the issue of legitimacy did not turn on formal legality. Foreign policy authors Robert Tucker and David Hendrickson define the general circumstances succinctly:

> Legitimacy arises from the conviction that state action proceeds within the ambit of law, in two senses: first, that action issues from rightful authority, that is, from the political institution authorized to take it; and second, that it does not violate a legal or moral norm. Ultimately, however, legitimacy is rooted in opinion, and thus actions that are unlawful in either of these senses may, in principle, still be deemed legitimate. That is why it is an elusive quality. Despite these vagaries, there can be no doubt that legitimacy is a vital thing to have, and illegitimacy a condition devoutly to be avoided.[32]

Where in Nicaragua under Somoza there had been only stagnation, corruption, and repression the FSLN showed compassion. They demonstrated to the Nicaraguan people that Somoza's sultanism violated both legal and moral norms, and successfully convinced them that the use of force against him was legitimate. Equally important was Somoza's loss of legitimacy internationally among Latin American nations, the media, and the U.S. Government, albeit with unresolved ambivalence. To use Max Weber's formulation, Somoza had traditional legitimacy; people accepted him largely without question because he possessed authority and vice versa. In other words, he had legitimacy because he had power. This legitimacy, however, rested on a narrow base. Tacho Somoza inherited Nicaragua that his family had run for over 60 years, but the exercise of his power was essentially arbitrary, and Nicaragua was hardly a state of law. He was nominally an elected leader, but elections were contrived and his political organization, the traditional Liberal Party, had become a façade coopted for his personalistic and authoritarian military rule. The National Guard on which he depended to exercise his authority enjoyed complete impunity. Anticommunist nationalism was another source of legitimacy used to justify all forms of violence against the population, and in exchange for which he had long received the support of the United States. In addition to this traditional legitimacy, the psychological dimension of his leadership was also critical. Somoza believed that the Nicaraguan people loved him rather than despised him and that as President he had an inherently justified personal right to take any action or possess anything he desired. He was mistaken about this "charismatic legitimacy," as Weber called it, and his confusion was a key vulnerability that contributed to his rigidity in the face of attack and ultimately produced his downfall.

The Sandinistas, on the other hand, acquired charismatic legitimacy at Somoza's expense by questioning his authority and by challenging him—heroically—in the eyes of the people. To some extent, their legitimacy was also traditional, in the sense that the Sandinistas embodied the romance and possibility of revolution that was deeply embedded in Latin American political culture. It was also highly circumstantial. As the factors that made the insurrection possible coalesced, the legitimacy of this small and marginal group of Marxist–Leninists grew until it became their principal strategic asset, proving crucial during the offensive period between the seizure of the National Palace in the summer of 1978 and their victory on July 19, 1979. Soon after, their charismatic legitimacy began to wane. Once they were in power and it became apparent that the FSLN directorate was a grimly socialist "caudillo with nine-heads instead of one," in Sergio Ramírez's description, their legitimacy narrowed to the minority mandate of true revolutionary supporters and their possession of authority. The subsequent imposition of police state authority was not sufficient to overcome gross errors of governance and the new counterinsurgency war that was imposed on them, and a decade later their own loss of legitimacy was reflected in a crushing electoral loss.

Among the political factors that form this critical strategic dimension of irregular war, legitimacy is at the top of the list. The Sandinistas had many things working in their favor, most importantly a despised dictator as their adversary and a facilitative international environment. But this small and dedicated revolutionary group still needed to emergence from clandestinity, implement an insurrectional strategy, and ultimately control events sufficiently to put themselves in power. "Political competence" is a fitting term that helps explain how the Sandinistas achieved their revolutionary reversal. In Israeli strategic theorist Chaim Kaufman's formulation, political competence is,

> The degree to which each side's leadership is committed, uncorrupt, and disciplined, as well as whether it commands sufficient loyalty and obedience from subordinate institutions and agents that its strategy can actually be carried out.[33]

Competence also includes having at least circumstantially superior knowledge, judgment, skill, and strength, qualities that also include legitimacy. Once the FSLN achieved internal unity, they demonstrated political competence that was both absolutely and, more importantly, relatively greater than Somoza's. Theirs was the harder task and the greater accomplishment. Somoza's challenge was to muster sufficient political competence to retain and defend his regime; the Sandinistas had to create another way out through armed overthrow even though they were the inferior side. As a general principle, the side that exhibits greater relative political competence in an irregular war, independent of military strength, is the most likely to succeed.

Legitimacy, or as Kaufman defines it, the "command of sufficient loyalty," is the key operating requirement for political competence. Command of loyalty in war is critical across three types of fundamental relationships: the relationship between the government and the military, between the people and the government, and between the military and the people. This concept has its echo in Clausewitz's famous depiction of war as:

> ...more than a true chameleon that adapts its characteristics to the given case. As a total phenomenon its dominant tendencies always make war a paradoxical trinity composed of primordial violence, hatred, and enmity, which are to be regarded as a blind natural force; of the play of chance and probability within which the creative spirit is free to

roam; and of its element of subordination, as an instrument of policy, which makes it subject to reason alone. The first of these three aspects mainly concerns the people; the second the commander and his army; the third the government.[34]

Michael Handel distills the triangular structure of these relationships, observing that they vary in relation to each other and are rarely of equal weight, which the specific and unique nature and circumstances of each war must determine. Thus, "In representing guerrilla warfare...the role of the people takes precedence over the role of the professional military (at least in the war's initial stages), while the role of the government is as important as in a conventional war."[35] Naturally, the complexities of society make it essential to further discriminate within each of the three elements of the triangle to determine which subgroups are of greatest importance.

The Nicaraguan triangle rested on a narrow base. Government was a cosmetic democracy, but in reality, it was a military dictatorship where Somoza held all of the power and the National Guard, the country's only strong institution, was his enforcer. Somoza's critical vulnerability was his link to the population, including to political and economic leaders who were not cronies or otherwise beholden. As his legitimacy and authority slipped, the already tenuous ties between the government and the people broke. Given the repressive as opposed to protective nature of the National Guard, the inherently weak ties between the military and the people also broke under the impact of violence.

It is a correspondingly simple matter to adapt this triangle of relations among people, government, and army to an insurgent force, with the insurgent organization (or organizations) assuming the role of the government and their armed element(s) that of the army. In this case, the FSLN began the Nicaraguan civil war fractured into three factions with limited military capacity and miniscule popular support. Once unified, their principle task was to build a revolutionary movement by exercising superior political competence, constructing their own triangle and correspondingly destroying Somoza's own. To accomplish this they focused on breaking Somoza's weak link—his lack of legitimacy with the Nicaraguan people fueled by the alienating violence of the National Guard—while strengthening their own. The two key elements of their insurrectional strategy served this purpose perfectly: They exploited the absence of a political opening from above to seek tactical alliances with the noncommunist opposition, including traditional political and economic elites, and conducted insurrectional activities that demonstrated the potential of armed opposition while winning popular legitimacy. In the final phase, despite the false start with the call to insurrection in September 1978, the bond between the FSLN and the population strengthened, and the bond between the guerrilla army and the people in arms flourished. It was the building of these political linkages that made military action in the final offensive possible and the second call to insurrection in June 1979 a success.

There was of course nothing predetermined about this outcome, just as military factors in and of themselves were not decisive. Rather, the FSLN won the Nicaraguan civil war through exercising political competence that contrasted entirely with

Somoza's political incompetence. In political negotiations, Somoza offered nothing but prevarication, and in responding to popular opposition he offered nothing but repression. Exclusion, suspicion, and insecurity poisoned the political environment, and the National Guard's firepower became counterproductive and even irrational. The relationship between the government and the military—between Somoza and the Guard—remained strong until the end, but the relationships between the military and the people and between the people and the government broke under the strain of violence. Provoked, the people did find another way out, national mutiny via the FSLN-led insurrection. Somoza's critical errors were political not military. Had he not rejected offers of international mediation and foreclosed the possibility of elections, he likely could have preserved Nicaragua from revolution, even though the cost would have been a timetable for him to relinquish power. In another, important sense, however, Somoza was not the sole instrument of his own destruction, but a victim, and there is some merit in the bitter rant of his memoir, *Nicaragua Betrayed*.

DILEMMAS OF INTERVENTION

The role of the U.S. Government surrounding Somoza's overthrow and the beginning of the Sandinista revolution demonstrated once again how U.S. policy and strategy made at the intersection of good intentions and power so often finds misfortune. The dilemmas of intervention in internal conflicts that the Carter Administration encountered were classic; the response is an object lesson in political incompetence. To Somoza, no one was more to blame for his ignominious downfall than President Jimmy Carter. In his view, not only had Carter and his policymakers abandoned and betrayed him, they had intentionally handed Nicaragua over to the FSLN. The accusation surely misplaces fault by attributing his fate to conspiracy. Yet still there is something to it. The United States was after all Nicaragua's traditional patron, and Carter broke the mutual anticommunist protection pact by turning against Somoza. Doing so without having a ready alternative violated the wing-walker rule of not letting go of one thing until you have a firm grip on something else. In consequence, not only did the United States leave an ally exposed, it contributed directly to destabilizing the country. For the Sandinistas, like August Sandino in the 1920s and 1930s, the *Yanquis* were the enemy just as much as Somoza and his National Guard, and they were competently prepared to take advantage of the situation.

As a candidate, and once he entered office in January 1977, Carter declared that his "new foreign policy" would shun the militarism that had led to disaster in Vietnam, reject the amorality of the Nixon–Kissinger era, and avoid "inordinate fear of communism." Instead, benevolent intercourse with the Third World would replace preoccupation with East–West confrontation and concern for human rights would shape relations with governments of all types, including traditional friends. In Latin America, the United States would disassociate itself from authoritarian military regimes and their dirty wars, eschewing intervention, where support for the 1973 overthrow of Salvador Allende in Chile stood out as a notorious recent instance. Negotiation of a treaty to divest semicolonial U.S. sovereignty over the Panama

Canal would be a constructive initiative of high symbolic value both in the region and to the world. Jimmy Carter's approach to America's role in essence echoed Woodrow Wilson's deeply moral vision that was focused on the world as it should be rather than as it is. These post-Watergate and post-Vietnam ideals found strong support both in the American public and among the eighty to ninety liberal democrats recently voted into Congress.

In early 1977, Nicaragua emerged as a test case of this new foreign policy. It seemed to be a good choice. Somoza ran a blatant dictatorship with an atrocious human rights record, and, more importantly, Nicaragua was small enough that any countervailing costs to the United States would be negligible. At first, the approach appeared to work when Democratic Congressman Ed Koch, soon to be mayor of New York City, took up an initiative to cut $3.1 million slated for the National Guard from the security assistance budget. To appease the Americans, Somoza feigned acquiescence by lifting state a siege, releasing some political prisoners, and freeing up the press. He did not have much to worry about at that moment; the National Guard had decimated the Sandinistas in its latest counterguerrilla offensive and killed FSLN leader Carlos Fonseca. After proposing even stiffer conditions than Congress had proposed, then contradictorily defending Somoza, the Administration released the military aid. This early skirmish cast the die, and as NSC Latin American advisor Robert Pastor recounts, "Small and rather haphazard decisions in Washington...blew down on Nicaragua like a hurricane."[36]

In fact, a policy tug of war between factions in the White House, the foreign affairs bureaucracy, and Congress, abetted by nongovernmental groups such as the Catholic Church and magnified by the media, would ensure that Washington remained deeply schizophrenic about Nicaragua. The Carter Administration was itself divided from the start. Secretary of State Cyrus Vance, supported by officials such as Deputy Secretary Warren Christopher and Assistant Secretary for Human Rights Patricia Derian, tended to advocate liberal positions that were conciliatory and sought a third way in foreign policy. Their orientation reflected the President's own deeply held commitment to morality and principle in foreign policy, which included his belief that the many U.S. invasions and occupations over the last century in Latin America were a "stain on the nation's character."[37] It was to prove much easier to denounce human rights violations in Nicaragua and declare a policy of nonintervention than it was to actually try to deal with the situation. Remaining true to these principles meant trying to convince a head of state to resign, while being reluctant to pressure him to do so. It also meant adhering to multilateralism, even if doing so greatly complicated matters and led to stalemate or worse. To set out unilaterally to rearrange the politics of Nicaragua would have violated the intentions of the new foreign policy, reviving an undesired role of protector and saddling the United States with responsibility for ensuring that the outcome worked. More forceful means of getting rid of Somoza such as coup plotting were entirely out of the question. In contrast, National Security Advisor Zbigniew Brzezinski was a more traditional Cold Warrior, and his more hard line positions regularly made him odd-man out in the White House, at least until the consequences of U.S. reversals began to accumulate toward the end of Carter's

Administration. His proposals for more aggressive action that focused exclusively on preventing Nicaragua from becoming another Cuba did not prevail.

The Administration, fully supported by Congressional liberals, became determined to have Somoza replaced during 1978, but again adherence to principles limited the courses of action it was willing to pursue when Somoza dug in and refused to go. An almost equally strong group of conservatives in Congress, led by two House Democrats, Jack Murphy and Charlie Wilson, believed that the United States should not abandon its stalwart anticommunist ally Somoza and served as drags on effective action from the opposite position. At one point, they ginned up a letter to the President to that effect, which 100 members of Congress, including Speaker Jim Wright, signed. Murphy and Somoza had become friends when they both attended La Salle Military Academy and West Point, and Murphy remained loyal to the extent that he was present at Somoza's side when U.S. Ambassador Lawrence Pezullo first came to tell him it was time to go, much to the Ambassador's surprise. Both congressmen gave the Administration pause at various junctures, Murphy by using his position as House Merchant Marine Committee Chairman to threaten Panama Canal legislation, and Wilson by using his position on the House Appropriations Committee to hold foreign aid bills hostage. (Wilson was to become better known when he turned his romantic anticommunist affections to the Mujahedin and the CIA after the Soviet invasion of Afghanistan.[38])

Public reaction also had its effect. Most importantly, the June 1979 cold-blooded execution of ABC correspondent Bill Stewart, filmed and broadcast on the evening news, caused instant and universal revulsion. The incident turned Nicaragua overnight from a foreign policy issue into, "one that evoked the deepest and angriest emotions in the American body politic [and]...quieted the thunder from the right."[39] An early example of the CNN effect, it also reinforced the timidity of the Administration as the Vietnam syndrome kicked in.

The combination of this fractured configuration in the government and blind dedication to principles produced strategic confusion in Washington. The consequence was failure of "change management" in Nicaragua, which in turn permitted the various other protagonists to continue their politics by means of war. The ideal time for a political-diplomatic effort to ease Somoza out would have been in 1977, when United States disavowals had encouraged the emergence of a moderate and nonviolent opposition. At that point, most Nicaraguan opposition leaders were extremely wary of the then-weak Sandinistas and were virtually begging the United States to help them form a coalition. It was only as violence increased in 1978 and the situation developed from tension into crisis that the Administration engaged. The strategy at first remained limited to quiet diplomacy and "constructive engagement." Somoza quickly detected that Carter was trying to get rid of him, which merely deepened his determination to hold on to power. By the fall of 1978, when crisis had fully developed into emergency during the September FSLN offensive, the United States did launch a complicated, prolonged, and agonizing initiative involving OAS-sanctioned multilateral mediation between Somoza and an opposition umbrella group, the Broad Opposition Front (FAO). The objectives were to get Somoza to relinquish power and allow a transition to a moderate government that would exclude or at least restrict the Sandinistas. None of the parties was eager or had much of an incentive to negotiate, and the effort died in early February 1979 after nearly 6 difficult months. In the end, U.S.-led diplomacy had the opposite effect from intended and merely, "served as a resting place on the road to revolution."[40] Somoza frustrated all efforts to convince him to go by making cosmetic gestures, such as a promising to step down and then deliberating endlessly over a plebiscite, but in reality he simply remained obdurate. The fractious FAO that had galvanized around the initiative splintered when it found itself left with no choices but to acquiesce or radicalize. Most of its members then adhered to FSLN, which took full advantage of the collapse in diplomacy to regain the initiative. Internationally too, regional countries intensified their opposition to Somoza, and drew closer to the FSLN with less regard for the consequences than they would have had the United States remained in the lead.

Only after mediation ended did Carter decide to impose sanctions, terminating all military assistance, cutting economic aid, withdrawing the Peace Corps, and drawing down the Embassy. However, hesitation to take stronger measures left the decision on whether to stay or go up to Somoza, while the U.S. disassociation from him further eroded Somoza's legitimacy without altering his regime's behavior. The real if unintended impact came several months later when the military aid cut left the National Guard weakened for the final showdown with the FSLN. The Administration had foresworn intervention on moral grounds, assuming that this rectitude pleased the Latin Americans. This was not necessarily the case, and within Nicaragua many moderates would have welcomed it. As a frustrated Alfonso Robelo, one of the most prominent opposition leaders who later aligned with the FSLN, explained it, "First the U.S. came and told everyone they would pressure Somoza to go. They created false expectations. When Somoza's reaction was to say, 'Come and [remove me] physically,' they backed down."[41] Virtually everyone in Latin America—including the Cubans and the FSLN—fully expected that the United States would use its power eventually to remove such a troublesome dictator who owed his existence to Uncle Sam. Many would have protested the principle, but most would have been relieved at the outcome.

The one thing President Carter was not going to contemplate, however, was unilateral American intervention, either to remove Somoza or to forestall a Sandinista victory. Ironically, the closest the United States did come to taking military action during the entire period was not in Nicaragua itself, but against presumptive allies. By September 1978, the Latin American leaders who were the most committed to seeing Somoza gone, Perez, Torrijos, and Carazo, were frustrated that the United States was not being more decisive. They cooked up a plan to provoke the Administration into action by placing Venezuelan Air Force planes in San Jose and letting the United States know they planned to bomb Managua. The gambit definitely woke up the White House, which put U.S. Southern Command in Panama on alert, weighed deployment of the Air Force to intercept any air strikes, and began a round of crisis phone calls to their counterparts. Torrijos, doing his mercurial best to play the Americans, pointedly told him, "President Carter, you have a great deal of prestige on this continent; there is nothing you can't solve if you work on it."[42] Carter promised the United States would get more involved, and, insisting on nonintervention, won agreement from Perez and Torrijos to contain the conflict to Nicaragua. The ultimately futile diplomatic initiative that lasted until February 1979 began shortly after.

Once the Sandinista offensive seriously heated up in June, crisis meetings of the Policy Review Committee, the SCC, and other high-level discussions on Nicaragua accumulated rapidly. The ambivalence and inertia that had seized the Administration after mediation collapsed in February shifted to fear of the domestic and international implications of a Cuban-backed revolutionary takeover. After the OAS rebuffed the U.S. proposal to send in a multilateral peacekeeping force, and it was clear that the Latin Americans were concentrating on ushering the Sandinistas in, Brzezinski attempted to convince the President that military intervention was necessary. He argued, "We have to demonstrate that we are still the decisive force in determining political outcomes in Central America and that we will not permit others to intervene."[43] It was a modern rendition of the Roosevelt Corollary to the Monroe Doctrine, with containment as rationale and honor joining fear as underlying motives. Carter, joined by Secretary of State Vance and Secretary of Defense Harold Brown, refused to consider it and opted instead to try and craft a transition strategy using only U.S. political influence. In such exceptional circumstances, the principled notion that a simple presumption of U.S. power would suffice without actually being prepared to use it was a serious lapse that left the field to those who felt no such constraints. Diplomacy could only accomplish so much in the absence of adequate positive or negative incentives among participants, and, despite periods of intense negotiations, this was certainly the case in Nicaragua between September 1978 and July 1979.

U.S. military views at the command level accorded with President Carter's and Defense Secretary Brown's. No one was dusting off counterinsurgency manuals, and there was absolutely no appetite for reviving the Vietnam nightmare by sending U.S. troops to Nicaragua, or anywhere else in the Third World for that matter. Concern about a Castroite takeover was hardly absent, but the extrinsic national security interests at stake hardly merited distraction from the main show against the Soviets in Europe to which the U.S. Armed Forces had returned. From a U.S. military perspective, the moral sensibilities and complexities of finding a middle way that drove the broader Washington deliberations did not figure. As the Joint Chiefs of Staff representative put it in a meeting of the White House SCC, the issue reduced to a simple choice of: "Which is worse Somoza or the Sandinistas?"[44] Nicaragua was a Cold War battleground, and policy hinged on this either/or choice, but the means for addressing the challenge should stop short of getting the United States involved in actual fighting.

This did not mean that the U.S. military was uninvolved in Nicaragua. On the contrary, they were integral to the U.S. role in Nicaragua's civil war in multiple ways. It was very clear which side the antagonists were on. Because the National Guard had remained closely intertwined with the United States since the days of its formation under tutelage of the Marines, the Sandinistas greatly feared U.S. military intervention to defend Somoza, and with good reason. The United States was Somoza's patron and ally, a relationship that an anticommunist ethos had underpinned since the outbreak of the Cold War. A more formal structure followed the Cuban revolution, with the signing of the U.S. instigated hemispheric security pact, the Rio Treaty, in 1961, and formation of CONDECA for the mutual defense of Central America. One standard exercise featured scenarios to repel an invasion of Nicaragua by Cuban sponsored guerrillas. It was to his fellow commanders in CONDECA from El Salvador and Guatemala that Somoza made his vain midnight appeal for assistance as he was about to flee the country after that scenario became a reality. Had the United States given them the green-light, then the story of the Nicaraguan rebellion would have been different.

President Somoza was a West Pointer. He spoke and acted like, and essentially considered himself an American Army officer. For him, the U.S. military was the real power. U.S. Southern Command (SOUTHCOM), then headquartered in Panama adjacent to the Canal, was America's military overseer in the region, and in December 1978 when the SOUTHCOM Commander, Army General Dennis McAuliffe, asked for an urgent meeting, Somoza responded immediately as if he had received an order. The United States was in the midst of its mediation effort, and McAuliffe accompanied Special Envoy William Bowdler to Managua to tell Somoza on behalf of the Joint Chiefs of Staff that, "peace will not come to Nicaragua until you remove yourself from the presidency and the scene." Somoza, who taped the conversation, claimed that the message "burned" into his mind. However, he did not accept that he was being kicked off the U.S. team, but rather concluded that Jimmy Carter was using the General in a devious scheme of "extreme intervention."[45]

The rest of the Nicaraguan National Guard regarded itself as a close cousin of the Army. Virtually all officers were thoroughly oriented to the United States through training, contacts, and careful cultivation, with anticommunism the ineluctable coin of the realm. One effect of the suspension of U.S. military assistance in 1977 was an almost immediate deterioration of these long-standing ties. As the FSLN offensive burgeoned into full-blown insurrection in July 1979, the Administration correctly perceived that the National Guard was the only barrier to a Sandinista victory. Increasingly desperate U.S. preoccupations narrowed to casting for a way to preserve the National Guard by recruiting officers who might shepherd a post-Somoza transition. By then, lack of access to potential candidates and a means to influence them complicated this extremely delicate if not very sophisticated exercise in military politics. Somoza, who as might be imagined, had experience neutralizing coup plots, was not pleased. When the U.S. military attaché, whose sympathies were with the National Guard, set out under instructions to canvass officers about possibilities after Somoza was gone, the officers immediately reported back through his son Tachito. Somoza put an end to it by calling Army Chief of Staff Edward "Shy" Meyer to complain that U.S. Ambassador Pezullo was trying to get him killed. The Administration was completely mistaken in the belief that the Guard could still be vested with legitimacy. It was far too late. The realization that the United States had lost altogether its ability to decide outcomes in Nicaragua came with difficulty. Somoza and his high command were preparing to leave for Miami on July 17, when Ambassador Pezullo presented him with a list of six officers the United States would consider acceptable commanders. Somoza chose one. Like the scenario for the transition as a whole, this handover was a fantasy. The Sandinistas simply dismissed the effort as another attempt to preserve Somocismo without Somoza. The National Guard, undefeated, collapsed as thousands of offices and men fled in a dramatic rush to the Honduran border or on commandeered boats from the Pacific port of San Juan del Sur to El Salvador.

The U.S. failure to manage change in Nicaragua contributed to the "insolvency" of Carter's foreign policy.[46] The policy failed on two counts: It achieved neither its positive aims of advancing human rights and finding a middle way, nor its negative aims of preventing the FSLN from seizing power and containing Cuban and Soviet influence in Central America. Although the Sandinista victory did not directly affect the global balance of power, this first significant reversal in Latin America in over 20 years added to the sense of America in decline by accumulating with other mishaps, including the fall of the Shah and the hostage crisis in Iran, along with Soviet advances in the Third World that culminated in its invasion of Afghanistan. These mishaps tended to overshadow significant successes that included peace between Egypt and Israel, the normalization of relations with China, the Carter Doctrine that established a U.S. military commitment to defending the Persian Gulf, and the Panama Canal Treaty.

The Carter Administration's misadventures in Nicaragua were also symptomatic of more general problems and dilemmas that redundantly feature when the United States tries to come to grip with revolution and irregular war. Although Nicaragua was not a military disaster like Vietnam, it was a misfortune of war that resulted from an aggregation of failures to learn, to anticipate, and to adapt.[47] These lapses deserve explanation. The claim that the Administration was distracted by other world events may be true, but it is not an adequate justification. In Central America where the United States was after all predominant, the problem was not lack of power, but lack of competence. The first U.S. deficiency lay in failing to understand the nature of revolutionary war and therefore failing to conceive of effective ways to deal with the challenges that emerged in time to do anything about them. The second major deficiency lay in failing to counterbalance adherence to principles with reality, and then in not recognizing or taking responsibility for the consequences. This was the critique, most eloquently expressed in Jeane Kirkpatrick's article "Dictatorships and Double Standards,"[48] that exercised the Reagan Administration, at least until it fell victim to its own ideological excess, also in Nicaragua, just a few years later. By condemning Somoza without having an idea of what might replace him, the Carter Administration promoted regime change just as certainly as if the United States had intervened militarily, except that it yielded control over subsequent events.

There was an element of self-deception at the heart of this incompetence. These were also failures to 'know the enemy and know yourself,' to which could be added, 'know your allies.' Somoza's fall was a lesson in the dangers of delinking from an ally, however despicably authoritarian, without having a viable plan for transition and an alternative that does not result in a loss of control. Somoza was "our son-of-a-bitch"; it was a formulation that had held for 45 years. This made it easy for him to manipulate us, difficult for us to see beyond him, and in the end to do anything beyond trying to convince him to go. As Robert Pastor recounts, it was not until July 7, just 10 days before Somoza fled and 12 days before the Sandinistas took over, that Washington recognized the military balance had shifted against the National Guard.[49] By this time, Somoza was on his way out and the United States was struggling to preserve the National Guard, it was far too late. One particularly effective action the United States did take was the arms embargo. Unfortunately, it cut supplies to Somoza, but had no effect on supplies to Sandinistas. Politically, when the United States abandoned Somoza it undercut his legitimacy and the legitimacy of his armed opposition correspondingly rose.

The Cold War in Central America was no fantasy that could be wished away by good intentions. President Carter could reverse standards of U.S. behavior on principle by unilaterally choosing not to intervene. However, this did not mean that the other protagonists at the hard end of the Cold War and revolution, where politics and force had always gone hand-in-hand, were prepared to do the same. Somoza and the Sandinistas had been fighting a long and dirty war. The insurgency may have been weak, but it was also serious. For the Nicaraguans who believed that Marxism–Leninism was the only hope for the future and gave their lives willingly for that cause, their ideology was like a religion. Somoza and the National Guard who killed to excise the communist cancer from Nicaragua and then found themselves fighting for survival were no less committed. Take your pick, whether it was fighting against gringo imperialism or defending the free world, the United States was part of the mix from the beginning. It is no wonder that hapless diplomacy was the result when the United States jumped into the vortex assuming that there was a moderate, negotiable way to transfer power and maintain the status quo in the middle of a war. This merely combined poor timing with nonexistent leverage and vastly overestimated the power of the United States to determine outcomes.

The approach that the United States took toward Nicaragua in 1979 was essentially the same as the equally fruitless efforts to find a middle way during the Mexican and Russian Revolutions. There are also echoes of the debate between liberals and conservatives that first erupted over "who lost China?" following the undoubtedly prudent U.S. decision not to intervene in the Chinese Civil War. When it became apparent that moderation was not going to work in Nicaragua, the Carter Administration attempted to follow two contradictory polices by trying to accommodate the inevitable Sandinista victory while at the same time trying to prevent them from coming to power. Before Ronald Reagan arrived in 1981 to turn up the heat in Central America, the Carter Administration had another chance to get it right, this time in El Salvador which was already on fire even as the flames of revolution engulfed Nicaragua.

Matagalpa Nicaragua, 1978. Muchachos await a National Guard counterattack. Susan Meiselas/Magnum Photos.

Masaya, Nicaragua. 1979. National Guardsmen trapped on the main street. Susan Meiselas/Magnum Photos.

Jinotepe, Managua. 1979. Body of National Guardsman, killed during insurrection, being burned with the official state portrait of President Somoza. Susan Meiselas/ Magnum Photos.

Managua, Nicaragua. July 20, 1979. Sandinistas enter the central plaza to celebrate their victory. Susan Meiselas/Magnum Photos.

San Salvador, El Salvador. 1979. Members of the Junta of the Revolutionary Government. (L–R) Mario Andino, Col. Jaime Abdul Gutierrez, Guillermo Ungo, Col. Adolfo Majano, Ramon Mayorga Quiroz. Susan Meiselas/Magnum Photos.

San Salvador, El Salvador. 1981. "Tiempos de Locura." Susan Meiselas/Magnum Photos.

San Vicente, El Salvador. 1981. Peasant guerrillas train in the countryside. Susan Meiselas/Magnum Photos.

El Salvador. 1983. Extreme rightist ARENA leader Roberto D'Aubuisson. Copyright Harry Mattison.

San Salvador, El Salvador. Ambassador Deane Hinton in the U.S. embassy. Copyright Harry Mattison.

San Salvador, El Salvador. A voter dips his finger in indelible ink after voting in the 1984 presidential elections. Copyright Tom Johnson.

La Palma, El Salvador. 1984. FMLN delegates speak at peace meeting called by President Duarte. (L–R) Facundo Guardado, FPL; Guillermo Ungo, FDR; Ferman Cienfuegos, FARN; Ruben Zamora, FDR; Nidia Diaz, PRTC. Susan Meiselas/Magnum Photos.

Washington, DC. 1984. Salvadoran President Napoleon Duarte visits Ronald Reagan in the White House. Official U.S. photo/Library of Congress.

Managua, Nicaragua. 1985. Daniel Ortega and Fidel Castro during Ortega's inauguration as President. Susan Meiselas/Magnum Photos.

Suchitoto, El Salvador. 1985. U.S. trained and equipped Army troops operating against the FMLN stronghold on Guazapa Volcano. Jean Gaumy/Magnum Photos.

Jalapa, Nicaragua. Sandinista troops respond to a Contra attack. Susan Meiselas/ Magnum Photos.

La Rica, Nicaragua. 1990. Contra commander "Franklin" with his troops. Susan Meiselas/Magnum Photos.

Honduras. 1987. U.S. troops at support base during the Contra War. Stuart Franklin/ Magnum Photos.

5 ─────────────────────────────

Reform with Repression in El Salvador

> The sufferings which revolution entailed...were many and terrible, such
> as have occurred and always will occur as long as the nature of mankind
> remains the same....
>> —Thucydides, *History of the Peloponnesian War*

THE VORTEX

The involvement of the United States in El Salvador's civil war between 1980 and 1992
was America's deepest and most sustained foreign intervention between the
Vietnam War and the invasions of Afghanistan and Iraq following the September 11,
2001, terrorist attacks. Naturally, there are great differences among these conflicts,
but the problems and dilemmas that the United States came to face in each of them
are disturbingly similar. Setting aside for the moment dissimilarities in geography
and international context, as well as the characteristics of the adversaries and the nature
of the internal conflicts themselves, there is one outstanding distinction between the
interventions in Vietnam and the greater Middle East on the one hand and El Salvador
on the other. Whereas Lyndon Johnson had ordered combat troops into Vietnam
assuming that victory was predetermined, the U.S. failure there made direct military
deployment to El Salvador a decade later a political impossibility. That inhibition
had faded when George Bush made his intervention decisions in the early 1990s.

Common motives and justifications for all three interventions can be found in
fears of localized threats to national security from globalized aggression, desires to
defend and enlarge U.S. power and prestige, and the protection of interests declared
at the time to be vital. The military dimension of strategy was elemental to each
intervention, but the United States also found itself equally entangled in undertak-
ings that strived for political, and in essence, national transformations. Many of those

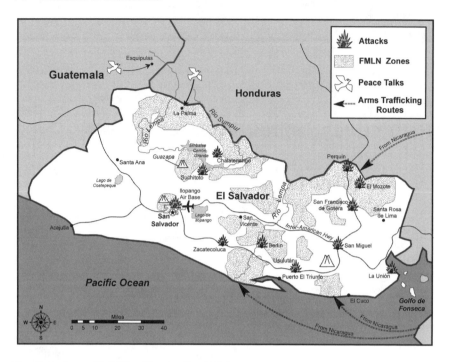

The Salvadoran Civil War. Map by Knutt Peterson.

who have had roles in the most recent interventions participated in the earlier ones, although the lessons construed by experience among neoconservatives and liberal internationalists vary widely. Domestic controversy, national ambivalence, and the problem of faction came to complicate each of them, sooner in the case of El Salvador, later in the cases of Vietnam and Iraq. If the U.S. experience in El Salvador is nearly forgotten today, the principal reason is because by not using American forces its direct costs remained low. Another lesson at the dark heart of El Salvador is how in pursuing our aims, the promise of democracy collided with the terror of the Death Squads.

The Nicaraguan and Salvadoran civil wars were closely related, and there is also much to compare between them. In both countries, authoritarian military regimes had long-ruled and effectively opposed any form of serious political reform. In the late-1970s, this backward form of governance began to break down as sectors of the population agitated for change, but found revolution to be their only recourse in the face of obdurate repression. The United Sates, after giving these regimes relatively unquestioning support in the name of anticommunism for decades, withdrew that support beginning in 1977 under the human rights policies of the Carter Administration without promoting any alternative, and thus abetted the sudden evolution of radical opposition movements. In El Salvador, the July 1979 victory of the Sandinistas next door gave an enormous inspirational and material boost to the revolutionary organizations that were burgeoning there. The Farabundo Martí National Liberation Front (FMLN) was essentially an analog to the FSLN. Augustín Farabundo Martí fought with Augusto Sandino in Nicaragua, and like Sandino he died a martyr. Both organizations originated by breaking away from more conservative communist parties and spent years as factionalized groups that posed little threat, until they unified with the advice and assistance of Cuba. The FMLN also attempted to capitalize on widespread popular unrest by repeating the FSLN's strategy of popular armed insurrection. Despite these similarities, the outcome in El Salvador, instead of a rapid evolution from civil disturbance to insurrection to overthrow, was a brutal guerrilla war that ground into stalemate and ended in negotiation more than a decade later.

The story of El Salvador's civil war differs from Nicaragua's in more than duration; it is much more complex and involved on multiple levels. The how's and why's of these differences stem equally from the history and courses of action chosen by its major protagonists—the FMLN, the Salvadoran Government, and the United States—and bear important lessons about the nature of irregular warfare and intervention. Nicaragua was not only an inspiration to El Salvador's revolutionary left; Somoza's downfall terrified the military and the conservative right that traditionally had dominated national government, and jolted the United States into ensuring that it would not repeat the mistakes that had led to the loss of Nicaragua. Few countries would have seemed a more peripheral target for U.S. intervention than tiny El Salvador. Certainly no one when the U.S. Government began worrying seriously about El Salvador in 1979 would have predicted how prolonged, difficult, and at moments central it would become. When U.S. representatives stepped into the vortex of El Salvador's civil war it may have seemed possible, given the great disparity in power, simply to take charge. Rather it was the United States that became associated with El Salvador's own dark and violent history, and became complicit in it. Far from Washington wielding determining influence, let alone force, it was interaction between the two nations in contest with their adversary, the FMLN and its allies, that determined the course of events.

Historical and sociocultural factors are critical to understanding. El Salvador may have been a small and poor country with a semimodernized agricultural economy and a primitive authoritarian government, but it was no mere banana republic. It was a full-fledged nation-state, where leaders and the people alike were deeply imbued with nationalism; possessed deeply ingrained practices, norms, and institutions; and were more likely to resist than to comply with external pressures. A salient feature of national life was (and is) the Salvadoran culture of violence. Although such statistics are always subject to debate, the murder rate traditionally was in the in the 100 per 100,000 range, placing El Salvador at the extreme high end globally.[1] Some attribute this violence to population density, which is the highest in Latin America, at over 600 per square mile in a country of 6 million, famously the size of Massachusetts. Others claim that the country's extreme violence originated with social and economic repression. It is common for Salvadorans themselves to explain congenially that they are, after all, descendants of the pre-Colombian *Pipiles,* fierce warrior-traders who migrated south from Mexico and brought with them the blood cult shared with their close relations, the Aztecs.

Whatever the reason, El Salvador's propensity for violence predated the 1979–1992 civil war, just as its particularly virulent version of anticommunism was not a product of U.S. Cold War influence. Both are tied to one traumatic and bloody historic event, *La Matanza,* the massacre of 1932. In that year, the Salvadoran Communist Party under the leadership of Farabundo Martí secretly organized a mass revolt that the government thwarted by indiscriminately slaughtering between 8,000 and 30,000 peasants and workers.[2] El Salvador's dictator at the time was General Maximiliano Martínez Hernández, a highly autocratic mystic and admirer of fascism whose idiosyncrasies included filling the street lights of San Salvador with colored water to protect the city from a small pox epidemic. By ordering and supervising the 1932 massacre, El Salvador's elites became beholden to him for "saving the country from communism." The Salvadorans were also proud that their effectiveness allowed them to demonstrate to the United States and other powers, whose gunboats had arrived outside the port of Acajutla at news of the rebellion that, unlike Haiti, the Dominican Republic, Cuba, and especially Nicaragua, there was no need for foreign intervention. Martínez used *La Matanza* to consolidate his rule, but also unlike Nicaragua, he was El Salvador's last personal caudillo when he was removed from office in 1944. What he left behind was an enduring project of government that political scientist William Stanley called "the protection racket state."[3] Essentially a form of despotic militarism, under the terms of the protection racket state, the Armed Forces of El Salvador (ESAF) controlled political life, ran the government, and kept order on behalf of the small oligarchy, known generically at the "Fourteen Families," whose wealth was founded on coffee, cotton, sugar, and unchanging exploitation of the largely *campesino* population. The military functioned as a large repressive apparatus; it was divided into the Army that was nominally in charge of national defense, and the security forces, consisting of the National Police and the Treasury Police that controlled the cities, along with the National Guard that kept order in the countryside, often brutally, by manning small detachments among rural villages and plantations. Their *modus operandi* consisted of a simple formula: maintain authority through physical presence and the threat of force, use an intelligence networks to identify "subversives," and eliminate them. In exchange for their services, the Salvadoran officer corps received status as a ruling caste outside of the law with access to economic benefits corresponding to rank. Each graduating class from the military academy formed a *tanda,* "a sort of West Point Protective Association gone berserk,"[4] in which officers swore loyalty to each other and advanced together without regard to professional competence, a practice that would become a critical liability when it came time to fight a real war. Tension between the military and economic elites often pervaded this reactionary system. Beginning in 1948, in cycles of about 10 years, presidents who had come to power by coup or manipulated elections and junior officers who identified themselves as the "*Juventud Militar,*" the Military Youth, would get the idea that they should develop some independent political legitimacy among the population and open the regime by announcing reforms such as expansion of social services, land reform, and state-led economic modernization. Inevitably, conservative factions within the military would conspire with members of the oligarchy to suffocate the movement. The paranoid lesson of 1932 was that reform—or any social change—threatened violent revolt behind which communists lurked. Like other misruled regimes, this rigidity was a curse that provoked its own instability, set the stage for revolution, and ultimately aroused the furies of war.

THE SEASON OF MADNESS

Where the Nicaraguan insurrection under Sandinista leadership had spread suddenly like a brushfire after years of burning slowly, in El Salvador, the movement deepened and grew for a decade until civil disturbance exploded onto the streets in the late-1970s. By mid-1979, El Salvador was on fire. This was the beginning of the *"tiempos de locura,"*[5] the season of madness between 1979 and 1981 when the nation disintegrated into violence and instability, and the grueling civil war that was to last for another 12 years began. For over a year, a burgeoning epidemic of popular opposition—sure enough with radical revolutionaries behind it—had spread throughout much of the country, and especially in the capital San Salvador. Universities and even high schools, labor unions, peasant organizations, and political parties, joined by much of the Catholic Church, all became centers for increasingly open and extreme demands for change.

The Salvadoran revolution had its formal origin in 1970 when a small group broke away from the lethargic pro-Soviet Communist Party to form the Popular Liberation Front (FPL). The military openly stole national elections in 1972 and 1977, delegitimizing the electoral process and driving many participants into more radical opposition. Catholic priests and catechists, primarily Jesuits who had adopted Liberation Theology, formed tacit alliances with Marxist–Leninists and politicized primarily rural communities to struggle for "social justice" against determined enmity. Four, and ultimately five guerrilla groups formed, each with a corresponding mass organization of students, workers, and *campesinos*. The July 1979 Sandinista revolution was a major ideological and material catalyst for the movement. By that time, the largest of the mass organizations, the Popular Revolutionary Bloc—aligned with the FPL—was able to sponsor demonstrations that brought as many as 100,000 people into the streets.

The conservative government, led by General Humberto Romero, a cavalry officer who owed his imposition in 1977 as President as much as anything else to the fact that he was an expert rider popular with members of the oligarchy, responded with habitual repression, including a Law for the Defense and Guarantee of Public Order that suspended the pretense of due process and prohibited all forms of opposition. Troops frequently confronted demonstrators in the streets, broke politically motivated strikes, and arbitrarily arrested and sometimes murdered activists who did not take refuge in clandestinity. Violence in the countryside was equally fierce, where the purpose of the National Guard, supported by ORDEN (spanish for "order"), a paramilitary auxiliary, was to eliminate anyone who appeared to threaten stability. It was during this period that the shadowy Death Squads, with names like Mano Blanco (White Hand) and the Maximiliano Martínez Hernández Brigade, named after the author of the Matanza, emerged.[6] And whereas the massacres of 1932 had taken days, the killings persisted, rising and falling with political currents throughout years of warfare. The Death Squads consisted of small groups linked to the security forces and associated with a growing ultrarightist political movement. They worked in secret, using lists of names typically drawn from denunciations to select their victims, seizing them during curfew hours, torturing them, and leaving their bodies in grisly tableaus at the entrance of San Salvador's barrios, along the roadsides, or in more remote dumping grounds. Their purpose was to eliminate thousands of suspected communists, most of them young males, and in the process intimidate the population with terror. This violence, which had neither proportion nor limit to the extent that it seemed irrational, did have deadly effect. But it also incited ever-greater disobedience, and with the Sandinista-led insurrection as inspiration, popular mobilization and revolutionary pressures grew until they threatened to overwhelm the government.

Out of this building chaos, on October 15, 1979, a newly revived *Juventud Militar* stepped in to overthrow the hapless Romero. The coup installed a military–civilian Junta and brought moderate and leftist political representatives, including some communists, into the government to break the power of the Fourteen Families and launch a reform agenda that would *quitar banderas,* literally "steal flags" from the left. But as terrified as they were that they could end up dispossessed like their Nicaraguan counterparts, the Salvadoran officer corps was deeply factionalized over this reformist strategy and the ESAF proved to be a poor institution to manage a serious transformation. To its conservative mainstream, the inclusion of representatives from the far-left was an intolerable sharing of power with their archenemies, and even the presence of moderate Social and Christian Democrats was suspect. The junta was able to initiate reforms of the banking and agroexport sectors, and it expropriated large landholdings from the oligarchy. Kidnappings and violence had already driven many of them to Miami and other locales, from where some of them began to organize the nucleus of a new extreme rightist political movement and finance the Death Squads. Beyond that the government was stymied.

Had the coup occurred 1 year earlier, perhaps it would have quelled the burgeoning insurrection, but by the time the reformists acted much of the radical left was firmly committed to armed revolt. The popular organizations and labor unions associated with revolutionary factions regularly seized factories, schools, and churches and shut San Salvador down several times with general strikes and street protests. In January 1980, the mass organizations celebrated their unification with a demonstration that numbered as many as 200,000. Neither could the reformists halt the predations of the security forces and the right, which claimed among its victims the Attorney General, several leaders of the *Juventud Militar,* and hundreds of members of the political parties that had actually joined the government. The ferocity of political killings attributed to state-linked forces in fact jumped immediately after the coup and reached nearly 2,000 per month by October 1980. Several infamous incidents sparked national and international outrage and contributed directly to the deepening of the civil war. In March 1980, a right wing sniper assassinated the outspoken "voice of the people" Archbishop Oscar Romero while he was saying mass; his martyrdom brought tens of thousands of shocked Salvadorans to the central plaza in front of the National Cathedral for his funeral where security forces fired on the crowd and in the ensuring panic dozens died.[7] The Salvadoran church, itself deeply divided, would play no role in mediation as it had in Nicaragua. In November, the Maximiliano Martínez Hernández Brigade supported by several hundred security force troops, seized the six prominent leaders of the FDR from the Jesuit High School where they were about to speak, and later left them to be found tortured and murdered. The FDR had just been formed as a coalition of nonarmed leftist organizations, and the assassinations effectively terminated any possibility of negotiations between the government and the opposition.

Throughout this period, a parallel structure of conservative officers from the *tanda* of 1963, with close ties to the extreme right, emerged to take control the high command and effectively prevent the *Juventud Militar* and the new government from consolidating their power. Within a year, they had cleverly engineered the dismantling of two successive juntas, resignations had stripped the cabinet of its center-left personalities, and the reformist officers had ceased to be a factor. As had occurred with these cycles in the past, the government resumed its conservative character as the military resiliently preserved their institution and the essence of the protection racket state. Except that this time it was different. With the regime remaining extremely shaky and the revolutionary movement growing, throughout 1980, anarchy appeared to threaten. The Christian Democrat Party (PDC) after its left-wing members split off to join the opposition, cast its lot in a pact with the military and remained in the government. The extreme right was well-represented within the Armed Forces, in several private sector organizations, and in an ultranationalist political movement, the Broad National Front, made up of military officers, businessmen, and other self-styled super patriots that was then coalescing in Guatemala. They bitterly opposed the arrangement, but for the first time found themselves on the outside. Coup plotting persisted right through 1980 and from time to time after that, but a majority of the senior officers acquiesced to the reformist strategy, which they recognized was needed to prevent revolution and in any case did not directly challenge their own interests. The PDC stayed to head the civilian government in tenuous alliance with the Armed Forces, reforms went fitfully ahead, and there was talk of elections even as the violence continued without abating. Before his murder, Archbishop Romero denounced the approach as "reform with repression."

El Salvador's descent into civil war was deep, prolonged, and extremely bloody. The extreme right and the extreme left mirrored each other, and although revolution and counterrevolution gave the killing and destruction its logic, the violence, especially during this period of madness often seemed irrationally divorced from its political purpose. Sure enough, there was plenty of fighting typical to guerrilla war—military sweeps, ambushes and counterambushes, bombings sabotage of infrastructure, and at times regular combat. But state terror was at the core of the dysfunction; intentionally targeting civilians, even if they were suspect, was a highly corrosive weapon that spread indiscriminate death, destruction, recrimination, and revenge. The left was more discriminating: Its assassinations numbered perhaps one for every ten of the security forces, usually described as "*ajusticiamento*" or "execution with justification." Nevertheless, the impact was to bring society itself to the fringe of anarchy as suspicion and insecurity born of violence became a way of life, and grief injured nearly every household of rich and poor alike. The population was at once shocked and inured, yet remained enormously resilient. It is difficult to grasp exactly what took place. Perhaps a fitting analogy is the impact of the September 11, 2001, terrorist attacks on the United States, but with violence repeated without warning or relief throughout the country. There is little doubt that the impact of the internal conflict was a universal process. As Thucydides tells of the Peloponnesian War:

> The sufferings which revolution entailed upon the cities were many and terrible, such as have occurred and always will occur as long as the nature of mankind remains the same; though in a severer or milder form, and varying in their symptoms, according to the variety of the particular cases. In peace and prosperity states and individuals have better sentiments, because they do not find themselves suddenly confronted with imperious necessities; but war takes away the easy supply of daily wants and so proves a rough master that brings most men's character to a level with their fortunes.[8]

The breakdown of moral and political norms, of social order itself, is a universal consequence of civil war. The longer the conflict persists and the more it approaches "total war," the greater the corrosion. The phenomenon is analogous at the strategic level to one of Clausewitz's most insightful concepts, that of friction, the "unseen all-pervading element" that makes every action in military operations, even the simplest, difficult.[9] Corrosion affects all of those who are a part of it, not only victims, but perpetrators and their allies alike. In a prolonged and total civil war like El Salvador's, only great resilience and perseverance can resist and overcome this corrosion.

It was into this "Manichean struggle completely alien to members of a secure and tolerant society" that the United States stepped in the summer of 1979 with its own fears and interests, and its own sense of propriety.[10] The Sandinista victory in Nicaragua had jolted the Carter Administration into a determination not to lose another Central American country to the communists. The decision to defend El Salvador from radical revolution was nothing less than a full-fledged reversal in which the human rights principles that had led the United States to distance itself from repressive regimes became secondary to national security and the containment objectives of the Cold War. El Salvador had attracted some prior U.S. criticism over specific human rights violations and in the new Annual Human Rights Report to Congress. This disapprobation had the principal effect of prompting the government to join Guatemala, Argentina, and Brazil in rejecting military aid in 1977. On the ground, despite a consequential reduction in military and intelligence presence, the U.S. Ambassador had in effect continued to support the regime's right to respond to armed subversion by cracking down. Fresh from the Nicaragua debacle, two U.S. delegations, one headed by Assistant Secretary Vaky and the other by Special Envoy Bowdler, paid urgent visits to El Salvador. Both were appalled that Romero's reactionary violence was leading him unawares directly down Somoza's path. They attempted without success to shoulder him onto an election track.[11]

THE JOINT VENTURE

The October coup came as a welcome event. Even though the Embassy did not play a direct role, it knew about the coup in advance, and the abrupt change of government became a crossroads that also marked the advent of U.S. intervention.[12] There had been nothing like it since Vietnam. The United States interfered deeply in the affairs of El Salvador for the next 12 years, but the basic terms of that involvement were established during this initial phase. It was a triumph for National Security Advisor Brzezinski's view of the world, that the Soviet invasion of Afghanistan in December 1979 reinforced. It was also a hard bullet for the Carter Administration to bite. After attempting so diligently to sustain a principled foreign policy that dissociated the United States from authoritarian regimes and unilateral interventions of the past, suddenly, for the sake of national security, the Carter Administration found itself compelled into complicity with a grotesquely murderous ally at its worst moment of crisis. To intervene was not to abandon principle altogether, on the contrary, but it proved one thing to proclaim a policy that placed human rights at the center of America's international concerns and entirely another to try and do something about it directly. The new Salvadoran Government ushered in attractive and conforming promises of reform and democracy. The strategy of stealing flags from the left had the pragmatic advantages of offering an alternative to Marxist–Leninist revolution as well as a potential way of stemming the violence. After a bit of hesitation, the Administration associated itself with the reformist project, and in the process took up halting human rights violations as its central cause, not only because state-sponsored terrorism was morally wrong, but because it was counterproductive. An outspoken Ambassador, Robert White, replaced the incumbent claiming no less of an objective than turning El Salvador's dirty war into a "clean counterinsurgency war."[13] Accordingly, the American project consisted of supporting reforms that would reduce the appeal of the left and build the government's legitimacy, reducing official violence by compelling the government to reign in the security forces, fending off coup attempts from the right, and building the political center by isolating radicals on both extremes. These goals amounted to nothing less revolutionary than transforming El Salvador itself. Three Administrations sustained the profound degree of material and political commitment that this ambition required. However, given the corrosive nature of the conflict, the resilience of the protection racket state, and the constraints placed on U.S. strategy, intervention also aggravated the war, the challenges remained severe, and the accomplishments were never exactly those intended. The loss of Nicaragua and a return to the Cold War in Central America answers the question of how

United States became so alarmed about such a small place. The question that super-seded it was: If the United States had the power to shape the world, why was it so hard to shape tiny El Salvador?

The commitment trap that the United States encountered in El Salvador was a foreign policy staple in propping up questionable allies throughout the Cold War.[14] It vexes the Bush Administration in Iraq today, and goes to the heart of the dilemmas and complexities of intervention in internal conflict. The Administration did not determine the conditions under which it reversed course and became the Sal-vadoran Government's ally during the final period of Carter's presidency. Unlike the reactive ambivalence that had doomed efforts to manage Nicaragua's transition from Somoza to futility, this time there would be no negotiations with the revolutionary opposition, no multilateral initiatives, no arms embargo, and no hesitation to inter-vene. The guiding assumption in El Salvador was that the armed left may have been a building danger, but did it not have the power to take over even if the government was extremely rickety. Therefore, the central problem of fighting a "clean" counter-insurgency focused inward on the problems of halting the counterproductive violence of the state while at the same time stabilizing the government. From the beginning, these objectives were frequently at odds, and struggling to resolve them involved the United States deeply in the politics of the Salvadoran military. The Administration had ended up in Nicaragua grasping at the straw of maintaining the National Guard only to watch it collapse as the Sandinistas rode into Managua. In El Salvador, the first order of business was to guard the unity of the Armed Forces. This was a cautious and fundamental bottom line that the United States and the Salvadoran high command shared. To achieve this end, the United States began its involvement by acquiescing as a cadre of conservative senior officers maneuvered the leaders of the October 15 coup out of position and reconsolidated their con-trol.[15] Unreserved support for human rights and reform would have required risky defense of junta President Col. Adolfo Majano and his fellow members of the *Juven-tud Militar,* who aspired naively and tardily to an arrangement with the revolutionary left. Instead, the Americans' new partner became Defense Minister Gen. Guillermo Garcia, who was neither a warfighter nor a strongman, but rather presided as the ESAF's senior military politician. Garcia, the commanders of the three security forces, and the rest of the high command collaborated to purge the reformists through transfers to outlying units, exile, a few murders, and finally in December 1980, by arranging a vote among officers that went 302 to 4 against Majano. They then unified behind a traditional set of priorities whereby defending the institution was their central purpose and fighting insurgents—their way—came second. Despite coup threats from ultrarightists who were seeded throughout the officer corps and lukewarm support for civilian government, the Salvadoran Armed Forces remained stable through three leadership transitions, respecting the arrangement with their American partners while a maintaining modified version of their protection racket until they peacefully and definitively withdrew from politics in 1992.

The concrete leverage that the United States would exercise over El Salvador derived from the promise and provision of economic and security assistance.

Through much of early 1980, as revolutionary agitation and violence built, the Carter Administration agonized over whether to resume military aid. The Pentagon and some in the State Department argued for full reinstatement. In the end, the White House put a tentative toe in the water by sending 300 Salvadoran officers to Panama for human rights training and won approval from Congress, despite the misgivings of liberal Democrats, to reprogram $5.7 million in aid limited to "nonlethal" items such as trucks and radios. Helicopters were promised. The argument was that in exchange for this backing, the Salvadoran military would support the reform program and forebear violating human rights.

The approach was a partial success. Many of the career officials involved in making and implementing policy had served in Vietnam, including in the CORDS Program, and they had learned there the fundamental irregular warfare lesson of the primacy of politics. The strategy implemented in 1980 set the stage for El Salvador's transition to democracy and remained in place for the next 12 years. It resulted in relative stability for the postcoup government, definitively ended the traditional military alliance with the oligarchy, opened the political system, and began the long process of building the democratic center. It was the United States that brokered the arrangement that brought the moderate PDC into government in a March 1980 pact with the ESAF. There were reasons for mutual suspicion, and it remained a shaky association that required constant American bolstering. The PDC was an authentic democratic party, but many on the right considered the PDC crypto communists, labeling them, 'watermelons: green (for the party colors) on the outside and red on the inside.' In El Salvador, this meant in effect that they were targets, and hundreds of PDC stalwarts died at the hands of both extremes. Jose Napoleon Duarte was a popular, although by no means universally loved PDC leader, and when he became Provisional President of the junta under the pact and later won the 1984 Presidential elections, he came to symbolize the democratic change in the system. His past made him a semimartyr. In 1972, the military had stolen the Presidency from him when it appeared that he had won national elections in coalition with two leftist parties. After he unwisely called for popular support of an attempted pro-democracy coup that had already failed, they had him arrested, beaten, and exiled to Venezuela. Nevertheless, when he returned to join the civil–military junta, Duarte held to his conviction that no change could come to El Salvador without the support of the Armed Forces. Enough moderate officers quietly supported Duarte or at least tolerated the PDC, believing that their presence in the government was necessary to prevent a leftist victory and keep U.S. aid flowing.

The same measure of accomplishment during this initial period of intervention cannot be claimed for the other U.S. objective, that of restraining state-linked violence. On this score, the leverage that was supposed to derive from the promise of U.S. support simply had no effect. Political killings attributed to Death Squads and the security forces remained incessant, and worse, came to include U.S. citizens among its victims. On December 2, 1980, a National Guard patrol abducted, raped, and murdered four American churchwomen from the Maryknoll order who they suspected of being guerrilla sympathizers. On January 3, 1981, two soldiers acting as hitmen under the direction of two rightist military officers and a businessman, shot dead the PDC head of the Salvadoran land reform and two American representatives from the major labor organization (AFL–CIO) who were dining with him in their hotel restaurant. As with the 1979 shooting of the ABC correspondent in Nicaragua, the murders of U.S. citizens made the conflict real for Americans, whereas thousands of Salvadorans had died only in the abstract. These two incidents, and particularly the "nuns' case," became public outrages that made the decision to support the government all the more embarrassing for the Carter Administration. The cases also starkly revealed what it was that limited U.S. influence over its ally. The nuns' case convinced a deeply affected Ambassador White that the Salvadoran military was beyond redemption. In possession of incriminating evidence, if not proof, he denounced the murders and threatened to cut off aid. Washington, however, was not prepared to take such a drastic step and instead urged the government to undertake a thorough investigation in cooperation with the FBI. The civilian government agreed, but the feeble judicial system lacked both integrity and security, as a series of judges and investigators were suborned or intimidated from their duties. The military, from Minister of Defense Garcia on down, staunchly defended the impunity that its members had always enjoyed by stonewalling. It was only through years of persistent U.S. pressure that the investigations made even slight progress.

The dynamics that arose over the issue of violence established the basic pattern of the relationship between the United States and the ESAF as a whole. Unlike Somoza and his National Guard, the Salvadoran military had never derived its legitimacy from U.S. approval, and had responded to Carter's "betrayal" over human rights by angrily rejecting aid. Officers were suspicious of the Administration, not beholden to it, and they understood perfectly from the beginning that the sudden U.S. interest in El Salvador stemmed from national security and not human rights concerns. They rested confident in their own priorities and methods, knowing that the United States was not about to risk a split with the Armed Forces much less abandon El Salvador to the communists. This was the crux of the American dilemma. As Bill Stanley observes, "When U.S. policy coincided with the interests of the high command, it was successful; where interests clashed, it failed."[16]

If the five decades of relations between the United States and the Somoza dynasty in Nicaragua fitted a traditional patron–client model, the more complex relationship that developed between the United States and El Salvador could be characterized as a joint venture.[17] For 12 years, between 1980 and 1992, the two countries maintained a strategic alliance that brought the United States deeply into the internal affairs of El Salvador for the specific purpose of preventing the spread of communism. Like allies everywhere, each acted on behalf of their own fears, honor, and interests, and each contributed assets and shared risks according to their respective strengths, weaknesses, and disparate but overlapping realms of power. The political scope of the joint venture, including its possibilities and constraints, was defined in 1980 under the Carter Administration, and remained in effect despite serious flaws and setbacks throughout the civil war during the tenures of Presidents Reagan and Bush I. The outline of the military relationship was also established, although the controversial policy reversal to support the Salvadoran Armed Forces while continuing to denounce their violent excesses did not amount to a coherent counterinsurgency strategy. Significantly it was President Carter who authorized sending arms in January 1981 as Ronald Reagan was about to take office.[18] Unhindered by official U.S. admonitions and encouraged by the promises of unhindered assistance they were receiving from the Reagan camp, the ESAF continued its own strategy of trying to eliminate its opposition through state terrorism and indiscriminate force. While reforms had stolen its flags and repression had suppressed open public support, the revolutionary left remained armed, dangerous, and determined to overthrow the government.

ANOTHER WAY OUT

El Salvador surely was among the nation-states in the latter half of the twentieth century that deserved a revolution. Whatever the dismal socioeconomic inequities and the external influence of Cuba, the Soviet Union, and Nicaragua, it was the outmoded, rigid, and authoritarian government that brought instability on itself. Radical Marxist–Leninists were certainly not the only ones who believed in the need for change, but they possessed the language of revolution, and they were the ones who were willing to take the extreme measures needed to find another way out. The structure and origins of the Salvadoran revolutionary movement were in this sense analogous to their FSLN cousins in Nicaragua. However, the trajectory of the FMLN was more complex and violent. When they attempted to replicate the success of the Sandinista insurrection in January 1981, their strategic pattern veered onto an entirely different course than they had intended. Transformed into a tough and proficient guerrilla army dedicated to prolonged peoples war, they nevertheless could not discover a strategic solution to the problem of decisive force.

The development and organization of El Salvador's revolutionary movement followed a classic path. Communist organizing and Marxism–Leninism were central influences on its formation, but these were by no means the only factors. Religion, and particularly Catholic liberation theology, as well as direct experience of repression and social injustices were equally important. A shared belief in the illegitimacy of the government and the need to replace it by force united the radical left's various leaders and supporters, but the problem of faction hindered unity of effort from the time the FPL first broke away from the Salvadoran Communist Party to take up arms in 1970. Tens years later, five distinct revolutionary groups, each with their own guerrilla and mass organizations, were competing, at times violently, over leadership, ideology, and the relative importance of political versus military strategy. The five factions achieved a major advance when they formed the FMLN in 1980. Collaboration was shaky in the beginning and each retained their individual identity, but coordination grew more effective. The FMLN General Command retained overall authority that lasted throughout the remainder of the war. Each of the groups had several layers of clandestine structure, both rural and urban, and in the initial phase, its corresponding mass organization. The FDR was the FMLN's companion political umbrella. After the assassination of its original leaders, the FDR found itself reduced to three small center-left parties, the Social Democratic Party, National Revolutionary Movement, and Popular Social Christian Movement, and it became little more than a façade for sustaining international legitimacy.

To briefly summarize the FMLN alphabet, the oldest and largest of the factions, the FPL, was originally dedicated to prolonged popular warfare and had organized base areas in the relatively remote northern departments of Chalatenango and Cabañas. The only senior comandante who had been alive during the 1932 massacre and was not a middle class university student was FPL leader Cayetano Carpio, a Communist baker who liked to refer to himself as the "Ho Chi Minh of El Salvador."[19] Carpio caused a scandal within the FMLN and among his Sandinista hosts in 1983 when he murdered Ana Maria Montes, his second in command who had disputed his inflexible orthodoxy, and then committed suicide. Disillusioned young PDC members formed the Peoples' Revolutionary Army (ERP) following the 1972 electoral fraud. Operating principally from the mountains of Morazán Department in Eastern El Salvador, the ERP came to emphasize militarism over ideology, followed the FSLN *Tercerista* faction in pushing for armed insurrection, and ended up becoming the most powerful guerrilla faction under Joaquin Villalobos, first among equals of the FMLN *comandantes*. The Armed Forces of National Resistance (FARN) broke away from the ERP in 1975 after Villalobos and other leaders accused Roque Dalton, prominent poet of the revolution who wanted to be Ché, of being a CIA spy and had him executed. The FARN was known for its kidnappings, but was also the most amenable to negotiations. After its original leader Ernesto Jovel disappeared in a suspicious plane crash, the FARN rejoined a tense alliance with the ERP and other guerrilla factions. The smallest and most obscure of the factions was the Central American Workers' Revolutionary Party (PRTC). It also splintered from the ERP over its preference for region-wide revolution. The last group, the Armed Forces of Liberation (FAL), formed in 1980 when the Communist Party (PCS) decided it had to become part of the armed movement or be left behind. Its leader, Shafik Handal, was a dedicated, hardline communist who provided a valuable conduit to the Soviet Union and, until his death in 2006, used his superior political skills to dominate the FMLN after it became a political party in the 1992 settlement.

The three principal breeding grounds for the revolution were the universities, labor organizations, and the Catholic Church. Coalitions of students, rural and urban laborers, and professional groups, as well as the political parties of the left, formed the coalitions of popular organizations linked to the guerrilla factions that mounted strikes and mass demonstrations, at least until repression took hold. Eventually, most of the public and private sector unions, as well as peasant and agricultural workers' organizations, became bases of political agitation under radical leftist control or influence. The National University in San Salvador was the entire movement's coordinating center until the National Guard violently shut it down in mid-1980.

Ideological, religious, and ethnic motivations are elemental to irregular wars. If winning legitimacy is a key strategic objective, then it becomes critical to understand how these factors, along with others such as cultural identity and socioeconomic status, are interwoven and influence the loyalties—the "hearts and minds"—of a population. Religion was a central feature of El Salvador's ideological civil war, to a greater degree than it was in Nicaragua, although ethnicity was not a significant factor as it was, for example, in neighboring Guatemala. The "religious awakening" that brought a significant element of the Catholic Church into a tacit and in certain cases specific alliance with the left was central to the intellectual formation and mobilization of the revolutionary movement. Archbishop Romero was by no means a political activist, but the violence of the regime was his particular abhorrence and social justice was his cause. These were the consistent themes of his widely disseminated weekly homilies, and in his role as voice of the people—then their martyr—he influenced millions of Salvadorans with a moral message that was in implicit sympathy with the left. The Jesuit-run University of Central America in San Salvador provided sophisticated intellectual underpinning for the revolutionary left, as well as a clandestine sanctuary, especially for the FPL. Proponents of liberation theology, again with Jesuits prominent among them, applied their linkage of spiritual well-being with social activism on behalf of the poor to raise political consciousness among *campesino* villagers throughout the countryside. Overlapping networks of covert guerrilla collaborators and politicized catechists mobilized tens of thousands of peasants who became the rank and file of the guerrilla armies and their supporters. They joined a Marxist–Leninist insurgency, but most remained Catholics who understood revolution in the language of religion.[20]

Religion became both an agent and a victim of the civil war's corrosion. In fundamentally Catholic El Salvador, the extreme right concluded that the church, which was in fact deeply divided, had reversed its traditional conservative role and was supporting the communists. They responded by targeting priests, nuns, the Archbishop himself, and anyone associated with the left wing of the church. Their attempt to portray religion as the enemy of nationalism was crystal clear in a 1977 leaflet from the White Warrior's Union Death Squad: "Be a patriot! Kill a priest!"[21]

As was the case in Nicaragua, Clausewitz's "moral forces" were a determining factor in the long and grueling Salvadoran civil war. This was especially true for the dynamic relationship between politics, religion, and revolutionary violence. Although in principle political beliefs are malleable and reversible in ways that religious conviction (or ethnicity) is not, the assumption that ideology is somehow "softer" than religion can be misleading. Late in the struggle when FMLN leaders knew they could not win and were positioning themselves for negotiations, ERP commander Joaquin Villalobos began to emphasize that the insurgency was not a religious movement and therefore was less inclined to fanaticism.[22] Prior to arriving at this conclusion, however, the FMLN relied on both religious fervor and ideological firmness to justify its violent methods and to sustain dedication to the war as a whole. At the social level, Marxist–Leninist ideology and its global mythology of revolution blended with Catholic faith and liberation theology to cement the insurgency together. At the individual level, ideological conversion can be as powerful and as deeply ingrained as religion. Certainly this was true for the tens of thousands of Salvadorans who sustained the insurgency for over a decade in spite of loss, hardship, and failing odds, not to mention the Salvadoran youths who believed that revolution was the only hope for the future and gave their lives willingly for that cause.

Throughout the war, support for the insurgency was widespread. The FMLN could count on perhaps 14,000 guerilla fighters at the highpoint of their capacity in the early 1980s, and another 50,000 active militia and mass supporters.[23] Sympathizers were present in all fourteen of El Salvador's departments, but tended to be more prevalent in the remoter North and East, along with significant populations in the central departments of Usulután and San Vicente, as well as the poor barrios of San Salvador. They were much sparser, and there were virtually no permanent operational bases, in Western El Salvador where the impact of La Matanza 50 years early had been the strongest. Even in highly organized areas, revolution was not the choice of the majority. Many Salvadorans openly opposed the FMLN or supported them only when convenient or coerced. Many others, perhaps a quarter of the population, fled to safer areas, most importantly the land of promises, the United States.

Until 1979, the Salvadoran insurgent groups were largely limited to petty terrorism—kidnappings, assassinations, extortion, bombings, bank robbery—intended to draw attention to their cause, gather funds, and attack their enemies: the Salvadoran regime and its patrons in the oligarchy. The armed left also used terrorism, but it was never a primary method, and they went to extensive lengths to discriminate and justify violence against civilian targets. Their guidebook was *Fundamentos Económicos de la Burguesía Salvadoreña,*[24] also known as "the kidnappers' guide to El Salvador." The book documented the kin structure and businesses of the so-called Fourteen Families, and established the rationale for appropriating their wealth and attacking their political control. Although the early insurgent groups did target the security forces who they considered directly responsible for repression, until 1978, they avoided attacking the Army in the belief that the *Juventud Militar* was an ally. Among their most prominent assassination targets were moderates and reformers, for example, Mauricio Borgonovo, a Foreign Minister from a wealthy family who was widely considered to be politically enlightened, and later, dozens of PDC mayors and other civil officials who courageously took office in small embattled towns. This violence of the left mirrored the violence of the right in these early days, and the progressive elimination of the moderate center was increasing the polarization of Salvadoran society.

The season of madness from 1979 to 1981 was as critical to the Salvadoran revolutionary movement as it was to the government. Prior to that time, in their formative phase, the guerrilla organizations suffered from a strategic political–military dilemma. While rural strongholds and several undemarcated pockets along the border with Honduras offered relative sanctuary, the lack of arms and organization inhibited them from undertaking major military operations; at the same time, small-scale attacks by urban commandos exposed their mass organizations to devastating reprisals.[25] The three successive juntas that followed the October 1979 coup neither controlled the repression nor offered a peaceful alternative, which would not in any case have seriously interested the radical left even if negotiations had been feasible. The guerrilla organizations' preferred way out was a mass insurrection, culminating with the Final Offensive of January 1981. This was not, however, entirely a strategy of choice, and rather than the victorious overthrow of the Salvadoran Government, the unintended consequence of the FMLN's course of action was the long and bloody continuation of the civil war. The situation that came to a head during the final months of 1980 and into the New Year was also a crossroads between the internal conflict and the international dimension. These were the waning days of the Carter Administration when American influence helped keep the government together, albeit with serious antagonisms over reform with repression, and the approval of security assistance had yet to have a material impact. The extreme right celebrated Ronald Reagan's election in November and the Death Squads worked overtime as the government waited what they assumed would be unrestricted military support. But the impact on the left would be far different.

Revolution had had a long dry spell since Cuba in 1959, and the Sandinista victory in Nicaragua spawned great expectations for the overthrow of governments and the defeat of Gringo imperialism in all of Central America. In Managua, the FSLN Directorate and their advisors from the Cuban DGI moved quickly to make something concrete out of revolutionary solidarity with their Salvadoran comrades. Within days of taking power, the FSLN Minister of the Interior Tomas Borge hosted the first meetings with the FPL to discuss support for the armed struggle in El Salvador. By December 1979, Havana was brokering talks among the guerrilla factions and mobilizing external support. As he had done with the Sandinistas, Castro conditioned aid on unity. In several stages, the Salvadoran factions overcame their deep ideological differences and the blood that divided them; first, the popular organizations formed the Revolutionary Coordinator of the Masses (CRM) in early 1980, followed by formation of the FDR political front. Then the Communist Party formed its armed wing, the FAL, and joined the ERP, FARN, and FPL in the Unified Revolutionary Directorate (DRU). The organization was finally complete when the small PRTC joined the FMLN in October 1980.[26]

With the Sandinistas in power, Nicaragua's location next door made it an ideal base of operations. An arms buildup was the indispensable first order of business, and a thoroughly organized operation got underway involving Cuba as the principal source and clearing house and Nicaragua as the logistics base for transshipping arms into El Salvador by air, by sea, and overland across the Honduran border. This network was to sustain the FMLN throughout the war. Beginning in 1979, a relatively low level of arms had started flowing to the Salvadorans through the Costa Rican network left over from the Sandinista offensive, but by the time that the FMLN radio station *Radio Liberación* broadcast the call to national insurrection from Managua on December 15, 1980, an estimated 600-ton panoply of military supplies was on its way to El Salvador. Most of this materiel was the fruit of a mid 1980 shopping trip that Salvadoran Communist Party leader Shafik Handal took from Managua to Havana, then to Moscow, and with Moscow's imprimatur to its allies in Vietnam, East Germany, Czechoslovakia, Bulgaria, Hungary, and Ethiopia. The donated weapons consisted primarily of small arms and ammunition and were of Western manufacture for deniability, for example, Belgian-made FAL's left over from the

Batista days shipped from Cuba where they were replaced with Soviet offsets. During this early period, there were some sensational arms captures, including shootdowns of small planes and the interception of a semitrailer with secret compartments containing American M-16's from the Vietnam War. Subsequently, FMLN logisticians and their Nicaraguan counterparts became more adept at clandestinity, shifting primarily to sea routes, and the relatively sparse interdictions that came from great efforts on the part of the United States and Salvadoran military became a source of embarrassment for the remainder of the war. El Salvador's revolution may have grown up at home and the Soviets more fishers in troubled waters than scheming puppet masters, but assistance from Cuba and other Eastern Bloc countries was the FMLN's mainstay, and Nicaragua was the insurgency's staging ground. There were also contributions of training, funds, and other support, all via Nicaragua, from the PLO, Angola, Algeria, Vietnam, and virtually every revolutionary organization in Latin America with the exception of Peru's Shining Path.

THE "FINAL" OFFENSIVE

The FMLN developed its plan for seizing power in collaboration with and at the urging of Nicaragua and Cuba. Logically their strategy was based on the same insurrection formula that had been the path of victory for the Sandinistas. Filled with wishful triumphalism, the Salvadorans and their allies convinced each other that the wind of revolution was at their backs. In reality, two interrelated conditions, one internal and one international, made the FMLN's decision to launch their Final Offensive in January 1981 more of a reactive move than a seizing of strategic advantage. In the first place, on the urban front, time was not on their side. The presence of a reformist government in the national palace and the devastation of the popular organizations were rapidly draining the "social energy" necessary to mount an insurrection. The death toll in 1980 was on the order of 15,000, and mass protests had subsided almost entirely during the second half of the year. Even though there were perhaps 4,000 in the guerrilla and still significant numbers of cadre and supporters ready to follow the call to rise up, the security forces and the Death Squads had ravaged the mass organizations to the point that soon there would be no survivors to lead the uprising, and state terror had driven much of the population away in fear. As FPL commander Facundo Guardado put it, "If we didn't go on the offensive, the military was going to finish us off."[27] In other words, repression was having its effect. The other factor that led to the Final Offensive was the election of Ronald Reagan in November 1980. Prior to that point, the Sandinistas were torn to some degree over assisting their Salvadoran colleagues. The Carter Administration had been seeking accommodation and was offering badly needed economic assistance, but tensions were growing over Nicaraguan support to the Salvadorans. Confronted with evidence of clandestine arms shipments from Nicaragua to El Salvador in October, the FSLN suspended them over howls of protest from their Salvadoran comrades. However, the calculus changed in November after Reagan's election. His promise to draw the line against communism in Central America led to the conclusion that there was nothing left to lose, and arms shipments resumed in full force after a month. The FMLN was determined to launch its insurrection in order to present President Reagan with an irreversible *fait accompli* in El Salvador when he took office in January.[28]

An assessment of the Final Offensive provides valuable insight into the interaction of political and military dimensions in irregular war. The FMLN's objectives were to defeat the Salvadoran military and overthrow the government. Their plan for insurrection followed the Nicaraguan pattern with some modifications. It consisted of three elements: a general strike combined with mass uprisings in the cities, coordinated attacks on military targets across the country, and defections from within the Salvadoran Armed Forces. Offensive actions took place for 3 weeks beginning on January 10 when the FMLN announced:

> At 5:00 this afternoon the offensive was launched. The enemy is lost; we have him surrounded. Popular justice is at hand....The General Command summons the people to set up local powers throughout the country, alternatives to the municipal authorities, and to erect barricades and provide water to the popular combatants....People of El Salvador, we have begun the national liberation. The moment has come to take to the streets....[29]

Over 500 military actions took place throughout El Salvador. The FMLN partially occupied eighty-two cities and villages, including four departmental capitals and twenty significant towns, and attacked eighty-one military posts and garrisons.[30] But government repression had already won the battle of San Salvador, and the mass uprising simply did not take place there or in any other city. Rather than turning out to help, people by and large closed their doors to the guerrilla columns that infiltrated the cities to set up roadblocks and attack government and military installations. The general strike had limited success, with only about two dozens factories closing and 20,000 public employees walking off the job. The government had prepared for the offensive well in advance by declaring a strict curfew, militarizing utilities, and other critical workplaces, and detaining or eliminating union leaders and other activists who remained within their reach. Although forced to withdraw temporarily from numerous small outposts, in general, the Army and Security Forces responded effectively. It lost no garrisons and forced guerrillas to withdraw from most urban centers within days.

Among the FMLN's most egregious miscalculations was its expectation that soldiers and officers in several key barracks, constituting perhaps one-quarter of the troops, would rebel and sow distrust and disorder among the remainder of the Armed Forces. This presumption was based on supposedly confidential contacts with sympathetic officers in the *Juventud Militar* who had been sidelined, and on the expectation that soldiers would recognize their fellow peasants and workers in the guerrilla represented their real interests. As it was, most of the officers did not act and military intelligence detected the plots, with a single paltry exception. In the garrison of El Salvador's second city, Santa Ana, two captains killed the Second

Brigade executive officer who was in command, but were then forced to flee with their companies when the rest of the base refused to rebel. Many of the troops who initially followed with them returned to the barracks, while loyal troops hunted and summarily executed all the rest they could find. The captains and their few surviving troops made it to Morazán on the other side of the country, where the ERP made them into propaganda heroes.[31] Within the ESAF, the two rebellious officers became widely reviled as traitors and the Final Offensive itself, rather than disrupting the Armed Forces, reinforced its integrity.

In their own after action reports, FMLN leaders acknowledged that operational coordination among the five factions was tenuous and that unity of effort, let alone of command had eluded them. The Final Offensive was largely the ERP's idea; the FPL and the FAL were not entirely enthusiastic about it, the PRTC had only a few combatants, and the FARN did not participate at all. Critically, there had been virtually no political preparation for the insurrection, where it was expected that spontaneous uprisings would take place instead. Most of the urban cadre had been withdrawn from the cities and incorporated into the guerrilla forces without adequate training or arms. In other terms, consolidation of the FMLN triangle failed and they were unable to break the critical links among the Salvadoran Government, the military, and the people. As Mexican author Gabriel Zaid concludes it was the "abstainers," the vast majority of the population that did not necessarily side with the government and definitely did not side with the guerrillas, but feared the violence of both that truly determined the misfortunate outcome of the insurrection.[32] Guerrilla commanders concluded that rather than having the wind at their backs, they had missed the wave by at least 1 year.[33]

The Final Offensive was a political failure and therefore a strategic defeat for the FMLN. However, it was not a decisive military disaster. In this sense, its impact was the opposite of that experienced by the National Liberation Front in Vietnam following the devastation of the Viet Cong during the 1968 Tet Offensive. The FMLN, its will to fight still intact, reassessed and adapted quickly, and the Salvadoran civil war entered its guerrilla phase. Although they would attempt another Final Offensive very much along the same lines in 1989, the FMLN would never regain political ground, and the civil war would largely take the form of a confrontation between two armed forces. For the remaining 12 years, as the two sides struck terrible blows at each other, the FMLN would resist and survive, but it could not win.

RONALD REAGAN AND THE PROLONGED WAR ARRIVE TOGETHER

It was not mere supposition that had led the FMLN to conclude at the end of 1980 that they had nothing left to lose. In reluctant acceptance that the Cold War was a reality, the Carter accommodation policy toward Nicaragua had collapsed, and containment had hardened in El Salvador. Ronald Reagan did not say much about Central America during the election campaign, but it was clear that a crossroads was approaching. People associated with the Reagan camp were eager to draw the line against what they saw as Soviet expansion in America's backyard, precisely in El Salvador. The problem was that those who wer[e] were also signaling that it was not going to matter much line got drawn. This was an opportunity to put the th[...] Standards" into practice, and its author Jeanne Kirkp[atrick] Senator Jesse Helms and others of a like mind wer[e] contacts on the right not to worry, that the new Ad[...] tap. Reagan seemed to side with their approach when the press, "I don't think you can turn away from som[e] they don't agree with our conception of human righ[ts] other Carter officials were decrying violations and s[...] President Duarte got a cold reception when he tra[...] with the transition team. The Salvadoran right to[...] plotting to overthrow the suspect PDC picked up their peak. Kirkpatrick, soon to be UN Ambassa[dor] "going to the source" as Secretary of State, both justification for the December 2 murder of the Kirkpatrick put it, "The nuns were not just nun[s] behalf of the Frente [FMLN–FDR]...."35

The failure of the Final Offensive decisively [...] Salvadoran civil war. Repression had effectively and any other nonclandestine resistance, the A[...] including in the USG, believed that the reb[...] staunch blow did not destroy the FMLN. A[...] increase military assistance to El Salvador, the[...] *pli,* headed for the hills. Several thousand y[...] ranks, and the conflict entered its prolonged within sight of San Salvador, in FPL-contr[...] ment, and especially in Northern Morazán ragtag forces that had overoptimistically [...] piñata party, turned themselves into the[...] America. Thousands received training in [...] that was their life blood became more s[...] sustained this relationship throughout th[...] burdens and strategy. As the war length[...] comandantes groused that they had little[...] the Cubans or the Nicaraguans, but rath[...]

El Salvador may have been a small[...] prolonged insurgency were ideal. Cour[...] Monitoring guerrillas was next to imp[...] ventional military units through mou[...] cumbersome. Major cities, including and inaccessible mountains where g[...] logistics routes. For example, Ferm[...] spent years of the war continuou[s]

immedi… rthern edge of the capital city without detection. In 1982, a
"flying … eral hundred guerrillas managed to move undetected from
Morazár… te, seize and hold the provincial center of Berlin, then after
slipping … ESAF arrived, continue to the Western part of country and
disperse … paign that lasted six weeks and covered 150 miles.

The S… rilla army that matured during the early 1980s remained a
capable a… l organization until it disbanded under the 1992 peace agreement.
ment. Eac… ILN factions retained its own structure and general areas of
operation… s predominant among them due to its military proficiency
and the fa… from Nicaragua and Cuba, but the FMLN General Command
mand pro… body for coordinating strategy, operations, and logistics.
Guerrilla f… f strategic mobile forces, select special forces, local guerrillas, militia… supporters, or the *masas*. Local guerrillas and part-time
militia gen… n their home areas to provide security, harass government
forces, and… e. The mobile forces, organized into columns, battalions,
and brigade… as many as 800 experienced, full-time troops capable of
conducting… erations throughout the country. The special forces were
small elite… Cuban-trained sappers and urban commandos who
doubled as … enior FMLN comandantes. They carried out some of
the most sp… FMLN's operations that included destroying half the
Salvadoran A… tack on its main base in San Salvador and blowing up
the two large… Lempa River that linked the eastern third of El Salvador
to the rest o… erritorial dispositions between the FMLN and the
government t… ly static throughout the war. The western quarter of
El Salvador, f… rrilla supply routes and with a generally low level of
popular supp… quiet. The remaining three-quarters of the country
remained inse… he war. The Armed Forces could operate and assume
temporary dor… e, but guerrilla territory, where the government permanently cont… sons and towns, extended to fully one-third of the
country. The F… Salvador into five main fronts and four sub-fronts,
each main fron… ple a strategic rearguard, a defensive zone, and an
expansion zone… d enter zealously defended FMLN rearguard zones,
especially in the… ntrolled areas along the Honduran border, only at
very high cost. M… fighting throughout the war amounted to a contest
for authority ov… territory in the so-called expansion zones, which
served as source… cruits for the insurgents, but which in fact never
grew much beyo… e rearguard and defensive zones (see map).

To summariz… amics of the conflict, there was a brief respite
following the fail… ffensive in early 1981. The FMLN then quickly
adopted a form o… rfare they call Prolonged Popular War, after the
Vietnamese mod… then gained the initiative roughly from mid-
1981 to mid-198… fort to liberate territory and defeat the Armed
Forces. They succ… major incursions into cities and seized several
smaller towns, b… ins was lasting. More seriously, the FMLN

inflicted major blows on the ESAF in numerous main force attacks on garrisons and counterattacks on cumbersome conventional military operations. These defeats brought the Salvadoran military to its nadir. At the end of 1983, casualties had doubled from the previous year to over 5,000, totaling one-fifth of the force structure, and it appeared to many that the Armed Forces risked collapse.[36] From that point the initiative shifted, as U.S. security assistance kicked in, allowing the ESAF to grow with the addition of new counterguerrilla units, increased firepower, and air mobility that made it relatively more effective and robust. Air power gave the military the capability to react to and disperse large concentrations, forcing guerrillas to operate in smaller units or to combine only for lighting attacks. As a result, from 1985 through 1989, the Prolonged Popular War ground into a prolonged war of attrition. During this period, the FMLN continued offensive operations, some of them extremely effective but generally on a smaller scale, and shifted to an emphasis on economic sabotage and the extensive and less costly (to them) use of mines. It was not clear to many at the time that even though the FMLN retained relatively secure territory and weapons continued flowing, attrition became a dominant strategic determinant. Despite constant and energetic recruiting, including forced conscription, the FMLN was steadily declining without hope of reversal from its high of perhaps 14,000 effectives in the early 1980s to probably fewer than 7,000 by the late 1980s. In the meantime, the Armed Forces was growing from 20,000-minus at the time of the Final Offensive to 56,000 in 1987.[37] The civil war had become a stalemate, with neither side able to defeat the other. Faced with this situation, the FMLN again opted for an insurrectional strategy and attempted a second Final Offensive in November 1989. With its failure, both sides effectively acknowledged that there was no visible military solution, and in exhaustion began the 3-year long termination phase dominated by the search for a negotiated solution.

STALEMATE

There were to be many tragedies and many up and downs during the 12 years of El Salvador's civil war. What was not evident at the time, but is now perfectly clear, is that the real prospect for revolution was over before the Final Offensive of January 1981 began. The one possible exception would have come about, probably during 1983, had the FMLN forced a collapse of the Armed Forces, but even then a bloodbath would have been the almost certain prelude to an uncertain outcome. Unlike the case in Nicaragua, the dynamics between politics, force, and foreign intervention did not break in favor of the left, and relative competence made the difference. In Nicaragua, Somoza had rigidly resisted demands for change and alienated virtually the entire society; the United States was out of step and acted ineptly. The Sandinistas gained the advantage of political legitimacy, and backed with a generous arms supply, carried off their insurrection strategy. By contrast, in El Salvador, bloody repression eliminated overt support for rebellion and a reform government with backing from the United States combined to drain legitimacy from the burgeoning revolutionary movement. Arms from Cuba and Nicaragua did not make the difference, and with the collapse of its insurrectional strategy the FMLN found its political evolution frozen. The intermediate outcome was a prolonged civil war in which the FMLN depended primarily on military action and the Salvadoran Government could not defeat the guerrillas militarily, but held the political initiative.

This devolution into a purely military contest might have worked. To put it in Maoist terms, the FMLN came very close during 1982 and 1983 to achieving the third phase of revolutionary warfare by threatening to defeat the ESAF in a sustained near-conventional offensive. The initiative ebbed, however, as the Armed Forces held and America assistance began to take effect. The FMLN eventually recognized that they had overemphasized military action and declared a new combined political–military strategy. Beginning in 1984 and lasting through 1989, the FMLN carried out a "strategic-counteroffensive" with the objectives of sabotaging the economy, expanding the war throughout the country, bringing the war to the capital, wearing down the Armed Forces through attrition, and preventing the government from establishing authority in the countryside.[38] Each of these courses of action had effect. Sabotage caused over $2 billion in damage to infrastructure, production, and investment; guerrilla actions, ranging from road blocks and destruction of agricultural facilities to ambushes and raids on military targets, took place at least at some level in all fourteen departments; urban commando activities such as bombings and assassinations increased especially in San Salvador; military casualties remained high, and several major attacks against garrisons inflicted serious blows; and as late as 1989 civil authorities were absent from half of El Salvador's municipalities. The FMLN's strategic goals were to reveal El Salvador's democratic transition as a façade for repressive counterinsurgency, erode the will of the U.S. Congress to support the war, and provoke a broad-based popular uprising to overthrow the government and seize power. This political–military offensive had one fundamental problem. It was essentially a reactive and reformulated military strategy. The FMLN was indeed a strong guerrilla army and a dedicated popular movement supported it, but popular support remained within the limits of its preexisting constituency. What the FMLN could not achieve was critical mass in constructing the political linkages of its triangle. The left did have some success joining and even instigating protests, especially among labor organizations, as democratization began to open the political environment, but most of their efforts consisted of building popular support in the conflict zones where it already had control or influence. The FMLN maintained a putatively open attitude toward negotiations with the government, but rejected participation in elections, and instead demanded "power-sharing in accord with the correlation of forces."[39]

As a result, political strategy was excessively dependent on military force, and therefore the revolution remained prisoner of the decisive force problem. Once the possibilities of both popular insurrection and military victory were off the table, the FMLN still sustained a deep belief in the legitimacy of force. At the core of their will to continue fighting was what ERP comandante Joaquin Villalobos called "the communication of violence," a conviction that the effects of their aggression would somehow translate into popular support and eventually produce revolution.

They were mistaken. The contrary was the case, and the greatest effect of prolonged warfare was corrosion. The most perceptive criticisms came not from the anticommunist propaganda of the Salvadoran Government or the United States, but from those were considered to be among the intellectual authors of the revolution itself. To the Jesuits of the University of Central America, by 1984, the FMLN had become isolated and lost touch with political reality, as reflected in this sampling from an editorial published in their journal *Estudios Centroamericanos*:

> Today...there is a great tiredness; the illusion of a rapid change in the situation has faded....Opinion polls and behavior demonstrate today a great support of the masses for a project of negotiations and show that support for insurrectional violence is very small....The growing misery is attributed more today to the war than to structural injustice, and the war is attributed more to the FMLN than to the armed forces or the United States.[40]

Ultimately, it was not ideology alone, but external support from Nicaragua and Cuba, subsidized by the Soviet Union, that sustained the FMLN long after the prospect of winning sufficient popular support for their revolutionary project within El Salvador had faded.

THE JOINT VENTURE FINDS ITS WAY

The shared goal of saving the country from their mutual communist adversaries bonded the U.S. and Salvadoran Governments together. Their joint venture was a mutual dependency, but conflicting interests, methods, and perspectives simultaneously drove them apart. At the heart of the matter, the Americans believed they needed to save the Salvadorans from the excess of their own violence. Pulling in the opposite direction, the dominant conservatives in the Salvadoran military and political right simply would have preferred to use U.S. aid to unleash the maximum violence possible, confident in their recollection that this was the best way to eliminate communist terrorism. The two partners wrestled over this central tension through each phase of the civil war, and it colored their collaboration on counterinsurgency strategy from the moment when the United States first entered the scene during the *Tiempos de Locura* until the final negotiations that concluded the war in 1992. In the end, even if the war resulted in a costly, exhausting, and victory-less stalemate, the balance of political competence that divided success from failure rested not with the FMLN and its allies, but with the Salvadoran Government and the United States.

It took a while for the Reagan Administration to find its ground on El Salvador. The country presented a most unsatisfactory dilemma in early 1981: how to prevent a communist takeover while limiting direct intervention and avoid the taint of Vietnam? The tension between aggression and caution was evident in the president's consistent reassurances that he was not going to send in U.S. troops, even as he sounded the trumpet against further Soviet advances in Central America. Secretary of State Haig's pronouncements in these early days about "going to the source" were overtly militaristic, and the eager flirtation that some administration representatives were carrying on with members of the extreme right marked a sharp contrast with Carter's approach. Rather than reluctantly dealing with an unpalatable regime, they seemed to signal unconcern with human rights and willing United States complicity with murders of U.S. citizens, not to mention thousands of Salvadorans. Congress, alarmed and driven by liberal Democrats in the House, asserted itself in reaction to mandate highly restrictive provisions on U.S. aid to El Salvador.[41] To avoid any whiff of quagmire, the threat of invoking the War Powers Act, and above all U.S. casualties, the U.S. military presence in El Salvador was arbitrarily limited to fifty-five trainers—the term "advisors" was explicitly prohibited—who were restricted from carrying weapons or accompanying Salvadoran troops in the field. No direct assistance went to the Salvadoran Security Forces. In addition, the President had to certify every 6 months that the Salvadoran Government was making progress on reforms, human rights, and the investigations into the murders of American citizens. The bluntness and inefficiency of Congress as a constitutional means to control strategy and policy turned into micromanagement on aid to El Salvador, particularly from 1981 to 1984, when the bipartisan Kissinger Commission and reasonable success promoting democracy relieved controversy and provided a fragile platform for bipartisan consensus.

The political fires were to burn only hotter when attention shifted to Contra program in Nicaragua, but the tug of war among supporters and opponents in Congress and between Congress and the Administration over El Salvador continued. Even with determined opposition from a minority and widespread skepticism, Congress acted as a brake on U.S. involvement in El Salvador, but not a barrier. Legislative constraints such as the fifty-five man limit on trainers and caps on funding levels did ensure that El Salvador would not become an "American war." Still, security assistance levels climbed from the $5 million that Carter approved before he departed in January 1981 to pass a total of $800 million, with all forms of assistance—military, economic, and covert—reaching approximately $6 billion by 1992. The House in particular often insisted on withholding specific portions of aid and keeping the level below Administration requests with the intention of pressuring the Salvadorans, especially on murder investigations. But this did not mean that Congress was going to go to the extent of taking the blame for losing a country to communism by actually cutting aid altogether. For its part, the Administration readily cut corners, for example, by reprogramming emergency aid without consultations and claiming human rights improvements when there had been none. Bitter disputes between hardliners and pragmatists split the Reagan Administration within itself. Some in the Administration, such as Undersecretary of Defense Fred Iklé, focused primarily on countering the Soviet/Cuban threat and accused Congress of giving the Salvadorans just enough to keep them from losing, but not enough to win, "...a policy always shy of success."[42] Others were more concerned that improvement in Salvadoran performance and reigning in the Death Squads was the key, not just to getting money out of Congress, but to winning the war. Caught between conflicting senses of values and interests, ideology, and institutions, these views coexisted in an uneasy tension and resulted in a policy process that often seemed a muddle within a dilemma.

In practice, the Reagan Administration reverted and then stuck to the Carter Administration formula that attempted to combine and balance the political and military dimensions of counterinsurgency. Given the complexities of the joint venture, it is no surprise that the results were mixed. The closer one was to reality on the ground, the less use there was for the distorting lens of ideology. Reagan's first Ambassador, Deane Hinton, a tough and pragmatic Cold Warrior, became convinced of the need to get the Death Squads under control. Dissatisfied with the inconsequential effects of quiet diplomacy, in October 1982, he decided to go public in a blunt speech to the powerful Salvadoran Chamber of Commerce in which he labeled the link between the Death Squads and the oligarchy a "mafia," with the indictment that, "The gorillas of this Mafia, every bit as much as the guerrillas of Morazán and Chalatenango, are destroying El Salvador."[43] Not only was the Salvadoran right incensed; the White House repudiated the speech and along with it the threat to cut aid that Hinton had included to give it some stick. One year later, however, when it still appeared that El Salvador might be lost either on the battlefield or in Congress, the Administration had enough conviction to send Vice President George H. W. Bush to tell the High Command in December 1983 that they had to halt the violence or face an aid cut off. This visit famously did have some effect; what were delicately termed "extrajudicial killings" tapered off, but no officers on the well-corroborated list of Death Squad leaders linked to the extreme right that Bush delivered were charged or cashiered from the Armed Forces. The dilemma was that the officer corps knew, even as they became dependent on U.S. assistance, that their fight was our fight. Having declared its stand against communism in El Salvador, the Administration was honor bound and would not abandon them to the FMLN. American intervention penetrated into the heart of military politics, but threats thus compromised could not surmount the ESAF wall of impunity. The issue went deeper. Neutralization of the 1979 coup reformists had not rid the Armed Forces of its own factions. There were reformists in the High Command who wanted to fight smarter or at were at least more responsive to U.S. pressures, but they had to preside over a balance of power in which the extreme right still had many partisans and wielded powerful influence.

If the Americans consistently overestimated the amount of leverage they had over the Salvadorans, there was another serious problem: It was never entirely clear just how determined the ESAF was to win, either on American terms or at all. Questions of will, differences between the Salvadoran and U.S. militaries, and the dynamics of the relationship between the two institutions folded into this ambiguity. It should be no surprise that Salvadoran adaptation to what the United States believed represented proper professionalism and counterinsurgency doctrine was selective at best. The ESAF had been fighting communism in their own way since 1932, and had not hesitated to sever their formal ties with the U.S. military in 1977 over what they considered to be the indignity of the Carter human rights policies. The institution was in many ways a typical Third World military, consisting of a small elite officer corps that commanded paternalistically over hardened core of career soldiers and a large body of peasant conscripts. All officers from the most junior recognized with some cynicism that they were defending their *patria* on behalf of the United States. The experience of being a newly significant cockpit of the Cold War rendered a material as well as patriotic sense of value. As security assistance grew, the attributes of the protection racket state transferred to receiving and distributing the benefits and privileges of being a U.S. ally in the form of enhanced power and opportunities for income. If one is looking for reasons why counterinsurgency proved so difficult in a country as tiny as El Salvador, part of the answer lies in this unintended effect of U.S. assistance, which gave the Salvadoran Armed Forces an interest in prolonging rather than terminating the war.

The war was going badly enough in 1981 that an insurgent victory seemed very possibly on the horizon. The first priority of the Reagan Administration was to reverse this trend by ameliorating the shortcomings of the Armed Forces. To this end, the "Report of the El Salvador Military Strategy Assistance Team," also known as the Woerner Report, after then-Brigadier General Fred Woerner who led the team, became the baseline for expanding, equipping, and training the Salvadoran military.[44] The Woerner Report identified how woefully prepared the ESAF was to fight against a serious insurgency. In 1981, the Armed Forces, including the Security Forces, had about 20,000 troops, fewer than twice as many as the FMLN and hopelessly below the 10:1 ratio of counterinsurgents to insurgents conventionally cited as ideal. To the extent that the Salvadorans had a strategy, it was to maintain fixed bases in population centers with small detachments guarding infrastructure and smaller settlements. The security forces operated on the principle of "identify and eliminate," erring on the side of suspicion, and engaging in small unit *gato y raton,* "cat and mouse" patrols and ambushes. As for regular force doctrine, the army spent most of its time garrison-bound and infrequently ventured into guerrilla held zones in the countryside on large, cumbersome "hammer and anvil" operations of short duration. FMLN guerrillas found these operations easy to avoid, but it was not so easy for rural populations whether sympathizers or not, who often found themselves the victims, especially when accompanied by indiscriminate aerial bombardment. Chain of command was dispersed among fourteen Departmental Commanders who typically represented the highest de facto authorities of the entire government in their operational areas, and in some cases operated essentially as war lords with consensual relations to the High Command in San Salvador. The three security force commanders each had their own troops stationed throughout the country, and there were other fiefdoms, of which the Air Force was the most important. Commanders used any number of kickback schemes, ghost soldiers, and control of transport to add to their personal incomes.

U.S. security assistance had a major impact on the ESAF. In the first place, it permitted expansion of the Armed Forces to 56,000 by the late-1980s, thus more than evening the ratios from about 1.5:1 in 1981 to 8:1 by 1987, as FMLN forces correspondingly declined. New weaponry and a frequent abundance of ammunition greatly increased firepower. The training and equipping of three Rapid Reaction

Battalions, several Hunter Battalions, and Long-Range Patrols (PRALS), and the adoption of more aggressive tactics, combined with new air support and helicopter airlift greatly increased the counterinsurgency capabilities of the Salvadoran military. U.S. intelligence support, including the Central America Joint Intelligence Team (CAJIT),[45] an innovative fusion center located in the American Embassy, greatly improved Salvadoran response capabilities. The outstanding feature of this assistance was the limitation of the direct U.S. presence, represented by the fifty-five-man ceiling on military training teams that were restricted to bases and for whom being protected from casualties was highest priority.

Assessments of "low-intensity conflict" in El Salvador conclude that U.S. assistance made it possible for the Armed Forces to persevere, but not to prevail. Most important among them are the so-called Four Colonels' Report written by four active duty Army officers in 1988, and the RAND study by Benjamin Schwartz, descriptively titled *"American Counterinsurgency Doctrine and El Salvador: The Frustrations of Reform and the Illusions of Nation Building."*[46] As the introduction to the Four Colonels' Report noted in 1988, "American involvement in El Salvador marks a milestone in the U.S. effort to devise an effective military policy in the aftermath of Vietnam....The essence of that approach has been to provide a besieged ally with weapons, ammunition, and other equipment, economic aid, intelligence support, strategic counsel, and tactical training—while preserving the principle that the war remains *theirs* to lose."[47] The Salvadoran military certainly became more proficient at combating guerrillas, but there were serious limits to the transformational influence of the United States. Even as the Salvadorans evolved, "clean counterinsurgency" never quite fit into the picture. They absorbed counterinsurgency advice selectively and controlled indiscriminate violence at their own pace and only under extreme pressure. The security forces remained relatively untouched; Death Squads continued to operate, although at reduced levels; search and destroy operations continued their generally ineffectual grind; and the officer corps stayed wedded to the *tanda* system. This is not to suggest that the Salvadoran military simply failed to absorb much of the counterinsurgency wisdom that the United States had to impart. Rather, American advice and assistance itself was an interactive aspect of irregular warfare that made the U.S. a partner on complicit with the darkest side of the Salvadoran conflict at the same time it was trying to reform how it was fought.

THE "OTHER WAR" AND LIMITS ON THE DARK SIDE

The most egregious example was the El Mozote massacre, the largest single atrocity to occur during the civil war, or anywhere in Latin America during the second half of the twentieth century. The extended rampage took place over 3 days in December 1981, when the elite Atlacatl Rapid Reaction Battalion, under the command of the Army's most effective guerilla fighter Lt. Col. Domingo Monterrosa, put their brand new U.S. training and equipment to use by torturing, raping, and executing at least 767 noncombatant men, women, and children.[48] The Atlacatl Battalion was on one of its first operations, ostensibly taking the war to the ERP in the remote mountains of Morazán Department. The villages in the area of El Mozote were known not to support the guerrillas, and in fact the Army had sent word out in advance that those gathering there would be safe. It was a wanton act of violence, disconnected from any coherent purpose, and never adequately explained. Monterrosa himself reportedly once admitted to a fellow officer that the massacre was, "A page I would have torn from my book of life."[49] Word inevitably began to seep out, first from FMLN clandestine Radio Venceremos and Tutela Legal, the church-linked Salvadoran human rights organization, and then from reports by Ray Bonner in the *New York Times,* that included photos by Susan Mieselas, and Alma Guillermoprieto in the *Washington Post* who the guerrillas escorted to the massacre site in January. Their articles made the front pages on January 26, 1981. Despite this thorough and credible documentation, the Armed Forces denied that a massacre had taken place.

The reaction in Washington was a study in the dilemmas of intervention, which author Mark Danner described as "a central parable of the Cold War" in his 1993 book on the subject.[50] The day after the story broke in the press, President Reagan certified that the Salvadoran Government was making "a concerted and significant effort to comply with internationally recognized human rights." In order to justify the certification and to forestall any effort to cut aid to El Salvador, several U.S. officials, including then-Assistant Secretary of State for Human Rights Eliot Abrams and Assistant Secretary of State for Latin America Thomas Enders cast doubt on the massacre by attributing any killings to combat with guerrillas in testimony to Congress. Liberals were incredulous. During an interrogation of Enders before the House Subcommittee on Western Hemisphere Affairs over body counts and methods of documenting what was actually taking place in El Salvador, an incensed Democratic Congressman Stephen Solarz criticized the, ". . . Orwellian tones of this certification, in that the President seems to be saying the human rights situation is getting better, when everyone else says it is getting worse." Efforts to invalidate the certification and to cut off aid did not prosper however. Confronted with the hard edges of counterinsurgency and the dark side of humanity, too much was at stake to compromise the Cold War joint venture by distinguishing between casualties and victims.

The contradictions between the fighting war and the "other war," as the Four Colonels' Report termed it, [51] were deep and systemic. U.S. Army trainers who worked with their Salvadoran counterparts carried the mixed message themselves. "*De Oppressor Liber*" read the Special Forces motto on their uniform patches, but some of the tee shirts they stripped down to during the heart of the day on the firing range read, "Kill them all and let God sort them out." This medieval ethic was one their Salvadoran pupils could more readily relate to. If some of them grasped that the essential objective of counterinsurgency was not chasing guerrillas but securing the support of the population, the lesson was generally beyond the competence of the Armed Forces as well as the government to actually implement it. Efforts to introduce counterinsurgency techniques such as psychological operations, civil defense, and civic action tended to be paternalistic, manipulative and superficial, while the presence of the EASF in the countryside was more often a source of fear rather than security. One account of a civic action program is unintentionally revealing:

Clowns, a mariachi band and skimpily clad dancers perform between speeches by Salvadoran army officers and social workers calling on peasants to reject the guerrilla. Meanwhile army barbers cut hair, and soldiers pass out rice, dresses, and medicine.... "You see the army winning heats and minds," [a U.S. advisor] says, "This is low-intensity conflict doctrine in action."[52]

Unlike in Vietnam, the United States conceived correctly the nature of the Salvadoran conflict. The strategy that it consequently adopted, while filled with contradictions and controversy, avoided the more costly errors committed in Southeast Asia. However, as the microcosm of clowns entertaining peasants illustrates, the sum of American concepts and Salvadoran methods did not necessarily add up to effective prosecution of "the other war." The National Campaign Plan, an American initiative launched in 1983, was an attempt to win popular support and regain government control over contested zones. The Plan was a coordinated civil–military initiative that called for a surge of troops in carefully selected contested zones, beginning in two departments, Usulután and San Vicente. The military would provide a shield behind which the government would demonstrate the positive material impact of siding with it. Backed by generous provision of U.S. advice and resources, Civil Defense units were to be recruited, peasant cooperatives organized, schools and clinics opened, local administration reestablished, and development projects implemented. Once secured and established, the Plan would then progress to the next department. After an initially promising start, the effort collapsed for lack of resources, coordination, follow-through, and above all will.[53] The extra battalions went elsewhere, and the concentration of resources in two departments provoked jealousies that led to redistribution of patronage nationally, thus ensuring that not enough got done anywhere. In the end, the Plan was unsustainable politically.

It would be myopic to attribute these shortcomings exclusively to Salvadoran deficiencies. The National Campaign Plan embodied a distinctly American can-do approach founded on solid accumulation of lessons learned from other counterinsurgency experiences and codified in the U.S. Army's Internal Defense and Development Doctrine, also known as Foreign Internal Defense (FID). The only problem was it would have been a stretch for even the most developed nation to carry out, let alone an underdeveloped country in the midst of a guerrilla war and political transformation.[54] The National Plan, however well-intentioned and conceived, was made in the USA and was simply beyond the scope and competence of the Salvadorans who were expected to own and implement it. Subsequent efforts on a broader scale to impose a schedule for transforming the nation drawn up in Washington, complete with creation of a Salvadoran National Commission for Reconstruction (CONARA), along with milestones and benchmarks for critical actions such as holding elections, writing a constitution, implementing land reform, privatizing state enterprises, improving tax collection, and respecting human rights, met a similar fate.

This is not to suggest that U.S. attempts to influence El Salvador in the name of counterinsurgency were entirely misguided, but rather that the important changes that did take place tended to be gradual, indirect, and often unintended. These changes are best appreciated at the strategic rather than the operational level, where both the civil war and American intervention were interactive engines of transformation. Misconceived American policy had contributed to instability in Central America in the first place, and had the falling domino of revolution in Nicaragua not threatened, the United States never would have had sufficient interest in El Salvador. If the negative aim of preventing further extension of Soviet influence in Central America had been the sole consideration, simple reinforcement of military efforts to eliminate the FMLN in El Salvador would have been the most direct course of action. As the Reagan Administration itself recognized, such an option would have been unwise and infeasible. With the Vietnam syndrome in effect, Congress constraining U.S. involvement, and the Salvadoran Government already on the verge of collapse, it became politically necessary and good counterinsurgency strategy to emphasize the positive aim of building Salvadoran democracy while limiting the direct American role. This led the United States to "ally with the devil it had to subdue" [55] and to form a joint venture in support of reform with repression.

TO ELECT GOOD MEN

The real goal became political success not military victory. It might have been preferable to defeat the FMLN, but it was not necessary; stalemate was acceptable even if it meant prolonging the war. The direct linkage of political and military dimensions in El Salvador was critical. SOUTHCOM Commander Gen. Paul Gorman and Ambassador Deane Hinton agreed that, "The purpose of U.S. military assistance to El Salvador was to protect the democratic process and give it room to grow."[56] The Kissinger Commission report, the most comprehensive statement of U.S. goals in Central America, affirmed that support for democracy was the key to achieving regional security. In El Salvador, democracy promoted "at the point of bayonets" as Mark Peceny termed it,[57] was a pragmatic, hands-on experience. Necessity had provoked the entire project. It was a gamble, and the rhetorical idealism that characterized USG pronouncements faded before the country's political realities. Earlier in the twentieth century, it had been a matter of course to organize elections with the notion of teaching the beneficiaries of U.S. interventions, "to elect good men." An entire chapter of the Marine Corps *Small Wars Manual* was dedicated to the supervision of elections.[58] International election monitoring and democracy promotion efforts are common place today, but El Salvador was to be the first country where the United States would take on such an experiment since Vietnam.

To many Americans on both the right and the left, it seemed madness when elections were scheduled for March 28, 1982, to elect a Constituent Assembly that would form a provisional government and draft a new constitution. The civil war was raging. The FMLN had recovered from the Final Offensive, was attacking the Armed Forces in large units, and U.S. assistance had only begun to have an effect. The ruling junta had barely stabilized from the 1979 coup and it remained weak in transition. But even as the military situation hung in the balance, the elections definitively transferred the political initiative from armed revolution into the democratic realm. The FMLN–FDR consistently presumed that they had taken the high ground by advocating a political solution to the war through dialogue. What they meant by this was power-sharing negotiations, an approach that had international appeal, including among liberal members of Congress who opposed U.S. policy, but no viability within El Salvador. With elections on the table, the United States and the Salvadoran government insisted that the insurgents should lay down their arms and participate in the process. It was a strategic dilemma for the FMLN. Confident in their revolutionary legitimacy and military advantage, the FMLN stuck to their frontal strategy, deciding to shoot up the elections and threaten those who went to the polls that they would "vote today, die tomorrow." If the ballot did not exactly prove to be the coffin of the revolutionary movement—the war was to continue for another 10 years through five national elections—the critical process of garnering popular support shifted to the democratic process, except among committed supporters and what proved to be fairly limited populations who the FMLN was able to prevent from voting. Not only did El Salvador demonstrate the incompatibility of elections and revolution, the FMLN was ignoring their own forerunner, Ché Guevara, who may have been feckless as a guerrilla practitioner, but also recognized that, "Where a government has come into power through some form of popular vote, fraudulent or not, and maintains at least an appearance of constitutional legality, the guerrilla outbreak cannot be promoted, since the possibilities of peaceful struggle have not yet been exhausted."[59]

The 1982 elections were a striking success. The popular legitimacy of having the opportunity to express free choice was self-evident in the long lines at polling centers in all corners of the country, including tens of thousands of peasants who walked long distances braving hostile fire and threats from guerrillas to vote. For once, the military received praise for having provided security and refraining from interference. The phenomenon was to repeat, itself and extensive international monitoring gave successive Salvadoran elections free and fair evaluations, although there were some mars on the process. Voting was technically compulsory, the actual size of the turnout in the 1982 elections came under question, and subsequent elections saw declines. Many Salvadorans were not necessarily voting because they supported the government, nor did the elections make the country into a democracy. Rather the 1982 elections set a precedent that signaled strong popular desire to end the civil war and a broad repudiation of the armed left. Thus, democratization attacked the strategy of revolution and shifted the political center of gravity away from it. Not incidentally, those images of voting lines did more than anything to convince Congress and relieve deep public skepticism about U.S. policy, to some degree offsetting the damage of the Death Squads.

The central problem of holding elections in the midst of a civil war was not the FMLN. The radical left had in fact contributed to the relative cohesion of Salvadoran elites and society more broadly with the government, the Armed Forces, and the United States. Despite the traditional ravages of military intervention in politics, El Salvador's partisan configuration was surprisingly robust. But it was deeply polarized, and the problem of faction retarded movement toward the center while extremism risked counterproductive results. On the left, the absence of the three small parties of the FDR, serving then as the political front of the FMLN, left the field to the PDC, who were widely favored to win a majority. Although it had split over the decision to ally with the Armed Forces and remain in the junta, the PDC retained an authentic national base on the center and center-left, with junta President Napoleon Duarte as their leading figure. On the right, the former official party, the National Conciliation Party (PCN), retained a significant following despite its association with the discredited system of military rule. But it was the rapid emergence of a party on the extreme right, the National Republican Alliance (ARENA) that provided an unexpected political development as well as a potential threat to the political process itself. ARENA emerged first in 1980 as the Broad National Front from a small founding group in Guatemala. It was as a well-financed venture by members of the mostly self-exiled oligarchy, but its constituency proved to be much broader. ARENA was profoundly, almost religiously nationalistic, anticommunist, and pro-free market. The businessmen who formed its principal cadre identified strongly with the Republican Party and Ronald Reagan, but its platform and underlying ideology assumed a right to rule and an emphasis on state authority that bore greater resemblance to other corporatist parties of the right in times of instability and violence. ARENA's message was a militaristic promise to restore order and end the civil war by eliminating the communist terrorists and subversives. ARENA's founders did not need to educate the population or emulate foreign models; their historical reference point was the 1932 Matanza, and their instruments were the Death Squads and a close alliance with the Armed Forces.[60] ARENA coalesced around a charismatic leader, Roberto D'Aubuisson, a hyperkinetic former Major who was one of the few officers dismissed as a threat immediately following the October 1979 reformist coup.[61] D'Aubuisson's ties to repression and the security apparatus were deep. As one of National Guard Commander Gen. Jose 'Chele' Medrano's "three assassins," he had been closely involved with the "National Democratic Organization"—ORDEN, the paramilitary organization was thoroughly familiar with the Death Squads that had also emerged under Medrano's leadership. Later he had headed the National Agency of Special Services of El Salvador (ANSESAL), the CIA-linked intelligence organization located in the Presidency. D'Aubuisson emerged to prominence as an agitator of the several coup attempts that occurred during *Tiempos de Locura* and began making television appearances in which he used files lifted from ANSESAL to denounce "communists" by name. Many of them, including prominent PDC and church figures such as the Archbishop, subsequently turned up dead. D'Aubuisson's militarism made him appear a national savior rather than anathema to many. With D'Aubuisson's spell-binding speeches and ample financing from the business community, ARENA came from nowhere to gather votes from all walks of life in all parts of the country in the 1982 assembly elections. The PDC won a plurality of twenty-four out of sixty seats, but ARENA won nineteen, which allied to the PCN's fourteen seats, was enough to create a majority and poise D'Aubuisson to become provisional president. (Two small centrist parties won the other three seats.)

The 1982 elections were a vindication for the United States and a crossroads in El Salvador, but they required a final twist of intervention. When it appeared that the election's success was a victory for the extreme right, the bloom suddenly faded in Washington where ruling Democrats in the House threatened to cut aid if D'Aubuisson came to power. It was in these circumstances that Ambassador Hinton, aided by a visit from famous Cold Warrior, retired Gen. Vernon Walters, diverted the looming disaster by engineering the selection of Alvaro Magaña as President and the naming of a national unity government in an agreement with the High Command. Magaña was a public nonentity. However, his status as a banker who had controlled financial accounts of the Armed Forces made him acceptable to both the military and ARENA's private sector backers. D'Aubuisson had his supporters within the military, but a balance of officers recognized that the return to violence ARENA was promising offered no solution and accepted the decision. D'Aubuisson had to settle for Presidency of the National Assembly, a position from which he and his stalwarts were able to obstruct reforms and even run a Death Squad, while at the same time they began to accept the give and take of democratic practices. ARENA leaders also learned from this bitter experience that the trust they assumed they could put in the United States—even the Reagan Administration—was misplaced.[62]

By the March 25, 1984, presidential elections, the joint venture was fully in operation, and even though the war had stalemated, what could be called the experimental phase of U.S. policy had proven a relative success. Jose Napoleon Duarte's victory over Roberto D'Aubuisson by 53.6 to 46.4 percent—abetted by covert U.S. aid just to keep a thumb on the scale—validated the centrist strategy. Assembly elections 1 year later in which the PDC gained a majority marked an evolution of the democratic process from fragile transition to consolidation. Another critical transition took hold during this period as the Armed Forces began to withdraw from politics, reduce human rights violations, and to accept the democratic process. The impartial security and logistical support they gave to the elections garnered the military unaccustomed popular approval and helped define their proper role vis-à-vis the government and society. Duarte and sympathetic military reformers, in tandem with U.S. pressure, had some effect on cleaning up the security forces. A few notorious officers were sent into golden exile, Death Squads in the National Police and the Treasury Police were disbanded, and killings of civilians in 1986 declined 90 percent from their highpoint in 1981.[63] Even if the National Campaign Plan was a failure and mutual suspicion remained between soldiers and politicians, an influential coalition of officers came to recognize the logic of political liberalization as an indispensable element of counterinsurgency strategy, or at least of maintaining U.S. aid. In a series of showdowns, a small group of senior commanders, including Minister of Defense Gen. Eugenio Vides Casanova, ensured that professions of loyalty to Duarte replaced instigation of insubordination from hardliners. By the mid 1980s, the tide had turned. Even Col. Sigifredo Ochoa, an effective guerrilla fighter who had nevertheless been retired for his outspoken political agitation claimed, "The Armed Forces do not want to execute coups d'etat or return to the past. I believe the democratic system is the best system."[64]

Duarte certainly played a critical role, but he hardly got a free ride from ARENA, the military, or ironically the United States, and his Presidency was no triumph of democracy. The constraints on him came from all directions. ARENA was vituperative in opposition and did everything it could to derail legislation. Support from the Armed Forces did not extend to ending impunity for abuses, to negotiating with the guerrillas, or allowing FDR leaders to return to the political process. Likewise the United States wanted no part of negotiations, while it pressured Duarte to investigate and prosecute human rights violators and imposed economic austerity measures as the price for aid that eroded the PDC's support among the working class and contributed to a revival of huge demonstrations. The war remained mired in stalemate, and Duarte's inclinations were to end it by dealing with his former colleagues in the left and responding to the regional dialogue initiatives that had begun to spring up. Meetings with the FMLN–FDR began with a dramatic 1984 celebration in the rural hamlet of La Palma. They continued even after the FMLN kidnapped Duarte's daughter Inez in late 1985, bringing the government to a standstill for 40 days and exposing Duarte's vulnerabilities. Predictably, a total of six encounters produced nothing in the end, because both sides believed they retained the military strength to prevail and thus had no incentive to relent.

Faced with multiple pressures and unaccustomed to rule, by the time of the 1989 presidential elections, the PDC had wasted itself with infighting, incompetence, and corruption. Demoralized and alienated from its base, the party nearly disintegrated in a nasty fight over Duarte's successor candidate. The PDC's misfortunes did not translate into military advantage or political support for the FMLN, whose supposed strategy of prolonged people's war was hardly prospering outside the zones they already controlled. On the contrary, it was ARENA that benefited, but only after it had undergone a transformation of its own. With the threat of a guerrilla takeover more remote, the appeal of militaristic populism seemed less urgent, and the party began to move away from its more extreme edge although it retained its decisively right wing and anticommunist complexion. A group of relatively moderate and sophisticated businessmen who had associated with the party after its founding prevailed over the inflexibly extremist oligarchs, and selected Alfredo Cristiani over Roberto D'Aubuisson as their candidate in the 1989 elections. Cristiani beat his Christian Democrat opponent 53.8 to 36.0 percent, and ARENA took thirty seats in the Assembly, which in alliance with the PCN's seven seats, gave it a solid majority over the PDC's twenty-four. With the right firmly and legitimately in power, El Salvador was as polarized as it had ever been, but exhaustion with the civil war had set in, and the most urgent business was finding a way to end it. As long as U.S. assistance kept flowing, the Armed Forces remained oriented to fighting on, but the protection racket state had begun to seem outmoded. Finding a way out of the deadlock with the FMLN was going to be an extremely delicate task, and ARENA was to prove reasonably competent at achieving it. However, there was another chapter in the Salvadoran saga yet to go.

The Contra War

We too have seen the crossroads. . . .
                    —Nicaraguan President Daniel Ortega, 1986

THE LOWBALL OPTION

All interventions are controversial. Some are more controversial than others, and the American-backed counterrevolution by the guerrilla army known as the "Contras" against the Cuban- and Soviet-backed Sandinista Government in Nicaragua was an extreme case. The Contra War, which lasted for roughly a decade from 1980 to 1990, offers no particular enlightenment on the strategy and policy of irregular warfare. If anything, the Contra insurgency and the FSLN counterinsurgency serve in a number of ways as negative examples. This nearly forgotten small war does, however, offer valuable insights into the utility of peripheral strategies as practised through proxy war and covert action, alternative if less celebrated American ways of war.

Washington politics drove the strategic dynamics of the Contra War. There is no need to recount the epic struggle between the Reagan Administration and Democrats in the Congress that ruled the national political scene during much of the 1980s, and culminated in the Iran–Contra scandal that nearly consumed the Reagan presidency. Likewise, the unresolved competition between the so-called hardliners and pragmatists within the Administration resulted in major confusion and disagreement about the purposes of the Contra program and the importance of sustaining Congressional support. The body of literature that depicts the various dimensions of this enormously complex small war is substantial, and Robert Kagan's *Twilight Struggle* is the definitive account of this story.[1] Three overlapping motives drove U.S. intervention in Nicaragua and shaped its nature: First, the United States had a

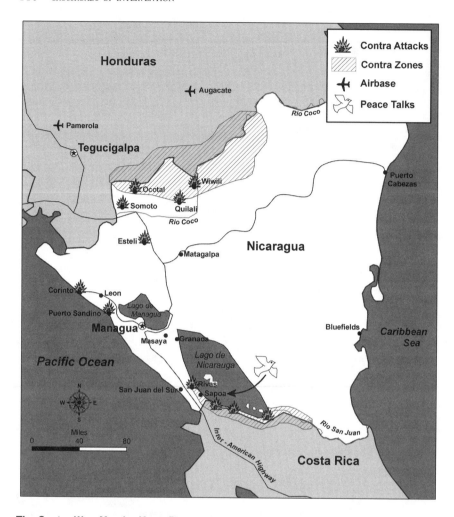

The Contra War. Map by Knutt Peterson.

propensity to intervene because it was the dominant great power in the region, the presence of hostile foreign intervention violated the Monroe Doctrine, and prior U.S. behavior in Central America, and Nicaragua in particular, set a precedent. Second, global Cold War competition with the Soviet Union provided the determining justification for intervention and established its value. Third, the etiquette of U.S.–Soviet confrontation in the Third World that inhibited escalation, combined with ambivalence about the use of force resulting directly from Vietnam, reduced the acceptable cost of U.S. intervention to a minimum, and thereby limited its nature and scope. Under other circumstances, penetration of a hostile power directly into the traditional U.S. sphere of influence would almost certainly have been considered enough of a threat to international prestige and the regional balance of power to justify much stronger direct intervention. What resulted instead was a divisive and often feckless mix of U.S. policies that combined high ideological declarations of vital interest with what was termed the "lowball option." Whatever else it may have accomplished this proxy insurgency made America a contentious belligerent in an indecisive cycle of violence that wracked Nicaragua for over a decade.

Armed resistance to the Sandinistas also had roots that pre-dated direct U.S. involvement. It was not a mercenary enterprise. In the wake of Somoza's July 1979 collapse, a remnant of the National Guard had fled into Honduras where they formed the loosely organized September 15th Legion, named after Nicaragua's Independence Day. Led by sergeants and a few officers, the 500-odd force amounted to bands of marauders who conducted small hit-and-run attacks against the Sandinistas, but in a pattern they would maintain for the rest of the war, spent most of their time in camps in the sparsely populated border region. Their natural leader was former National Guard Col. Pablo Salazar, "Comandante Bravo," who had legendary appeal because he had fought undefeated against the Sandinista's. When the FSLN managed to assassinate him in 1980, former Nicaraguan Representative on the Inter-American Defense Board in Washington, Col. Enrique Bermudez, became senior commander of the military resistance for the duration of the conflict. By 1981, various groups that rejected Sandinista rule had begun to congregate. Dispersed groups of Miskito Indians in the Caribbean region were already suffering FSLN dislocation and repression. They took up the anti-Sandinista banner along with a group of Nicaraguan exiles who formed a reluctant alliance with the ex-Guardsmen called the Nicaraguan Democratic Force (FDN). This core group of early Contras, soon joined by supporters that ranged from Miami exiles to aggrieved campesinos, formed the basis of an authentic peasant army that would come to number in the thousands. They enjoyed initial support from two sources. The Honduran security forces were concerned to do something against the threat of Sandinista aggression on their southern border, and Police Commander, and later chief of the armed forces, General Gustavo Alvarez Martinez became the Contra's local host and America's man in Honduras. Not incidentally Alvarez had attended Command and General Staff School in Argentina, and the other group assisting the Contras came from Argentine Army Intelligence Battalion 601. They were hunting Argentine revolutionaries who had fought with the Sandinistas and taken refuge in "free Nicaragua," including members of a commando unit of the Argentine Revolutionary Workers' Party who had assassinated Anastasio Somoza on September 17, 1980 in Paraguay where he had fled. It was this group of anticommunist counterrevolutionaries who had formed a nexus in Honduras to contain Sandinista aggression on which the United States was to build.[2]

The Salvadoran and Nicaraguan wars were intimately connected, and as was the case with U.S. policy in El Salvador, the origin of American opposition to the new regime in Nicaragua began not with Ronald Reagan, but with Jimmy Carter. The hardening against the Sandinistas occurred during a tense accommodation dance that lasted for over year. As the United States searched for moderates in Nicaragua it could support and held out the promise of normalized relations—explicitly including nonintervention—and a $75 million aid package, it insisted in exchange that the government halt its support for the Salvadoran FMLN and curtail its growing alliance with Cuba and the Soviet Union. It soon became painfully obvious that it was neither in the nature of the Nicaraguan revolutionaries to comply with U.S. wishes nor that those economic incentives and admonishments would suffice to change their behavior. The Sandinistas did temporarily suspend clandestine arms shipments to El Salvador prior to the November 1980 U.S. elections, but only when confronted with intelligence evidence, and they resumed them after Reagan's victory in time to prepare the FMLN for its Final Offensive. By then, the outlines of a totalitarian state were in place, and there were few moderates to be found. All non-FSLN members had been pushed from the ruling Directorate and civic opposition curtailed. The new state security apparatus had quickly replaced Somoza's National Guard with an Eastern Bloc model, and ministries had filled with Cuban, East German, and Soviet advisors. The foreshadowing of enmity came very late in the game. President Carter accepted the onus of a failed strategic rationale, admitting that "the scales fell from my eyes."[3] He embraced an older set of Cold War views and methods to contain Soviet influence, but only with great ambivalence, particularly because of his commitment to human rights and nonintervention. For Ambassador Pezullo in Managua, "The worst alternative took place, but maybe it was still a ballgame."[4] The Administration still intended to uphold goodwill by giving the $75 million in aid to Nicaragua, but had to stretch credulity by certifying to Congress that the Sandinistas were not helping Salvadoran "terrorists," only to turn around and quietly suspend the aid in January 1981 just before Reagan took office. Carter had also rediscovered covert action as a tool of American power, authorizing the ill-fated Desert One operation to rescue the Embassy hostages in Iran and initiating support for the Mujahideen to fight the Soviets in Afghanistan. In 1980, he also signed the first findings to back Nicaraguan opposition to the Sandinistas, and the CIA formed the Central American Task Force to oversee the program. U.S. support was designated for "democratic elements" and did not include paramilitary assistance to the then-nascent Contras, although some funds found their way to groups that were forming armed opposition. The program also included support to Honduran and Salvadoran security forces to interdict arms headed to insurgents in El Salvador, a purpose that would soon be used as a rationale for aiding the Contras.[5]

Contrary to legend, the Reagan Administration's approach to Nicaragua was haphazard and rived with contradictions rather than a single-minded and aggressive anticommunist pursuit. Secretary of State Haig kept up saber rattling about going to the source through most of 1981, but it became clear that such bellicosity was not going to fly. If there was strategic logic in cutting off support for revolution in Central America by blockading Cuba, neither the White House nor the Defense Department, not to mention Congress or the public, had any taste for using U.S. troops or risking confrontation with the Soviets. Neither was there any enthusiasm for taking direct action against Nicaragua. With options thus constrained, arguments that there was a deal to be had between the United States and Nicaragua would remain lodged at the heart of the policy dispute over coercion versus accommodation.

All an agreement would require was for the United States to reconcile itself to a Marxist–Leninist regime in Central America and for the Sandinistas to be pragmatic about their own interests by halting support for revolution beyond their borders and reducing their burgeoning armed forces to a level that did not threaten their neighbors. This was the essence of the approach that Assistant Secretary of State Thomas Enders took in a series of meetings with the Nicaraguan leadership between August and October 1981. The talks represented a crossroads. In the end, accommodation had insufficient appeal to hardliners on either side, and the diplomatic track between the United States and the Sandinistas that persisted for most of the decade proved fruitless.[6] It became clear to the Reagan Administration by the fall of 1981, as it had to the Carter Administration the year before, that defiant Sandinista leaders were going to require further persuasion.

The basic and lasting elements of U.S. strategy in Central America crystallized through extensive deliberation and were formalized in NSDD 17 and associated implementing decisions which President Reagan signed at the end of 1981. These included: increased economic assistance to the region, military assistance for El Salvador and Honduras, increased intelligence collection and surveillance, a public information program to build domestic support for the policy in the United States, strengthened military presence in the Caribbean, and a new plan for covert action against the Sandinistas. Despite his reputation for favoring aggressive use of U.S. power, Reagan was a cautious and reluctant war-maker. On Central America, not only did he decide that U.S. troops would not intervene directly, he even insisted that Secretary Haig talk to the Cubans first. Far from the unrestrained aggression of a superpower defending its sphere of influence, U.S. policy in Central America wended its way between the boundaries of contradictions in which belligerent anti-communism and determination not to lose El Salvador collided with restraints to direct intervention and post-Vietnam reluctance to use force. The decision to covertly arm the Contras was not the result of a thoroughly articulated and long-term plan, but rather a "lowball option" in Ender's phrase, arrived at by default. The pragmatics of U.S. politics drove the choice, and its initial advantage lay in requiring only the secret acquiescence of the two new congressional intelligence committees rather than more public deliberation. The Administration considered overtly supporting armed opposition at several stages, but doing so would have been tantamount to declaring war on Nicaragua, creating complex legal and political problems for which there was little appetite.[7] More fundamentally, if unspoken, the Contra program was like all insurgencies, a second best strategy employed in the absence of more direct and forceful alternatives. The Contras themselves were a low-cost disposal force, soldiers in a proxy war, and protagonists in a peripheral strategy of somewhat confused intent that nevertheless served global purposes.

THE CURSE OF IDEOLOGICAL FATALISM

When the Sandinistas chose a course of confrontation with the United States, they let ideology be their guide. It led them to their fate. Faced with the proposed terms of a deal, including the crucial demand to stop aiding the Salvadoran guerrillas, Daniel Ortega concluded, "We too have seen the crossroads. We have decided to defend our revolution by force of arms, even if we are crushed, and to take the war to the whole of Central America if that is the consequence. . . ."[8] In this they did not suffer much confusion, but the competence the FSLN leadership had mustered in mounting their insurrection failed them when it came to safeguarding and actually running their revolution. Given the choice of a settlement or looming hostility from the predominate superpower, nonalignment might have seemed an honorable option best in line with their own fears and interests. However, to the Nicaraguans, there was something more tangible than revolutionary confidence behind their will to defy the United States. After all, the enormous disparity in power had not prevented them form outwitting the United States and succeeding in the first place, and the constraints on U.S. policy gave them some assurance. More materially, their identity as Marxist–Leninist revolutionaries and enemies of the United States made them friends of the Eastern Bloc, and in fact the Sandinistas had made a strategic decision in 1980 to ally themselves with the Soviet Union in the belief that it was the ascending superpower and would shield and sustain them like it did Cuba.[9]

The Soviets proved to be much less enthusiastic about the prospect of adding another impoverished client to their list, but the Sandinistas were a target of opportunity and they plunged into a relationship that emphasized military assistance. Fidel Castro was much more disposed than his Soviet patron to push the long-range objective of extending revolution in Central America and to risk more in the process. At the same time, 20 years of experience had accustomed him to gambling against the United States, but he was fully aware of the strategic conditions under which Cuba survived. He urged the FSLN to pursue their socialist revolution with discretion by advising them to avoid provoking the private sector, the church, and above all, the United States.[10] Cuba also echoed Soviet caution in clarifying that their military assistance was intended only to help Nicaragua defend itself.

Molded as they were in the vision of the Cuban revolution, the Sandinistas were positively eager to align themselves politically and strategically with the Soviet Union, and certainly more eager than their prospective patrons.[11] The Sandinista triumph in 1979 came precisely when American power seemed to be at a nadir, and they believed that the "correlation of forces"—the favored term of socialist politico-strategic analysis —had brought the Soviets into a position of equal strength. Thus the Sandinista leadership was initially confident that Moscow would safeguard Nicaragua from the United States as well as assist their transition to socialism out of ideological identity. The reality was no quite so optimistic. The Nicaraguans found that the Soviets had interests of their own and would have less coming from their Russian patrons than they had expected. Nicaragua never advanced from receiving economic assistance to COMECON membership. Even as Nicaragua militarized during the Contra War and arms deliveries increased, reaching $600 million in 1986, 1950s vintage MIG 21's, promised in the first military assistance pact in 1980, were never delivered, even though Bulgaria had trained the Nicaraguan Air Force pilots and a landing field at Punta Huete built at enormous expense. When new Secretary of State George Shultz warned that introduction of MIGs would provoke a U.S. reaction, the Soviets simply rebuffed Nicaraguan request. It became clear after 1984 as Andropov and Chernenko became even more prudent and Brezhnev's aggressiveness faded, the correlation of forces had shifted once again.

The dogmatic logic of ideology made the Sandinista choice to help the Salvadorans a certainty that did not seem like much of a gamble at the time. There was no separation between their own revolution and the ones they were supporting across their borders. During this period, the Salvadoran revolutionaries formalized their close relations with the Sandinistas, In the language of their agreement, the Nicaraguans were to "adopt the Salvadoran cause as their own"[12] allowing the FMLN to establish extensive operations in Nicaragua with Cuban and Nicaraguan assistance. These included a headquarters and a logistics operation for arms supply into El Salvador by land, sea, and air. The Sandinistas provided the FMLN with their most important first tranche of arms prior to the final offensive by handing over U.S. weapons from Somoza's National Guard, that Cuba backfilled by supplying the Sandinista Army with new Eastern Bloc weapons. This arrangement remained in place for the duration of the war. By fueling the FMLN, they believed that they were being good Leninists and keeping the United States off balance next door.

Once the prospect of an arrangement with the United States hardened into armed hostility, the twin fear of Contra counterrevolution and a U.S. invasion caused "war psychosis" to seize the Sandinistas. Military logic, including a pure desire to have an Armed Force with tanks, artillery, air defense, and fighter aircraft as powerful as possible essentially took over.[13] To meet the Contra threat, they turned quickly from insurgents to counterinsurgents, and launched on a major conventional expansion to provide at least some comfort and deterrence to defend the revolution against the prospect of a U.S. invasion, with anti-imperialism as its rallying cry. The government imposed universal conscription in 1983, and by the mid-1980s the EPS had grown to about 80,000 troops, larger even than the U.S.-backed Salvadoran military, and had plans to grow to 150,000. The force was divided into two separate commands, one for counterinsurgency and one for conventional defense. Nearly 2,000 Cuban military advisors were working in Nicaragua, and in 1983, Castro sent his most experienced military advisor, Gen. Arnoldo Ochoa, to help with counterinsurgency strategy against the Contras. Ochoa did not bring with him any of the Cuban combat troops that he had recently commanded in Angola and Ethiopia, expeditions that were in principle more peripheral to Cuba than Nicaragua was. Cuban counterinsurgency assistance mirrored what the United States was providing to the Salvadorans, and included air mobile Irregular Warfare Battalions (BLIs) that conducted much of the fighting against the Contras. Bankrolling the military buildup which included tanks, antiaircraft weapons, helicopters, and MIG pilot training, although not the MIGs was the Soviet Union. Soviet security assistance peaked at $600 million in 1986 and totaled over $2 billion for the decade.[14] Much of this aid, including small arms and ammunition transshipped to the Salvadoran guerrillas, came from Cuban stocks that the Soviets then offset. The arrangement continued right up until the Sandinistas lost power in 1990. Moscow's largesse, which included fuel and other economic subsidies, it turned out was not free of charge. Nicaragua's debt when the Russians made an issue of collecting what Nicaragua owed to the old Soviet Union was calculated at nearly $4 billion.[15]

This was the fatal flaw in what Sergio Ramírez called their "ideological fatalism." "History must record that their brazen challenge to American hegemony was folly. If the Sandinistas had been sensible, they would have taken a moderate course from the beginning, especially in foreign policy."[16] However much principles or interests guided the Sandinista leadership, their chosen course of action would prove very costly. The adversary relationship with the United States and the accompanying Contra War would become an all-consuming challenge, and after nearly a decade of war, they would find themselves out of power and their revolution over in 1990.

A SMALL COALITION OF THE WILLING

American involvement with the Contras began as a small coalition of the willing in late-1981. Termed the "*Tripartita*," the CIA quickly recovered from its snake bit condition once the President had signed NSDD 17 to become the senior patron of an explicit if undocumented arrangement between the United States, Argentina, and Honduras. A full month before Reagan had approved the finding CIA Director William Casey flew to Buenos Aries to discuss coordination with Argentina's military regime, which had taken its recently concluded dirty war to distant Central America with some enthusiasm. Army Chief of Staff (and later President) Leopoldo Galtieri told him their biggest concern was whether the United States would stick with it and not abandon the Contras. Reassured, the venture got off to a solid start, with the CIA quickly standing up logistic and financial support and the Argentines in charge of training and operations. Ironically, it was Argentina that who ended up feeling betrayed when the U.S. sided with Great Britain in the 1983 Falklands/Malvinas war which put an embarrassing end to the partnership.[17] The Contras too would end up abandoned in the late-1980s when they no longer served U.S. purposes, much to the chagrin of Eliot Abrams and others who had fervently supported them.

Honduras was in an uncomfortable and complicated situation but did not have many options. The FDN was already present and had begun nascent operations into Nicaragua from the isolated and sparsely populated border region. Used to complying with U.S. wishes and vulnerable to both Sandinistas and Salvadoran guerrillas, President Policarpio Paz and General Alvarez quickly agreed to host the Contras. Initially they at least half-expected quick and decisive action from the United States to get rid of the Sandinistas. Instead, under the less ambitious terms of the lowball option Honduras would become a virtual U.S. protectorate, with Ambassador from 1981 to 1985 John Negroponte often referred to as the American Proconsul, and relations frequently strained, especially after a less pliant government took over in a 1984 coup. The United States needed Honduras to loan its territory and provide essential sanctuary for the Contras. This naturally invited FSLN incursions against the Contras, which inevitably provoked sensitive counteraccusations of crossborder aggression. In exchange for serving as the Contra support base, Honduras received greatly increased economic assistance and a de facto shield through the other critical aspect of U.S. strategy in Central America, an expanded and quasipermanent military presence in the region.

Conventional military deployments consisted principally of sustained "training exercises" in Honduras along with recurring naval maneuvers in the Caribbean. They complemented U.S. irregular warfare missions that supported counterinsurgency in El Salvador and insurgency in Nicaragua, and had multiple strategic effects. El Salvador and Honduras were ostensibly allies, and combined military coordination could have been extremely useful. However, relations remained tense as a result of the brief 1969 "Soccer War" in which El Salvador bested Honduras, and the United States was able to broker only so much cooperation. It was only begrudgingly that Honduras accepted and El Salvador sent its troops for training at U.S. bases in Honduras; the two countries rarely conducted joint operations in the several border pockets, the *bolsones,* leaving them as no man's lands that provided sanctuary for Salvadoran guerrillas throughout the war. More effectively, fear of reprisal from the U.S. military presence in Honduras did compel the Sandinista Army to carefully constrain crossborder operation against the Contras, while raising Sandinista paranoia of a U.S. invasion. Far from dreaming up offensive operations against its neighbors, the EPS sought Eastern Bloc support for a conventional buildup to help it defend against U.S. intervention. While U.S. forces constructed roads and landing strips in the border region and practiced backstopping Honduras against a tank and infantry invasion from Nicaragua, the Sandinistas exercised repelling U.S. landings on the plains outside Managua. The EPS also stockpiled weapons and ammunition, practiced mobilizing the population, and had detailed plans for the Army to disband into a guerrilla force to resist the invasion.[18] Their fears periodically took on a tangible edge. In October 1983, the United States invaded Grenada to remove the Cuban-backed New Jewel Movement from power, and in March 1988, President Reagan ordered two battalions of the 82nd Airborne to Honduras. Fear that this was prelude to direct intervention halted a major Sandinista offensive that was progressively wiping out Contra bases on the Honduran side of the border. The Joint Chiefs of Staff was never enthusiastic enough about Central America to permanently station a carrier battle fleet in the Caribbean or otherwise take steps to "seal off" Central America from Cuba as Al Haig had desired. However, recurring naval maneuvers did demonstrate American resolve and were enough to keep both Cuba and the Soviet cautious about the extent of their aid to Nicaragua and to make it clear that their intent was defensive in nature.[19] These U.S. military activities remained highly constrained relative to superpower capabilities, and none involved the direct use of force. However, they did help contain Nicaragua, ensure survival of the Contras, and guarantee respect for the limits of Cold War confrontation. At the same time, the conventional military presence in Central America did nothing to bring victory for U.S.-backed forces in the internal conflicts in El Salvador or Nicaragua. As has proved the case for America's experience with limited war at least since Korea, protraction and ambiguous results also generated great frustration. On the one hand, any hint of aggressiveness contributed to exaggerated sensitivity among liberals and moderates in Congress. On the other side, Reagan's plaintive and telling comment at a 1983 meeting that considered various military responses was, "How do we stop Castro with exercises?"[20]

The question of American purpose in supporting the Contras goes to the heart of the complexities and dilemmas of intervention and irregular warfare. Counterinsurgency, even though misapplied in Vietnam and revived only with controversy in El Salvador, is inherently defensive and stabilizing in intent. In contrast, it seemed novel, even radical in 1981 for the United States to consider using insurgencies to attack and destabilize sovereign nations. The idea entered the Reagan Administration from several sources. NSC Official Constantine Menges had written a paper in 1968 at the RAND Corporation suggesting that new Communist regimes were vulnerable to democratic insurgencies and could be used to counter Soviet advances in the Third World. Undersecretary of Defense Fred Iklé also picked up on the idea when he was at RAND, and the conservative Heritage Foundation had advocated it to put pressure on the Soviet system.[21] As a strategy, if the more orthodox U.S. support for counterinsurgency as was a tool of containment, U.S. support for insurgency harkened back to the greater aspiration of rolling back the Soviet Union with its origins in the 1950s and the Korean War. There were other precedents for CIA support to insurgencies, not all of them particularly encouraging, especially if one includes the misconceived 1961 adventure against Castro at the Bay of Pigs.

However, to the extent that the desire to stop and reverse Cuban and Soviet advances in Central America provided an overarching imperative, it is a deceptively simple one. Nothing about U.S. intervention in Central America was simple or easy, and as the experienced White House official Peter Rodman observed, "The confusion about motive was a ticking time bomb."[22] The debate that swirled endlessly, not in Central America, but in Washington, DC, more than anything else determined the nature and course of the conflict. What did the United States intend in sponsoring the Contras? Were they there to interdict arms supplies to the Salvadoran guerrillas? Were the Contras a bargaining chip in negotiations with the Sandinistas? Were they armed pressure to change Nicaraguan behavior? Was their real goal overthrow of the FSLN government? Were they a sideshow, or were they soldiers in the global struggle against communism, Freedom Fighters? Far from having a master plan as the Sandinistas feared, the Contras served all of these purposes as different factions within the Administration and between the Administration and Congress battled roughly between 1981 and 1989 over resources and control. Ronald Reagan did make a gaffe in a televised press conference on February 21, 1984 that, even if he was not out to overthrow them, he wanted to make them "say uncle."

If there was a bottom line to what the Contras actually did on the ground in Central America, it was ultimately their operational controller, the clandestine services of the CIA that defined it in terms of its own role and mission. Latin America

Division chief Dewey Clarridge put it most clearly in the plan he presented to CIA Director Casey in August 1981: (1) Take the war to Nicaragua. (2) Start killing Cubans.[23] As political leaders in the United States debated their higher purposes, this was, from the point of view of those who were designated to wield America's spear at this end of the Cold War, their lowest common denominator. It was hardly a strategy and as far from the popular model of the American way of war as one could get.

Ronald Reagan may have been guilty of hyperbole when he called the Contras "the moral equivalent of the founding fathers," but they were an authentic peasant army. They may not have thrived or even survived without U.S. sponsorship, the professional soldiers from Somoza's National Guard who led them, and sanctuary in Honduras and to a lesser extent Costa Rica. But the Contras were not mere mercenaries who fought for Uncle Sam's gold. From a few hundred who trained in the early 1980s with Argentines in Honduras and with Cuban exiles in Florida and California, their numbers swelled over several years to reach a peak of 16,000 by 1987.[24] A guerrilla army like that does not sustain itself without greater commitment; they had their own causes, both personal and philosophical, that motivated them to take up arms. They were mostly rural Nicaraguans, cattlemen and coffee growers, Miskito and Sumo Indians, Creoles from the Caribbean coast, Catholics and Protestants, members of the traditional Liberal and Conservative parties. They were diverse, divisive, and motley, but all of them had their grievances and had become disenchanted with Sandinista rule. They resented food rationing, collectivization of farmland, low fixed prices for crops, harassment of the church. Many were escaping forced recruitment into the peoples' militias. There was little toleration for political opposition in the midst of a Marxist–Leninist revolution. Whatever purposes their superpower patrons had in mind for them, one thing that united the Contras was a desire to see the Sandinistas overthrown.

As guerrillas, the Contras had no chance of achieving this militarily. They were, however, a serious insurgent force that took the war offensively into Nicaragua and caused the Sandinistas grave difficulties. The CIA program did not get fully underway until 1982, but by the first half of 1984, over 6,000 fighters had crossed the border into Nicaragua where they occupied significant swaths of territory and threatened several important rural towns. They were most effective when U.S. funding left them flush with arms and ammunition, and logistical support sustained them in the bush. Even during slack periods, small units were present in Nicaragua where they conducted hit-and-run attacks against EPS and militia outposts, launched ambushes, occupied small settlements, disrupted agricultural activities, and blew up infrastructure. In the Northeast and Caribbean region, virtually the entire Miskito population of 250,000 was hostile to the FSLN. When several prominent Sandinistas defected, notably hero of the insurrection Eden Pastora in 1982, they opened a Southern Front based out of Costa Rica which gave the Sandinistas a splitting strategic headache. In their most developed stage, the Contras could trouble the Sandinistas on three fronts, the FDN main force operating from the north, the Miskitos on the Atlantic Coast, and Pastora and his small Contra army, ARDE (spanish for "burn") from the South.

FROM INSURGENTS TO COUNTERINSURGENTS

The Sandinistas began confronting the Contras with confidence in the solidarity of their revolution and without much concern. The bulk of the EPS guarded the populated areas of the Pacific Coast against the expected Yankee invasion, while the Popular Militias defended rural areas, calling on army reinforcements when needed to help chase infiltrators back across the Honduran border. After 1982, as the U.S. program kicked in, Contra size and effectiveness multiplied and they began to penetrate deeper into Nicaragua, remain there longer, and attack with greater force. The Sandinistas recognized that although they were not in danger of military defeat, the Contra's capacity to wreak economic destruction, wear down resistance, and provoke dissatisfaction with the revolution made them a "strategic threat."[25] Inadequately prepared to deal with the military challenge, EPS Commander Humberto Ortega relied on his Cuban advisors and Soviet weaponry to adopt a more aggressive counterinsurgency strategy that in many respects mirrored the American sponsored effort in El Salvador. They introduced universal conscription in 1983 to expand the army from 12,000 to 60,000 troops in 1985, and supplied them with Soviet equipment, including trucks, artillery, tanks, and aircraft. New antiguerrilla units transported by MI-17 and MI-8 helicopters remained in the field and undertook major counteroffensives. By the beginning of 1985, and particularly with addition of Soviet MI-24 helicopter gunships, the EPS had become a more effective counterinsurgency force. In 1985 and 1986 crossborder operations against Contra camps generated great friction, with the U.S. warning Nicaragua and at the same time cajoling Honduras to stand up to them. The Honduran Government responded by insisting on relocating Contra bases to more remote areas. In the south, Costa Rica was caught between fear of growing Sandinista power and U.S. pressure. The government of Ricardo Arias found itself once again hosting Eden Pastora and his ARDE forces, this time as anti-Sandinistas, complete with CIA logistical support, and thereby inviting incursions they would rather have avoided. The EPS was partially successful in blunting Contra offensives and blocking infiltration routes, but was unable to halt large-scale incursions. It was not necessarily the effectiveness of the EPS, but the challenge of maintaining communications and supply lines that was the most important single factor in limiting Contra operations from penetrating deeper into Nicaragua.

The Sandinistas also addressed the political dimension of counterinsurgency. On the coercive side, they relocated thousands of peasants and Indians from their settlements in border areas to deny support to the Contras, but they also handed out land titles to give campesinos a stake in defending the government. Cuba was the model for a campaign to mobilize the population in defense of the revolution against "imperialist and Somocista mercenaries." The Nicaraguans also launched David versus Goliath diplomatic appeals to secure international restraint of U.S. aggression in the UN, the International Court of Justice, and the Contadora Group that was seeking a regional peace agreement. The U.S. rebuffed these efforts, although Congress did compel the Reagan Administration to name a Special Envoy for Central America and proclaim adherence to the "Contadora process" long after it had given up the idea of seriously negotiating anything other than acquiescence from the Sandinistas. If anything, the Nicaraguans found that their international initiatives placed themselves in the contradictory position of taking steps to avoid international isolation at the same time they were trying to implement a socialist revolution and adhere more closely to the Eastern Bloc. The desire for international legitimacy was an important factor in their decision to allow a limited political opening and hold elections in 1984, which they regarded as a necessary nuisance. In contrast to the process then underway in El Salvador, the elections were generally regarded as not free and fair. The Sandinistas followed with one of their periodic crackdowns by declaring a state of emergency and passing decrees suppressing the churches and press, thus undermining their domestic and international support. Similar to the situation in El Salvador, the war continued through periodic offensives and counteroffensives in which both sides suffered successes and setbacks, fueled by support from international patrons sufficient to ensure a military stalemate. What the Contra War did provoke was the political corrosion of the Sandinista revolution.

PATRONS AND CLIENTS

If the FSLN had at least temporarily possessed the political competence to place themselves in power, it was the one thing that the Contras never had. To the extent that strategic intent guided them, the Contras were a proxy military force, a classic guerrilla counterweight who could harass and bleed the Sandinistas and who the Sandinistas could not defeat. But unlike the Salvadoran FMLN, they were not the world's most crackerjack insurgents and never acted as a unified and coordinated force.[26] They spent much of their time inactive in their Honduran redoubts, making demands of their American controllers, for example, to support them by air rather than cheaper but more tiresome and difficult land routes. They gained the reputation of being brigands and brutes who raped women, executed prisoners, and enjoyed murdering unarmed civilians. They bickered and fought over leadership. The truth was as an insurgent political–military organization the Contras never amounted to much. A tinge of Somocismo and their murderous notoriety tainted them, but this was not just a problem of having a poor political image; they had no coherent political identity at all. They were insurgents and counterrevolutionaries, whose commanders and foot soldiers alike wanted to get rid of the Sandinistas. But beyond supporting this negative aim, they completely lacked a political program. Individual Contra commanders, like "Suicida," a former member of the National Guard special unit "The Rattlesnakes," were basically petty warlords who used charisma, the promise of American guns and money, and a chance to kill the hated Sandinistas as their recruiting tools. There were no political officers to catechize on the benefits of democracy, no cadres in peasant villages who secretly advocated the fight for freedom, and above all no political leaders to guide the organization or to inspire opposition to the Sandinistas and identity with the Contras more broadly within Nicaragua, much less spark a popular rebellion. Not that building the essential links between the people the insurgent army and the political organization is ever easy.

The original Contra politicians had certainly opposed Somoza, but they were mostly second rank personalities recruited by the CIA in Miami, where they had formed a like-minded brotherhood with anti-Castro Cubans. Most prominent among them was former Managua Coca Cola manager Adolfo Calero. For most of the war, Calero operated as the designated political caudillo of the FDN in league with the military structure headed by Enrique Bermudez and the general staff that came from the remnants of Somoza's National Guard. The smaller Southern Front may have made strategic logic, but its leader, mercurial former Sandinista Comandante Eden Pastora, was as much of a problem as a solution. He proved militarily inept and refused to work with the larger and better endowed Northern Front. These splits between former National Guardsmen in the north and former Sandinistas in the south, and between civilian politicians and the military hierarchy were endemic. The state department and CIA quarreled with their problem. Eliot Abrams as Reagan's assistant secretary for most of the 1980s and a dedicated neoconservative, tried especially hard to burnish the Contra's image and their democratic credibility in Congress. especially after suspicions of corruption made Calero and others in the FDN appear even more unsavory. Contra reform, however, was never much of a success. Most opposition figures with independent democratic credentials hesitated to entangle themselves with the CIA, and the CIA preferred to work with individuals they believed they could control. In the end, moderates like Alfonso Robelo, who had been a member of the FAO against Somoza, gravitated to the Contras because they found themselves betrayed and exiled from the Sandinista circle with no other way out and nowhere else to go. Arturo Cruz Sr., a forthright patriot who resigned from the early revolutionary junta, reluctantly allowed himself to be pushed and pulled over the years into association with the Contras, only to find himself manipulated by Americans and Nicaraguans alike precisely because he was honorable. In 1984, U.S. officials humiliated him by persuading him to run in the presidential elections as head of the opposition front, only to pull him out at the last minute to further discredit the FSLN sham. Beginning in 1985, the United States attempted to "moderate" the Contra image by grafting Cruz and Robelo onto the Contra structure, creating a front called UNO. FDN leaders Calero and Bermudez made the efforts torturous with resistance, the Nicaraguans never overcame their mutual distrust, and, although the machinations generated plenty of contention and press attention, the rickety political organization never amounted to anything credible.

It is unlikely that a strategy of building the center will work in an insurgent organization if political figures have no genuine authority or legitimacy and there is no political structure to capture the loyalties of an imagined popular constituency. In the case of the Sandinistas, political and military structures were unified, as represented by the leadership of the Ortega brothers, but adherence to democracy was a façade intended not to build a moderate center, but to further radical revolution. The Contras existed from the first to the last for military purposes. The CIA was the real political boss, and they came to cross purposes when U.S. officials tried to graft a political organization onto the guerrilla army. They may have been insurgents, but they fell easily enough into the traditional Nicaraguan pattern of patron–client relations with their American masters. It was a star-crossed relationship. On the one hand, U.S. officials found themselves deeply enmeshed and constantly vexed with the Contra's crippling internal problems and the Nicaraguan penchant for egocentric and conspiratorial politics. For their part, the Contras found the United States an equally fickle and complex patron. Instead of power emanating directly from the orders of the president, or better yet American might simply overthrowing the Sandinistas for them, the Contras had to contend with an Administration that proclaimed publicly the fate of the free world was in their hands, but insisted on clandestinity, was at once gung ho, but kept them dangling on a stop-and-go supply line. Instead of a clear chain of command, there was the State Department, the National Security Council, and above all, the "imperial sergeants" of the CIA among whom the incompatible mix of Contra political and military leaders maneuvered for favor in order to establish themselves among the rank and file.[27]

CORROSION

Covert Action proved a powerful but highly corrosive instrument of war in Central America. The CIA's stock in trade was manipulation and control, and this was how they approached the problems of Contra leadership. Their mission was to field a fighting force against the Sandinistas, and while they were effective at this operational aspect of the job, their limited vocation for building a serious political–military insurgency and consequentialist ethic undermined the Contras and led to excess. These institutional limits made the CIA a poor steward of policy in the absence of prudent oversight from elsewhere within the executive branch. In addition, the Contra program had received press attention almost from its inception, and the inevitable revelation of nominally clandestine activities in the media led to reactions of distaste while feeding the public appetite for scandal. To illustrate the effects of corrosion, it was almost as an afterthought driven by concern over problems in Congress that CIA Director Bill Casey suggested to his Latin America Division Chief Dewey Clarridge in 1983 that they ought to do something about the political and psychological aspects of the war. A principal product of this effort was a course and manual to train Contra guerrillas on political–military operations. As Clarridge notes, most of the material was "warmed-over Vietnam-era winning-hearts-and-minds-of-the-people advice," but when an unedited version of the manual that included instruction to "neutralize carefully selected" Sandinista officials leaked to the press, the CIA "Murder Manual" further tarnished the Contra image and even became an embarrassing feature of the 1984 Presidential campaign.[28]

So it was at the same time that controversy over El Salvador was easing, conflict with Congress over the Contras and U.S. policy toward Nicaragua was becoming a bone lodged in the Reagan Administration's throat. Political battles on the home front would have a critical impact on the war in Nicaragua, while at the same time Nicaragua became a highly divisive focus of national politics in the United States. Factions that divided Congress lined up as they had on El Salvador, with liberal Democrats who strongly opposed intervention in Nicaragua pitted against the Administration and their mostly Republican allies who were equally determined that U.S. support for the Contras was necessary to keep from handing Central America "over to the Warsaw Pact." In the battle of Washington, there were two irreconcilable extremes between those who believed that anything goes against communist governments who you do not deal with because they are inherently illegitimate, and those who believed that by virtue of winning a fair and square fight against the tyrant Somoza, the Sandinistas were legitimate while shadowy efforts to see them overthrown were not. Moderates from both sides sought compromises that would allow the Contra program to continue, but were generally uneasy with the policy and were quick to register their concerns over Administration excesses, especially once the inevitable press disclosure shredded covert deniability.

The liberals were determined above all to prevent the United States from entering, in Senator Chris Dodd's words, the "dark tunnel of endless intervention." Reinforcing them was the broad coalition of human rights activists and solidarity groups that had first emerged to oppose U.S. aid to El Salvador. They now coalesced around the "Coalition for a New Foreign and Military Policy" to oppose aid to the Contras on moral grounds, drawing attention to Contra human rights violations, and denouncing covert action to overthrow a government as reversion to the past sins of U.S. intervention in Latin America. Instead, they preferred to "give peace a chance" through regional diplomacy to end the conflict and prevent a repetition of U.S. folly in Southeast Asia, an approach that had wide appeal. Congressional attempts to pressure the Administration into negotiations through the regional Contadora process and later the Central Americans' own initiative fed into the internal dispute between the hardliners and the pragmatists. Whereas the hardliners in both Congress and the Executive regarded military action through the Contras as self-justifying in the name of the Cold War and wanted nothing to do with accommodating the Sandinistas, the pragmatists regarded the Contras as a means of pressuring the Sandinista regime into negotiations. Determination to compel the Administration into negotiating was so great in the House, where Democrats held the majority and the leadership adhered closely to liberal positions, that initiatives frequently verged on seizing foreign policy authority from the president. The extreme point came in 1987, when House Speaker Jim Wright conducted his own shuttle diplomacy with Central American leaders and tried to compel the Administration to accept a peace proposed sponsored by Costa Rica. After a public clash with Secretary of State Shultz, Wright's initiative produced an ill-fated compromise, the "Wright–Reagan Plan."

The fight over Contra aid was a legislative bed of thorns each year from 1982 through 1989. Lacking the votes to cut aid altogether in 1982 and 1983, Congress succeeded in restricting the funding level and aims of the program. Efforts in 1984–85 succeeded in cutting off funding, then limiting it to nonlethal aid only. In 1986, the Administration managed to reverse the cut and won $100 million for a program that was four times larger than previous funding. From 1986 to 1989, the program was again restricted to providing humanitarian support. Out of the resulting friction, unstable and shifting coalitions emerged in extremely convoluted funding battles, in which the House would vote on either side of the issue several times, while the Administration often acted as if it could ignore the House while relying on the Republican majority in the Senate (until the 1986 elections) to protect its positions in final legislation. Weak compromises blunted the exercise of national power, forced the Administration to take positions it did not agree with in order to keep the program alive, and when Congress did vote to halt Contra aid altogether, led them to go outside the law with scandal as the consequence.

The key reference points were two provisions contained in the 1982 Intelligence Authorization Act, authored by the moderate Chairman of the House Intelligence Committee Edward Boland. According to what became know as the first Boland Amendment, the aims of the covert action program were limited to interdicting arms going to the Salvadoran FMLN and no funds could be used to overthrow the Sandinista Government. This device was intended to split the difference between support for El Salvador against the FMLN and opposition to the Contras. Of course, the Amendment provided the program with technical legal cover, but it was also a practical fiction. The Reagan Administration could claim that intentions were within the law, but not only did the Contras themselves never interdict any Salvadoran arms, they denied they had an interest in doing so and consistently said their objective was precisely to overthrow the Sandinistas.

The first real vote on the covert program took place in 1983. The effort was both monumental and labyrinthine, and illustrates the appalling, complex dynamics that possessed the U.S. Government over Central America. By early 1983, news about the supposedly secret covert action program—complete with CNN coverage of Nicaraguan peasants killed in Contra raids—had begun to seep and then flood into the media. With polls showing that large majorities of Americans opposed U.S. policies on Central America, the program's legal veneer began looking thinner in the public light. Liberal members of Congress accused the Administration of violating the Boland Amendment, and moderates were increasingly questioning whether the Administration was complying with the law, especially after delegations from the House and Senate Intelligence Committees conducted visits to the region. In response to the growing disquiet in Congress and dire warnings from Jeanne Kirkpatrick, who had just concluded from her own assessment in the region that Soviet–Cuban influence was growing in Nicaragua and that El Salvador was on the brink, the Administration increased its uncompromising determination to stay the course. The White House launched a public affairs strategy focused on calming down fears of escalation and winning bipartisan support. Reagan spoke to a special session of Congress in late-April 1983, in which he denied any intention of sending troops, but threatened to blame Democrats for being soft on communism if defeatism won out "in the face of this challenge to freedom and security in our own hemisphere." They also announced formation of the Kissinger Commission in July, just prior to the Congressional debate. There were frequent press conferences and a major lobbying effort that amounted to a public diplomacy offensive. Other Administration actions that contradicted the benign message filled the headlines instead. The President himself said in an interview said that the Sandinistas were an illegitimate regime and for the first time called the Contras "Freedom Fighters." In the run up to the debate, news that the United States was planning to hold Big Pine II military maneuvers in Honduras and off both coasts of Nicaragua involving more than 5,000 troops—an inherent invasion threat—leaked to the press. An infuriated Secretary of State Shultz who was blind-sided, rightly consider them provocative to Congress. The Pentagon had also requested $168 million for Central American military assistance, an increase of more than 100 percent. Other reports surfaced that the CIA planned to more than double the number of Contras up to 15,000. CIA Latin America Division Chief Duane "Dewey" Clarridge and his boss Bill Casey were so openly contemptuous in briefings and hearings that confidence between the Administration and both the House and Senate Intelligence Committees essentially collapsed.[29]

It was in this contentious atmosphere that on July 19, the House held a secret session, only the fourth in its history, to discuss the Contra program. The House debated in a raucous and bitterly partisan session filled with moralizing by Democrats and red-baiting by Republicans for 2 full days from July 27 to 28. The proceedings became excessively Byzantine, with most but not enough Democrats opposing covert aid and the Administration pressing for unrestricted funding, while both liberals and conservative Republicans mutually resisted compromise. A stand-alone bill sponsored by Intelligence Committee Chairman Boland and House Foreign Affairs Committee Chairman Clement Zablocki had passed out of committee. It would seek balance by cutting off Contra aid, but providing overt assistance to regional allies for interdicting arms to the Salvadoran FMLN. A plethora of complicated amendments to the Boland–Zablocki Bill surfaced in the effort to discover a formula that could secure a majority. The Barnes Amendment ended funding immediately. The Mica Amendment delayed cutting off aid, but instead required the President to come up with a new plan for interdicting arms to Salvadoran guerrillas. The Boland–Solarz amendment to the Mica substitute amendment for the Young amendment turned Mica's proposal on its head by ending aid to the Contras immediately, but allowing Congress to reinstate it if after 30 days the President reported that Nicaragua was still aiding the Salvadoran guerrillas. With tempers flaring and bipartisan decorum in tatters, the parliamentary maneuvering reached its pinnacle when then-majority leader Jim Wright reintroduced the original bill saying, "I offer an amendment to the amendment as amended, offered as a substitute for the amendment, as amended."[30] The final House vote, 228–195 in favor of Boland–Zablocki, signaled deep Congressional misgivings about Contra aid. However, when the more conservative House appropriators finally compromised in November conference with their counterparts from the Republican-led Senate, the Administration received half of its request, $24 million for the Contras in fiscal year 1984. The program stayed alive, but opposition to it would only grow.

Each year from 1984 through 1989, the United States continued its fickleness over aid to the Contras. In 1984, Congress voted to cut aid altogether, then approved

$24 million in 1985, limited it to nonlethal aid, then in 1986 approved $100 million in lethal and nonlethal aid, then again restricted aid to humanitarian only for the remainder of the program from 1987 to 1989. In the process, the program was transferred from the CIA to the State Department, the when funding was prohibited the National Security Council created a semiprivate enterprise to evade the prohibition. When dollars flooded from Congress back into the program it was transferred back to the CIA, but by then it had veered into miasma of the Iran–Contra scandal. The impact on the war itself was fundamental, but hardly coherent, as Robert Kagan observes in *Twilight Struggle:*

> The rhythms of the war in Nicaragua followed a different pattern from the rhythms of the legislative process in Washington. Congress passed aid bills in the spring and early summer, which the President signed in late summer or early fall. The Contras began their offensives in the spring when the rainy season started, and ended them in the fall when the rainy season let up and the roads used by the Sandinista troops hardened. By the time the Contras received the first penny of "humanitarian" aid voted by Congress, therefore, they had already struck their blows deep inside Nicaragua and were on their way back to the safety of Honduras.[31]

It was not just a matter of rhythm. The consequences of the political battles were contrary to what both Congress and the Executive were trying to achieve. With the Contra program under such intense political scrutiny, CIA operations that might have been considered less sensitive elsewhere were inevitably portrayed as excesses. In 1983 and 1984, the CIA conducted over twenty White House authorized attacks against Nicaraguan facilities. The mining of Nicaragua's principal harbors at Corinto and Puerto Sandino, along with attacks on petroleum facilities, in 1984 was the most controversial case. After extensive high-level deliberation and planning, the President approved the plan over the objections of the Secretaries of State and Defense. It was intended as another means of bringing the war to Nicaragua through economic sabotage that would also raise maritime insurance rates, and several foreign cargo ships did receive damage when they struck mines. As instructed the Contras claimed they had laid the mines, but in fact the maritime operations were the work of a CIA special activities team that included Navy SEALS operating fast boats from a mother ship. When the mining became public and Nicaragua brought the case to the International Court of Justice, Congress reacted with outrage, both at inadequate notification and the subsequent Administration disavowal of the ICJ determination that the act violated international law. Even conservative Administration supporter and Senate Intelligence Committee Chairman Senator Barry Goldwater took CIA Director Casey to task in a fiery letter:

> It gets down to one simple phrase: I am pissed off. . . . Bill, this is no way to run a railroad. . . . This is an act violating international law. It is an act of war. For the life of me, I don't see how we are going to explain it.[32]

In consequence, in May 1984 both houses passed resolutions condemning the mining and voted the second Boland amendment which barred the use of U.S. funds for any military or paramilitary activities against Nicaragua. Ceaseless battles with Congress over the Contras and the Contras' lack of battle performance led some in the Administration to consider them a losing cause, but Ronald Reagan's own commitment did not waiver. As National Security Advisor Robert McFarlane recalled, it was the President's desire to hold the Contras together "body and soul" that gave others the determination to circumvent the Congressional aid cut off and keep them going.[33] Between 1984 and 1986, McFarlane and Admiral John Poindexter who succeeded him oversaw an exceptional and legally dubious undertaking to fund and supply the Contras that extended the NSC directly into operations well beyond its normally accepted role, and from which executive agencies, including the CIA, were partially or entirely excluded.[34] Efforts to raise money from alternative sources secured $32 million from Saudi Arabia and approximately another $16 million from Taiwan, Brunei, and private donors. (Approached first, Israel declined to participate.) Marine Lt. Col. Oliver North managed the activities from the NSC setting up a quasigovernmental effort that employed former U.S. military and other government employees to keep the Contras supplied by air, primarily out of Ilopango Air Base in San Salvador. Although third country support for the Contras had helped them survive, the resupply "enterprise," as its principal agent Richard Secord called it, proved both inadequate and counterproductive. Information and rumors about the effort had begun to leak out by October 1986 when a young Sandinista soldier got lucky and shot down one of the resupply planes with a surface-to-air missile, and the sole surviving crewman, Eugene Hasenfus, acknowledged the U.S. role. The next month, revelations about arms-for-hostages trading with Iran became linked with diversion of profits through secret bank accounts to the Contra operation, resulting in the Iran–Contra scandal. The affair further tarnished the Contras and so weakened the Reagan presidency that Robert Kagan concludes: "Indeed, those actions proved as unnecessary, and as futile, as they were ultimately destructive of the people and the policy they were meant to support."[35]

Incompetence and imprudence caused a second President's disgrace over the handling of conflict in Central America; Reagan's personal popularity, his greatest asset, dropped from 67 to 46 percent in November, the sharpest decline ever recorded, although he suffered nowhere near the same eventual loss that humbled Jimmy Carter. Multiple Iran–Contra investigations and their aftermath, including the spectacle of a bemedaled and flag-wrapped Oliver North bewitching Congress and the nation with his testimony, followed by perjury convictions of several officials, stretched through the remainder of Reagan's term and made funding for the Contras impossible, even though the Administration did not stop trying. Of greater irony, support for the Contras actually increased in Congress during 1986 before the scandal broke. A few months after voting to deny the Administration's request for nonlethal aid, Congress reversed itself and approved $100 million in lethal and nonlethal assistance to put the Contras and the CIA fully back in business with more than three times the amount of any previous funding. Although the program continued, the momentum that had led to bipartisan consensus collapsed, and Congress never again approved military aid for the Contras.

MARXIST–LENINIST JERKS VERSUS THE FREEDOM FIGHTERS

The Nicaraguan regime was too revolutionary for its own good, and the Sandinistas consistently offset U.S. excesses by doing certain damage to their own goals of getting the "Yankee imperialists and Contra mercenaries" off their backs. They had three avenues available to secure themselves: diplomatic appeals for protection from the United States, reliance on the Soviet Union and the Eastern Bloc, and domestic opposition to U.S. policy.[36] The FSLN found slight recourse among the international community, because there was neither sufficient interest nor will to challenge the United States in its own sphere of influence. The Soviets proved sustaining but recalcitrant and ultimately double-edged allies. When Daniel Ortega signed the first military and economic agreement with the Soviet Union in 1980, he had high hopes that newly revolutionary Nicaragua would soon join Cuba as a full member of the Warsaw Pact and COMECON. It was clear within a couple of years, especially once the Soviets entered their extended post-Brezhnev succession crisis, that the USSR was a criticizing and not particularly enthusiastic patron, and often a begrudging one when it came to providing hard currency loans, trade subsidies, and other economic aid. As they did with their other poor Third World clients, the Soviets substituted military aid for economic largesse. At the same time, they had no intention of running major risks with the United States, as the refusal to supply the Nicaraguans with MIG's, when pilots and mechanics had already been trained and airfields extended, clearly and bitterly demonstrated.[37] Gorbachev did consider Nicaragua enough of a strategic asset to provide military aid that surpassed $1 billion in 1985–86, and even signed a bilateral Five Year Plan that foresaw an increase of the Sandinista Army to an improbable 600,000. By then the Sandinistas could not have mistaken the evidence that the Soviet Union was a declining power, but still they clung faithfully to the Cuban example and their membership in the Soviet camp.

Unfortunately for them, their open identification with the Eastern Bloc contradicted their key objective of breaking the will of the United States to sustain the Contras. The Sandinistas certainly made no friends in Congress. Prominent Senators, such as Chris Dodd, and Congressmen, notably House leaders Tip O'Neil and Jim Wright, who were sympathetic took it personally when the Sandinistas betrayed them by making and then breaking promises, and running off to see the Soviets. The Ortega brothers got reputations of being "Marxist–Leninist jerks." Their 1979 promise to the OAS to democratize came to haunt them, and the patently biased 1984 national elections only damaged their international legitimacy. As a party with much to lose, the Sandinistas had no intention of negotiating anything away with the United States, like members of the Reagan Administration, they were leery of the Contadora process, and their intransigence upset the moderates in Congress who were trying to pressure the Administration onto the diplomatic track. The linkage between Sandinista behavior and Congressional support for the Contras was unmistakable.

In two instances, the impact was direct and dramatic. Nicaraguan President Daniel Ortega provoked a disastrous "stampede" away from liberals and the House leadership by traveling to Moscow shortly after an April 1985 vote that would have sustained the Contra aid cut of the year before. Sandinista Army incursions in February 1986 against Contra sanctuaries along the Honduran and Costa Rican helped swing moderates into supporting the Administration's request for $100 million to resume military aid that year. Thus the Sandinista's own behavior, and not just the excesses of the Reagan Administration, drove the inconsistency in U.S. support for the Contras. Poised between the liberals who opposed aid to the Contras and the conservatives who supported it, when the sizeable group of pragmatic moderates were in favor of the policy it went forward, and when they did not it stopped.[38]

It was not until 1985 when faced with the challenge of restoring aid to the Contras that the Administration finally articulated a fully developed policy and strategy for the insurgent program that balanced military and political dimensions. What became known as the Reagan Doctrine was much more than a public relations campaign to win congressional votes.[39] Its security rationale for supporting anticommunist insurgencies came from the heart of traditional American conservatism, but its moral appeal of supporting democracy added the element of neoconservative idealism. The President formally debuted the formulation in his February 1985 State of the Union Address, declaring that, "The United States must not break faith with those who are risking their lives on every continent, from Afghanistan to Nicaragua, to defy Soviet-sponsored aggression and secure rights which have been ours since birth....Support for freedom fighters is self-defense...their struggle is tied to our own security." The argument aimed to elevate the debate over shadow wars and covert action in peripheral countries to the higher plain of principled support for global freedom and democracy. Conceptually, the Reagan Doctrine transformed the Contra war into a metaphor for the Manichean struggle between the United States and the Soviet Union. The emphasis was no longer on military action to bleed Nicaragua, but on the political objective of changing Sandinista behavior.

The idea of supporting democratic insurgencies that had originally entered the Administration with Constantine Menges and Fred Iklé, was one element of a broader aspiration to demonstrate the ability of the United States post-Vietnam to use its power to roll back the Soviet Union in the Third World and to demonstrate that it could not prevail. Reagan had first floated the notion publicly in his 1982 speech to the British Parliament, and two 1982 NSDD's, 32 and 75, incorporated it into a general policy that would, "...contain and over time reverse Soviet expansionism by competing effectively on a sustained basis with the Soviet Union in all international arenas, particularly in the overall military balance and in geographical regions of priority concern to the United States."[40]

This was the tail end of the Cold War, although few understood it in 1985. Certainly, the President himself believed that the world was at a turning point, as did many around him, although more as an article of faith than from rational foresight. For some, and Bill Casey was most important among them, supporting insurgents who were fighting against communist regimes in the Africa, Asia, and Latin

America was not a peripheral strategy, but an extremely affordable way of pushing the Soviet Union to the tipping point. For Casey, who had experienced the World War II fight against Nazi fascism as an officer in the Office of the Strategic Services (OSS), this was not mere cynical fantasy. He often expressed the idea that, "When we win one, the whole house of cards will come tumbling down. It will set off a chain reaction throughout the empire."[41] It is perhaps highly dubious to have supposed that it would be possible to achieve such unlimited ends with such limited means, but the cost-effectiveness of supporting insurgencies is hardly in doubt. By conventional rule of thumb, if an irregular war requires ten regular troops for every guerrilla, the monetary costs alone to the Russians by one estimate reached $20 billion.[42] The United States and its allied patrons paid on the order of $1 billion to keep the Contras going. This is not to discount the costs in lives and well-being for the people of Nicaragua, or to enter the larger and more complex debate about whether a more accommodating approach to the Soviet Union would have served better. This was not the aim of the hardliners after all, whose intent was to defeat the Soviet Union, not live with it. As Fred Iklé, Undersecretary of Defense for Policy, explained in his widely publicized 1983 speech on U.S. Central America policy before the Baltimore Council on Foreign Relations, "We can no more negotiate a political solution with these people than the social democrats in revolutionary Russia could have talked Lenin into giving up totalitarian Bolshevism."[43]

The Reagan Doctrine, as it became known, was intended not only to reverse Soviet strategic advances in the Third World; it was rollback with a cause. A Big Idea, Wilsonian in scope, linking U.S. national security to freeing foreign peoples from tyranny was the heart of neoconservatism. The ideology became operational by advocating use of military action to extend democracy. As Peter Rodman recounts, more than any other individual, Eliott Abrams was responsible for transforming this line of reasoning into policy, first as Reagan's Assistant Secretary for Human Rights from 1980 to 1985, and then as Assistant Secretary for Latin America from 1985 to 1988, where the principal locus of his efforts would be Central America, and particularly support for the Nicaraguan resistance. Abrams had written in a 1981 State Department memo that:

> A human rights policy means...hard choices which may adversely affect certain bilateral relations. At the very least, we will have to speak honestly about our friends' human rights violations and justify any decision wherein other considerations (economic, military, etc.) are determinative. There is no escaping this without destroying the credibility of our policy, for otherwise we would be simply coddling our friends and criticizing foes. ...While we need a military response to the Soviets to reassure our friends and allies, we also need an ideological response. Our struggle is for political liberty...We desire to demonstrate, by acting to defend liberty and identifying its enemies, that the difference between East and West is the crucial political distinction of our times.[44]

This new and more sophisticated formulation offered the United States, and recalcitrant members of Congress in particular, the opportunity to identify with a goal beyond supporting, for example, ex-Somocistas as replacements for Sandinistas in Nicaragua. Still, the distance between ideals and reality was considerable. The Reagan Doctrine was proclaimed as a universal approach—the Heritage Foundation advocated applying it in Afghanistan, Angola, Cambodia, Ethiopia, Iran, Laos, Libya, Nicaragua, and Vietnam—but circumstances determined that insurgents would receive its benefits in only in three of them: Afghanistan, Angola, and Nicaragua. And only in Central America did democracy truly become part of the implementation, again as the result of broader conditions that made it feasible. When El Salvador followed Nicaragua to the verge of insurrection in 1980, the Carter Administration in its final days had rebalanced concern for human rights by supporting reform with repression to prevent a second loss. Successive elections and a strategy of building the democratic center then vindicated the continuation of counterinsurgency assistance that allowed the government to continue combating the FMLN guerrillas. The Kissinger Commission recommended in 1984 applying the approach regionally as a critical element of U.S. political, military, and economic assistance to resist further communist advances throughout Central America. As if in proof of the argument, by 1986, the regional dynamic had transformed; Guatemala, El Salvador, Honduras, and Costa Rica all had elected governments, even if only Costa Rica would qualify as a fully functioning democracy. The Sandinistas were clearly the odd man out, and the prospects for additional radical revolutions were remote.

The other large gap between ideals and reality were the problems the Reagan Administration had with the democratic credentials of their "Freedom Fighters." The strategic logic of the Reagan Doctrine made anticommunists recruits in the global struggle on behalf of the Free World, but when it came down to the ground, the Contras proved to be little interested in voting rights. The evident irony was that the Contras were being held to standards that did not apply to their fellow freedom fighters in Angola, and especially Afghanistan. At the same time that political controversy shredded the Contra program in Nicaragua, Congress encouraged rather than impeded U.S. assistance to the Mujahedin in Afghanistan. Of course, Afghanistan is far distant from the United States, and the Mujahedin were fighting directly against Soviet invaders. But our Afghan clients democratic credentials were less than zero and their respect for human rights was reprehensible. CIA Director Casey and other Reaganites were confused how it was possible to tap huge sums for Afghanistan—$50 million in 1984, the same year as the Contra cut off—when Ronald Reagan's personal appeals, so effective in other realms, yielded nothing. In fact, conservative Democrat Charlie Wilson of Texas, who had started his career as a Cold Warrior supporting Somoza, was busy forcing weaponry and money on a reluctant CIA as the Mujahedin's "maniacal champion." Wilson turned down Casey's pleas to help with Contras, calling them a "lost cause" because liberals felt so strongly. Tony Coelho, House Democratic Whip at the time, explained that Nicaragua became a cover for Afghanistan: "Most members didn't know where Afghanistan was, and the majority didn't care. Nicaragua was a vicious, bitter fight. We were so concentrated on Nicaragua that Afghanistan wasn't on the radarscope."[45]

In other words, when it came to applying the Reagan Doctrine in Nicaragua, principles certainly mattered, but a vision of what the Contras were supposed to represent was not a substitute for reality on the battlefields of Central America. The same was true on the domestic front, where neither Congress nor the public shared the Administration's passion. Long-time State Department Latin America Policy Planning Director Luigi Einaudi, who originally formulated the concept of building the center, suggested that a greater balance of prudence and ideology would have helped clear the way for a more stable consensus between Congress and the Executive on the Contras and resulted in a more effective strategy and policy. Perhaps there was nothing wrong in and of itself with aspiring to use an anticommunist insurgency as America's agent of transformation in Central America, but such great hopes could not change the nature of the conflicts any more than the CIA could make democrats of the Contras.

Not that the realists established a superior record for policy guidance when it came to the Reagan Doctrine. Promising to support anticommunist insurgencies was an offensive strategy that exceeded the defensive limitations implicit in Cold War containment. The proposition naturally provoked controversy between those who considered the Doctrine bold and those who believed it confused peripheral with vital interests and feared it risked escalation and possibly even disintegration of international order.[46] These fears proved to be unfounded, even if there were other unintended and unforeseen consequences, Iran–Contra and the birth of al Qaeda from the Mujahedin not least among them. Others, such as former-Carter NSC Advisor Zbigniew Brzezinski, recognized that U.S.-backed insurgencies could be useful tools in the global Cold War, but considered them potential tools for achieving balance and accommodation with the Soviet Union rather than instruments of overthrow. His proposal was to link regional conflicts in U.S.–Soviet negotiations to achieve "external neutralization and internal self-determination" by trading off U.S. support of the Mujahedin in Afghanistan for Soviet aid to the Sandinistas in Nicaragua.[47] Instead, although proxy wars remained perennials on the U.S.–Soviet agenda, superpower competition in the Third World tended to provide stronger motivation than any incentive to actually resolve them. George Shultz, among the Reagan Administration's most dedicated pragmatists, sought advantage, not balance through "constructive involvement" on Central America. Referring to the U.S. demand that Moscow, for example, halt military aid to the Sandinistas and FMLN guerrillas, Shultz said, "A litmus test of Soviet seriousness in response to our concerns would be whether they are moving seriously toward a real pullback from one of the positions gained in the 1970s."[48] The focus for the United States throughout both the Reagan, and later the Bush Administration was on cutting arms flows, not involving the Soviet Union in political solutions. Results were scant until the very end. Even Gorbachev stonewalled and kept arms flowing to Nicaragua long after the Cold War and with it Central America's strategic significance were waning.

The Reagan Administration was much too divided and undisciplined to sustain a strategy that might have adequately unified force and diplomacy in Central America. Much that did take place was pretense. Elaborate positions taken in response to peace proposals by the Contadora Group and the frequent shuttle diplomacy of the Special Envoy for Central America amounted to diplomacy "with an empty briefcase." Hardliners were always present to guard against initiatives that promoted diplomatic solutions for their own sake, and to ensure that serious efforts, such as the Enders two track approach to the FSLN, never went anywhere.[49] Except in his unguarded moments, the President, with one eye on Congress, was always careful in his statements to make it clear he was open to negotiations. The consistent themes of public policy emphasized political not military solutions in Central America, but support for the democratic center and respect for human rights whether regimes of the right or the left, although the option of directly military action never came off the table. Again, George Shultz was also the Administration's most sophisticated proponent of hitching the big idea behind the Reagan Doctrine to achieving pragmatic results. He became a forceful advocate of the Contras as a tool to compel the Sandinistas from their Soviet-backed radicalism: "We will welcome such a change in Nicaraguan behavior no matter how it is obtained. Whether it is achieved through the multilateral Contadora negotiations, though unilateral actions taken by the Sandinistas, alone or in concert with their domestic opponents, or through the collapse of the Sandinista regime is immaterial to us."[50]

What exactly were the effects of U.S. policy and strategy in the Contra War? In the first place, friction over Nicaragua resulted in extremely high political costs in the United States. Reagan and his supporters' passionate commitment to the Contras seemed out of proportion to any rational calculus or strategic value, while the liberals who desired above all to deflect the United States away from a militarist course were equally obtuse. But then ideological exuberance is a form of self-deception that can blind if it is not balanced with a good grasp on reality. The Sandinistas were equally afflicted. Their ideological fatalism compelled them to cling to an alliance with the Soviet Union, support fellow revolutionaries in El Salvador, and militarize their country even though this course of action meant incurring the irrevocable hostility of the regional superpower. However resilient they may have appeared, their revolution was an anomaly and their chosen course of action ultimately led to their own downfall. Unlike the contribution of the Afghan resistance, the direct impact of the Contras on the broader Cold War and the ultimate demise of the Soviet Union was almost certainly negligible. However, the Contras did serve their purpose, and this rather in spite of U.S. fickleness. They never had a hope of overthrowing the Sandinistas as they might have wished, but neither could the Sandinistas defeat them as long as they received aid from the United States and sanctuary in Honduras. This made the Contras key to creating the conditions within Nicaragua that led to the Sandinista's defeat in the 1990 elections. By the time all of this took place, however, the Cold War was ending and the Bush Administration was eager to downgrade Nicaragua to an annoyance.

7 ———————————————————————————

Every War Must End

> You lack the guts to do what needs to be done. . . .
> —Costa Rican President Oscar Arias to friends of the Reagan
> Administration, 1986

PEACE WITHOUT VICTORY

"Every war must end," Fred Iklé writes.[1] By the time the wars in Nicaragua and El Salvador ended, both seemed as interminable as they were inconclusive. But end they did, and both of them strangely. There were no military victories or surrenders. Yet after more than a decade of bitter fighting and the corrosion that accompanied it, peace came, definitively and with great relief. It has lasted ever since. There are two intertwined stories in how and why the contending protagonists in each conflict finally abandoned their arms. First, the two civil wars reached termination not in climax, but in stalemate, with the participants struggling exhausted and reluctant into negotiations. The outcomes, however, were consequential rather than sterile, and resulted in authentic political transformations that supplanted the causes for war. Second, these wars within a war ended only when the reason that drove external intervention disappeared. It would be true, but far too simple to say that when the superpowers stopped fighting, the fighting stopped in Nicaragua and El Salvador too. These savage wars of peace in Central America were also American wars, and although their prolonged and fitful termination hardly fits the triumphal myth of the American way of war, how they ended is very much a story of how the United States exited from its interventions.

The focus of this section is about the strategic dynamics that produced an end to these wars. Less attention is given to the instruments of the peace processes in Nicaragua and El Salvador or to the international organizations that were critical to its implementation, particularly the United Nations and the Organization of American States. This is not to downplay the importance of multilateral conflict resolution in untangling the internal wars and their participants. There are several excellent treatments of this subject, among them *The Central American Peace Process, 1983–1991* by Jack Child, *UN Peacekeeping, American Policy, and the Uncivil Civil Wars of the 1990's* edited by William Durch, and *Taming Intractable Conflicts* by Chester Crocker, Fen Osler Hampson, and Pamela Aall. Very thorough accounts of the processes that led to the end of these conflicts from the perspectives of direct Central American participants include *La Difícil Transición Nicaraguense* by Antonio Lacayo and *El Salvador: La Reforma Pactada* by Salvador Samayoa.

The internal Central American conflicts were proxy wars to the extent that their overall structure and dynamics reflected the wills of their external Cold War patrons. As long as both superpowers remained dedicated to expressing their animosity through militaristic competition in the Third World, the direct antagonists had reason to believe that they would prevail. Majorities in both countries were exhausted and desperately wanted the wars to end, but insurgents and counterinsurgents on both sides kept fighting as long as they received the means to do so. This was equally true for the FMLN, the Contras, and for their government opponents in El Salvador and Nicaragua. Throughout the 1980s, multiple diplomatic efforts of varying degrees of seriousness persisted in promoting peace without victory, but all of them lacked any mechanism for overcoming this underlying motivation. It was not until the final years of the decade when the Soviet Union under Gorbachev began to lose its grip and the regime changed in the United States from the Reagan to the Bush I Administration that the Central American civil wars were finally allowed to enter productive termination phases. The ambiguous but unmistakable diminution of the Cold War did not mean that the Soviet Union began to cooperate with the United States on Central America, nor did the United States simply relinquish its commitment to intervention. Neither did the direct combatants automatically give up trying to achieve their ends by force. On the contrary, the various motivations for fighting remained so deep and the cycle of violence so deeply entrenched that all of the participants had to be compelled in one way or another into accepting political means to end the conflict even after it became apparent that continued military action served little purpose. Democracy, reinforced by diplomacy, proved to be the ultimate way out in both Nicaragua and El Salvador, but the avenues each took to peace were very different.

The notion of resolving the Central American conflicts through negotiation and diplomacy had many advocates and played throughout in a kaleidoscope of formats both internal and international. The route of moderation naturally appealed to those who had less of a direct stake in the outcome, as well as to those who wanted to use force and diplomacy in tandem to achieve pragmatic aims. Unfortunately, motivations were often at crosspurposes and none of the proponents, including some very influential ones, possessed the power individually or in unison to produce results until fatigue and superpower attenuation changed the circumstances. After many false starts, the end game had its origins in 1987, but final results did not come until

1990 in Nicaragua and 1992 in El Salvador. At every stage, the direction, lack of direction, or misdirection of the United States was the crucial ingredient. The Carter Administration set something of a precedent with its hapless efforts to forestall revolution with moderation in Nicaragua, first in 1978 to ease Somoza out, and then in 1979 by trying to accommodate the Sandinistas at the same time it was trying to block them from coming to power. The dynamic reversed once Ronald Reagan was in office when hardliners made sure that the United States played the spoiler to any and all proposals, including from the pragmatists within the Administration. Given the view that Moscow and Havana were "behind the troubles in Central America," as Secretary of State Haig put it,[2] there was some point but little common ground for achieving anything with the Soviets on regional conflicts, either treated individually or linked to trade-offs such as Nicaragua for Afghanistan or even progress on arms control. Mexico also tried going to the source by brokering talks between the United States and Cuba. But there was even less basis for dealing directly with the Cubans than there was with the Soviets, and Haig's inconclusive November 1981 meeting with Cuban Vice President Carlos Rafael Rodriguez in Mexico City, followed by some desultory contacts with Castro, were as far as it went.

Regional efforts to resolve the conflicts diplomatically became a constant factor in the Central American wars, but to a predominant and determined United States, they were more of a track two complication and irritant than a solution.[3] An independent initiative by Mexico to launch the first Central American peace proposal in 1982, which the United States dismissed, evolved into a sustained regional approach when Mexico, Venezuela, Colombia, and Panama formed the Contadora Group, named after the Panamanian island where they first met in January 1983. The Contadora Group found common motives among complex national interests in their desires to assert regional influence, to prevent conflict from widening towards them, and above all to restrain U.S. interventionism. The resulting "Contadora process," to which various other Latin countries associated themselves from time to time, came to be based on a 21-point Document of Objectives that formed the agenda for negotiating binding treaties on political, economic, social, and security issues. The objects of these agreements, the Central Americans themselves, were highly ambivalent about the entire process, and signed onto the principles, but their motives were similarly tangled and at opposite ends.

The neuralgic clash of insecurity and ideology between the United States and Nicaragua was the heart of the matter. It would hardly do for the United States to give the impression that it was against diplomacy, and pressured by Congress, the Administration appointed a Special Envoy for Central America whose primary purpose was to demonstrate that it was open to negotiating while ensuring that nothing actually got done. Three successive ambassadors shuttled on endless consultations among the Contadora Group and the Central Americans, as well as the other Latin Americans and Europeans from time-to-time. Mostly this was for show. With great ambivalence, the United States responded to each Contadora round by maneuvering to control the process, especially working through its Central American allies behind the scenes to ensure nothing happened that might legitimize the Sandinistas, or give them any security advantage. The first priorities and perennial core issues were ending aid to the Salvadoran guerrillas, reducing the size of the Sandinista Army, and cutting ties to the Eastern Bloc. Special Envoys, Assistant Secretaries of State for Latin America, and the Embassy in Managua also kept up tense bilateral dialogue with the Sandinistas. When George Shultz made a serious stab at getting something going in 1984, the resulting series of sustained talks with the Nicaraguans in Manzanillo, Mexico led by tough and experienced Special Ambassador Harry Shlaudeman, came potentially close to reaching an agreement that would have linked up regional security guarantees with pressure for internal change in Nicaragua. However, domestic politics scuttled the effort just as Enders found when he tried the pragmatic approach in 1981. Administration hardliners bitterly apposed negotiating anything with communists which they equated to giving everything away in a "nonaggression pact," while simultaneously Congress outraged at Administration excess and especially CIA mining of Nicaraguan harbors, resulted in the third Boland Amendment that cut aid to the Contras and thus reduced U.S. leverage.[4]

As for the Sandinistas, they may have come to power in 1979 by masterfully manipulating the United States and other regional players, but when it came to getting Ronald Reagan's Uncle Sam off their backs, they were much less adroit and not so lucky. If anything, they were even more wary toward regional peace proposals than the United States, although they too felt obliged to play along. Nicaragua's Central American neighbors found the heavily armed Poland with palm trees next door more of a threat than an attraction, and it had turned out that the Contadora Group's first priority was not protecting Sandinista interests, regardless of Mexico's initial sympathy. Solidarity from Soviet, Cuban, and Eastern Bloc allies was of little help, although they did keep the arms flowing, but this and their support for the FMLN was precisely the crux of the problem. With the regional balance of power leaning against them, in May 1983, the Sandinistas appealed to the UN Security Council, where they held a seat, for relief from U.S. aggression. The Council, at U.S. urging, effectively boxed them in by unanimously referring Nicaragua to the regional Contadora process. The next year, Nicaragua did win the ICJ case over the harbor mining, but the United States chose to disregard that judgment at little cost to anything but principles. The Sandinistas simply refused to talk directly with the Contras. As rhetorically inclined Foreign Minister Miguel D'Escoto put it, "We do not talk to puppets. We would rather talk to the puppeteers."[5] And they were ever-ready to talk with the United States. However, the last thing they were prepared to negotiate away was their "revolutionary identity," which left pragmatists on either side very little to work with. Whether in dealing with Contadora, fellow Central Americans, or the United States, as at Manzanillo, it was only under threat from the Contras, and especially after the 1983 U.S. invasion of Grenada that FSLN defiance turned to flexibility. In the end, neither side was willing or able to unlink their foreign policies from their opposing ideologies.[6] Militarily, the great disparity in power limited what the Sandinistas could do other than support the Salvadoran insurgency and keep up the counterinsurgency slugfest. At the same time, domestic politics weakened U.S. leverage by constraining the exercise of power to the lowball options of keeping the Contras together body and soul while running threatening maneuvers and exercises. Thus honor bound but checked from taking more decisive action, the United States and Nicaragua found each other reduced to trading "proposals and insults."[7]

A DEEP DESIRE FOR PEACE

Comparable antagonisms prevented the Salvadoran civil war from moving out of its deep stalemate toward political resolution for nearly a decade. Throughout the 1980s, the FMLN and the Salvadoran Armed Forces remained locked in a death struggle of insurgent against counterinsurgent, each believing in their ability to prevail militarily. Interest in negotiations was largely, although not exclusively limited to posturing. Since 1981, the FMLN–FDR had made a show of maintaining that it was open to dialogue. Political representatives of the FDR with democratic credentials, such as Social Democrat Guillermo Ungo and former-PDC leader Ruben Zamora, traveled around the world presenting the soft side of the hard left. However, diplomacy was principally a shield for legitimizing force. The FARN was the only one of the four FMLN factions with a sincere interest in exploring possibilities for negotiations, and the dominant ERP was obdurately opposed. The supposed flexibility of the FMLN–FDR was in fact a left-handed demand to negotiate a "quota of power based on the correlation of forces."[8] Neither the Salvadoran right nor the Armed Forces, and certainly not the United States, had the slightest pretense of interest in offering anything, and maintained the counterposition that the insurgents should lay down their arms and join the democratic process.

However, while both sides wrestled unsuccessfully for a strategic solution in the military realm, a broader national and regional evolution was shifting the dynamics of the conflict into the political realm. A single event symbolized this transition. After his election as El Salvador's President in 1984, Napoleon Duarte moved quickly and dramatically to demonstrate his authentic desire to resolve the civil war. For him, the politics of sharing power was not an obstacle to talking; after all his PDC had gambled on a power sharing arrangement with an essentially hostile right and Armed Forces, and many leaders in the insurgency were former allies and even fellow-party members. Duarte's magnanimous announcement at the UN General Assembly that he was prepared to begin an unconditional dialogue with the FMLN contrasted starkly with the Sandinista's strident denunciations of military aggression and refusal to talk to the Contras. It took everyone by surprise. The Armed Forces, the rightist opposition, and the U.S. feared Duarte was a loose cannon. Many on the left sensed he was stealing another flag from them. Nevertheless, no one could afford to appear uninterested in peace without sacrificing legitimacy, and the first meeting took place with high theatrics and emotions as President Duarte and Minister of Defense Guillermo Vides Casanova sat across from two of the five FMLN Comandantes and two FDR leaders on October 15, 1984, in La Palma, a small town deep in what was normally an FMLN zone of control in Chalatenango Department. This extremely polite gathering produced nothing concrete. The United States and the ESAF, which was beginning to show increased counterinsurgency effectiveness, prevented Duarte from proposing a truce or cease-fire, and both sides stuck to their power sharing versus surrender to democracy positions. Two subsequent meetings disintegrated into extremism, and the process died with nothing further to talk about than whether to talk further or not. The absence of direct impact on the war did not mean that the attempt at resolution was without indirect effect. On the contrary, La Palma was a powerful political event, an appeal of passion more than reason that, like the 1982 elections, "touched a deep desire for peace in the Salvadoran population"[9] and furthered the evolution of democracy. Buoyed by the hope of reconciliation they had seeded, the PDC won a sweeping victory in the March 1985 assembly elections. The extreme right party, ARENA suffered badly as voters turned away from the militaristic message of Roberto D'Aubuisson, leading to his replacement with Alfredo Cristiani, a business-oriented representative of the private sector and comparative moderate. Even though the civil war ground on and Duarte's presidency ended 3 years later in failure as the PDC disintegrated in a miasma of corruption and infighting, he had revealed a glimpse of the elusive path from war to peace and presided over a significant advance for the strategy of building the center.

It is challenging to sift for enduring lessons of strategy and policy through the prolonged, convoluted, and often haphazard final phases that actually brought the Central American wars to an end. Most astonishing and perhaps unrepeatable was the conjunction of internal, regional, and global dynamics that made democracy an essential element of the solutions in both Nicaragua and El Salvador. In neither country did force result in lasting victory nor perpetuate an authoritarian regime, but rather democracy did come out of war by inducing the desire to end it. In other words, if these wars originated in the failure of politics, political solutions arose from the failure of war. The corrosive violence that made Central America a most inauspicious place in the hardest of times should not obscure the fact that by 1990, all of the countries of the subregion had joined the Third Wave of democratization in Latin America.[10] As for the United States, the prerogatives of power dictated pursuit of an outcome that favored its interests, and the role of principal warmaker often contradicted the role of democracy-promoter. In Central America, as occurred in Vietnam and other conflicts, domestic politics and regime change rather than enlightened policy-making and political competence led America once again to cycle in fatigue away from intervention.

DRAGGING TOWARD THE CROSSROADS

It was the Central Americans themselves who found the crossroads of peace by taking charge away from the patronizing Americans and Contadora countries at a moment when external initiatives had flagged. Their vehicle was the Arias Peace Plan, formalized in an agreement called Esquipulas II, after the town in Guatemala where the Presidents of Costa Rica, El Salvador, Guatemala, Honduras, and Nicaragua met to sign it on August 7, 1987.[11] Costa Rican President Oscar Arias proved to be the most politically competent player of the entire period. He began his peace offensive shortly after his election in 1986, and basing his plan on prior Contadora documents, maneuvered between a vindictive United States and the hostile Sandinistas, united the three other fellow Central American Presidents, secured broad international support, and won the 1987 Nobel Peace Prize for his efforts. Arias used Costa Rica's status as an exemplary democracy and claimed a popular mandate to seek peaceful resolutions of the Central American conflicts (which were dragging down Costa Rica's economy as well as destroying the rest of the region). He resolutely withstood heavy U.S. dissuasion—including threats to cut U.S. aid to Costa Rica—beginning with Ambassador Lewis Tambs, one of the conservative authors of the Committee of Santa Fe Report, all the way to President Reagan himself.[12] The Arias Plan incorporated Contadora provisions for regional security, and originally proposed negotiated resolution of the internal conflicts in El Salvador and Guatemala, but from the beginning the focus was on Nicaragua. At its heart, the Plan offered the Sandinistas a timetable and specific stipulations for the democratization of Nicaragua that would implicitly bring in exchange an end to U.S. aid for the Contras. The Central Americans united around the priority of extricating their civil wars from within the Cold War.[13] They were perhaps less taken with the project of establishing democracy as the governing norm for the region, and the Sandinista revolutionaries were positively determined to resist. However, when the Central American heads of state sat down in Esquipulas, all of them were elected except for Daniel Ortega, leaving him the odd man out. He signed the accord because he felt compelled to; although he denounced the Plan as intervention, he agreed to internal reforms as the only way he was going to end the Contra war. Support for the vision in the plan and willingness to help its implementation was widespread. UN Secretary General Perez de Cuellar offered good offices, the European Union signed on, Spanish Prime Minister Felipe Gonzalez prepared to play a special role, and even the Soviets and Cubans said they would abide by it. Everyone except the U.S. Administration was prepared to be satisfied.

The ambivalence and dilemmas that characterized U.S. intervention in Central America from the beginning were equally in operation as it came to an end. Restraints on the exercise of power conflicted with the desire for hegemony; factions competed to determine whether ideology or realism would drive policy; commitment to supporting insurgency and counterinsurgency remained, but the beginning of the end of the Cold War lessened its importance and rationale; the closest Central American allies resisted control from Washington even though the United States remained indispensable. At home, Iran–Contra had distracted the Reagan Administration, and in Congress, House Speaker Jim Wright was using the fight over Contra aid to seize unprecedented control of a foreign policy issue from the White House. In an effort to forge some kind of agreement on Central America, help ensure that any diplomatic efforts would remain under American control, and keep open the prospect for Contra aid, the Administration and Wright had rolled out the "Wright–Reagan Plan" after several weeks of negotiation on August 5, 1987, immediately before the Central American summit. Conservatives denounced it as a

White House sell-out, but it was in fact more of a negative diplomacy ploy that would restart military funding for the Contras if the Sandinistas rejected its strict American-dictated provisions on internal reform, which they did, calling it "a declaration of war." By signing on to the Arias plan in Guatemala 2 days later, the Central Americans superseded the United States, but it was only the prospect of renewed military aid to the Contras that pressured Ortega into agreeing.[14] As pragmatists, George Shultz and Special Envoy Phil Habib recognized that Esquipulas completed the strategic link between force and diplomacy, although by calling for simultaneous cease fires without specific conditions and not requiring direct negotiations between the FSLN and the Contras its enforcement mechanisms would require strengthening. Administration hardliners, however, who were viscerally opposed to a deal of any kind, remained wedded to military pressure alone and the Contras as a cause in themselves.[15] The common ground was an unwillingness to let the Contras disband before the Sandinistas had complied with the requirement to democratize. The Administration was unbowed by Congressional opposition and determined to follow up the $100 million voted for the Contras in 1986 with a $270 million request in 1987. The testy and convoluted struggle between the Administration and Speaker Wright continued for the next 2 years, and although the military program died entirely, Congress did continue humanitarian funding for the Contras.

The Administration's determination to keep the Contras alive was a tacit violation of the Esquipulas accord. Oscar Arias objected in public, and particularly decried the more extreme attitudes of the ideological hardliners. However, he also understood the relationship of force and diplomacy and recognized that the Contras were crucial to his plan. Ironically, what had motivated him into taking stronger multilateral action in the first place was frustration that the United States had in effect prolonged the conflict by being unwilling to take stronger unilateral action to win it. Arias told friends of the Administration that his diplomatic proposal was a second best choice, because "you lack the guts to do what needs to be done" by intervening militarily to remove the Sandinistas. President Carter had heard a similar argument from President Carlos Andres Perez in Venezuela and General Torrijos in Panama in 1979 when they explained they were supporting the Sandinistas in order to keep them out of Cuban hands, because the United States would not take stronger action to remove Somoza.[16]

Through slips, crises, impasses, and duplicity among Congress, the Administration, the Sandinistas, the Contras, and the other Central Americans over the next 3 years, one underlying strategic principle remained in effect: the existence of the Contras, combined with the latent potential for hostile U.S. action, coerced the Sandinistas into complying with the agreement. The war was as hard as ever at the end of 1987. The CIA program was at its peak, funded by the $100 million approved in 1986. Contra weapons now included antiaircraft missiles that helped neutralize Sandinista airpower, and clashes inside Nicaragua had risen from twenty-five to ninety per month.[17] Soviet and Cuban assistance along with universal conscription gave the Sandinista Army the wherewithal to fight back, but the cumulative costs were extremely high. The security situation in nearly one-third of Nicaragua was poor, the society was heavily militarized, half a decade of destruction (in tandem with FSLN mismanagement) had left the economy bankrupt and in hyperinflation. Most importantly, the war was corroding the revolution and the Sandinista's hold on power. There was no doubt that the Contras remained a substantial threat, even after the end of U.S. military support in 1988 essentially reduced them to a force in being.

Even if as rude rural guerrillas, the Contras were a political and moral disaster, they cannot be judged a failure; they served their purpose as an instrument of war. Only in an ideologue's dream were they truly freedom fighters or could they have overthrown the Sandinistas and cause the unraveling of the Soviet Union. They symbolized America's Cold War contradictions better than its principles, but in the end, communism rolled back in Central America. By bleeding Nicaragua, as the CIA and Oliver North directed them to do, the Contras did not execute regime change, but they did coerce change in the regime's behavior and indirectly provoked its downfall. Ronald Reagan's wish to make the Sandinistas say "uncle" came true, more or less.

It did not look that way to the Sandinistas, or to most outside observers right up until the results of the February 1990 elections came in. Daniel Ortega had agreed to join the peace process and hold elections in the certainty that the Sandinistas would prevail. Military and political dynamics were aligning to bring the end game into sight, even though there were many more twists and turns to come. The Sandinistas were not negotiating with the Reagan Administration, but still the clever tacticians, they were talking to Jim Wright and the moderates in Congress. As long as they held to their Esquipulas commitments, they were able to play opponents in Congress against the Administration to kill off the Contra program. The prospect of military aid died for the final time in votes on February 3 and March 3, 1988. Contras were filtering back to their camps in Honduras and fitful talks had begun with the Sandinistas. In early March, the Sandinista Army launched Operation Danto, crossing the Honduran border in a major effort to reduce the Contras in the field. The EPS Commander Humberto Ortega called the offensive off when the Reagan Administration ordered the 82nd Airborne to Honduras, and the Hondurans launched a few air strikes, even though at this point they wanted more than anything to rid themselves of the Contra blight on their territory. However, cut off, with supplies dwindling and CIA support shut down, "Contra leaders feared imminent destruction."[18] They went to negotiations with the Sandinistas at Sapoa in Southern Nicaragua feeling bitter and abandoned, but they were not yet totally defeated and held out some hope the United States would at least keep them protected. At Sapoa, the Ortega brothers and EPS Chief of Staff Joaquin Cuadra had to remain wary of further U.S. moves to support the Contras, but judged they were at their point of maximum military advantage. Thus offset the two sides arrived at a truce without surrender. In a first phase, they declared a temporary cease fire while the Contras disclaimed further U.S. military assistance and foreswore offensive operations inside Nicaragua, but remained armed inside their camps in Honduras. A final ceasefire, followed by disarmament and demobilization, was pending negotiation of an overall settlement, including political issues, which remained a contentious source of pressure on the Sandinistas through the 1990 elections.

Once Sapoa was in place, Congress quickly passed a humanitarian aid bill to sustain the Contras in their camps and effectively protect them from total destruction. The Administration publicly approved the agreement, but officials like Eliot Abrams who were most dedicated to existing policy set about to undermine it behind the scenes, as they had all other attempts to resolve the Central American conflicts. However, as the American tether began to loosen, the Contras began to unravel. The negotiations with the Sandinistas fueled a disruption between those who were now convinced it was time to join the opening political process and those who, like their conservative American sponsors, considered Sapoa a sellout and hoped that renewed aid would allow them to continue fighting. But this was the end of the Reagan presidency, and when George Bush I took office in January 1989, the Cold War was ending and the new Administration was eager to heal the "bleeding sore" of Central America.[19] Neither Bush nor Secretary of State James Baker had been among the hardliners on Central America when they were in the Reagan White House, and now that they were in charge ideology and maximalist positions that thrived on conflict gave way to pragmatics. One of their first accomplishments was a "Bipartisan Pact" between Congress and the White House. Although it hardly satisfied Republican conservatives such as Senator Jesse Helms, the Pact replaced previously irreconcilable divisions with compromise by signaling acceptance of the Arias Peace Plan, guarantying humanitarian assistance to the Contras, and focusing efforts on political rather than military transformation of Nicaragua, even in the expectation that this would require accommodation to the Sandinistas.

THE PEOPLE MAKE MISTAKES

"The revolution stays and Reagan leaves," Daniel Ortega declared vaingloriously at the celebration of the ninth anniversary of the revolution on July 19, 1988.[20] As it turned out, it was not enough to have survived 8 years of militant U.S. hostility, and the Sandinista's themselves had only one more anniversary to go before they and their revolution also departed. It was a risky decision to have accepted Oscar Arias' trade of peace for elections at Esquipulas in 1987. Old splits within the FSLN emerged as their own hardliners like Tomas Borge objected, and Castro, who cherished the Sandinistas like Reagan had cherished the Contras, warned that "The people can make mistakes."[21] It seemed like a good gamble, however, to the Ortega brothers, and the rest of the FSLN went along. Nicaragua was in desperate straights, diplomatically isolated and economically prostrate, with its superpower patron the Soviet Union on the decline and facing its own uncertain future. Most importantly, the Bush Administration had pledged to do what the Reagan Administration never would have done, normalize relations if the Sandinistas won free and fair elections, at least eventually. The Sandinistas even tried to make this promise a central element of their election campaign. It was, in fact victory seemed to them, a sure bet.

Except that it was not. Elections, like war, are a gamble, and this one the FSLN lost, badly. When 86 percent of the Nicaraguan electorate voted on February 25, 1990, the opposition coalition UNO beat the FSLN by 54.7–40.8 percent.[22] It was one of the most heavily observed elections to date, organized by the UN and OAS, with Jimmy Carter brokering every step, and hosting over 2,000 international observers. The reversal was shocking to many and widely unanticipated. The Sandinistas had run an elaborate American-style campaign that submerged the collective nine-headed Directorate, softened the edges of the revolution, and transformed presidential incumbent Daniel Ortega from a "dour commander to a smiling celebrity."[23] Opposing them was an unruly conglomeration of parties who cobbled together just enough consensus behind Violeta Chamorro, the politically unsophisticated widow of Somoza martyr Pedro Joaquin Chamorro. Many figured that Chamorro's campaign had committed suicide by refusing to disavow the Contras or the United States. But Chamorro's benign promise to end the Contra war and quickly repair relations with the United States had a popular appeal that the Sandinistas could not overcome. In retrospect, they recognized that they had done themselves in with a legacy of war and the militarization of the country, along with their own repressive and economically disastrous revolutionary mistakes.[24] Given a choice, the people of Nicaragua revoked the revolution and chose another way out.

The final pieces of the end game did not fall into place easily. When the Contras also got a say in their future, perhaps lacking wise advisors, they did not use the opportunity wisely. Military chief Bermudez and political boss Calero found themselves ousted in an internal revolt at the end of 1989. Most of the civilian figures who had associated themselves with the resistance had already returned to seek their fortunes in the opening political scene. The new Contra leaders refused to participate in the elections even though several of the field commanders were well-known and popular in their native northern zones. Many Contras did turn up to vote, but their principal contribution was to continue small-scale attacks that disrupted preparations and kept much of the border area insecure. Through two more Central American summits at Tesoro Beach in El Salvador and Tela in Honduras, Washington—with the complicity of Arias—had held up Contra demobilization to keep the pressure on the FSLN. The UNO election victory meant they now had to complete their negotiations with the new Chamorro Government in which they had no stake and over which they held little leverage. Initially the remnant commanders resisted demobilizing, until their erstwhile benefactor the CIA finally executed the coup de grace and told them it was time to shut down. They signed the Toncontín Accord in March 1990, and a joint UN/OAS mission, The International Support and Verification Commission (CIAV), created to support the Esquipulas II Peace Plan, then stepped in to assist with the demobilization, repatriation, and resettlement of the Contras. After this initial effort, there proved to be little enthusiasm for dealing with the "wild Indians" of the Nicaraguan Resistance, who found themselves pawned off to remote corners of Nicaragua where they became supplicants for international aid, while small bands of armed renegades roamed the countryside as re-Contras. A few diehard champions in Congress and from the Reagan Administration, such as Eliot Abrams, discredited by Iran–Contra indictment although pardoned by President Bush, lamented their plight, but their political notoriety was best quickly forgotten. With no more war or Washington controversy as fuel, and no political identity of their own, the Contras quickly faded from the news, as did Nicaragua itself. It was a dissolute end to a bitter insurgency.

Immediately following the February 25, 1990, elections, Nicaragua was at a cross-roads. It had neither entirely departed the realm of civil war, nor had it entirely committed to a road toward understanding. Dismantling the Contras was only part of achieving peace. There was a larger challenge. Mortification at the polls had temporarily demoralized the Sandinistas, and, without viable options, they relinquished the government with unanticipated grace. However, they were not prepared to simply abandon their revolution and fade away. Like good revolutionaries, they understood that power grows from the barrel of a gun and determined to hold onto to their arms, even if they had placed themselves before the eyes of the world in a way that made it impossible to use them. In addition to forming a powerful opposition bloc with thirty-nine out of ninety-two seats in the National Assembly and controlling the judiciary, the FSLN retained command of the Sandinista Army, the Ministry of the Interior and with it the police, as well as the intelligence service State Security (DGSE). As many as one-third of recent recruits abandoned the army after the elections, but there were still over 40,000 troops bristling with Soviet-supplied arms, and the revolution's most hardcore supporters could be found there and in the security apparatus. In addition, the party had handed out weapons and ammunition liberally among its civilian supporters.

The point man for dealing with the Sandinistas as well as the Contras was Minister of the Presidency and Doña Violeta Chamorro's son-in-law Antonio Lacayo.[25] Lacayo recognized that the government's electoral mandate gave it strong legitimacy, but that its direct authority was limited. Politically, the country was deeply divided. Radicals in both the UNO coalition and in the FSLN were making aggressive demands for immediate action. Lacayo, advised by former Venezuelan President Carlos Andres Perez who had returned to office in 1989, decided on a version of the strategy of building the center by seeking out moderates in the FSLN, especially those who held power. With President Chamorro's reluctant blessing, he began negotiations with Defense Minister and EPS Commander Humberto Ortega and his deputy Joaquin Cuadra, who had convinced ex-President Daniel Ortega and thus isolated intransigents among the FSLN leadership. Despite initially high tension and lack of trust, within a month they reached agreement on a Protocol of Transition that amounted to an anomalous form of political–military power sharing that would depoliticize and reduce the size of the military, civilianize the police, and recover arms from the population. In a very sensitive decision, Ortega remained as head of the military, thus guaranteeing that the government would not be in a position to take armed reprisals against the FSLN, while the party relinquished its formal role within the military. Conservatives in UNO, outraged at this accommodation to the enemy, abandoned the government, and went into opposition. Fidel Castro announced the end of military assistance to Nicaragua on March 8, 1990, and the last Cuban advisors quickly withdrew. The arrangement worked well enough that when Chamorro's term ended in 1995, Nicaragua was demilitarized and had completed its transition from dictatorship to democracy.

The United States could have made the government's power-sharing agreement with the Sandinistas untenable. This it did not do, choosing to acquiesce instead. President Bush's Assistant Secretary of State, Bernard Aronson, was a Democrat who had with some courage accepted a job that required making peace in Washington and promoting reconciliation in Central America. The Nicaraguan elections made both of these priorities easier since the Administration would not have to deal with a hostile FSLN government. Antonio Lacayo admits he had been naïve in expecting that this meant the United States would actually assist Nicaragua's democratic transition.[26] Instead, the United States missed the stabilizing significance of the pact between the Chamorro Government and the Sandinistas. Instead of helping nurture the delicate process, it hampered progress by reverting to a paternalistic approach, pressuring the government, and suspending most economic assistance for 18 months in an effort to divide the two. The ascendancy of arch-conservative Republican Jesse Helms to the Chairmanship of the Senate Foreign Affairs Committee, where he made Nicaragua his special cause, further perplexed U.S. policy by focusing on righting the wrongs of the past, such as restoring private property expropriated by the Sandinistas and bringing the murderers of several Contra leaders to justice. (Many Nicaraguans considered the 1991 shooting of former Contra military commander Enrique Bermudez to have been justice done and best forgotten.) Above all, the continued presence of Humberto Ortega and other Sandinistas in the Army and police caused deep suspicion, and with some reason.

END GAMES ON THE PERIPHERY

By the late-1980s, it was evident to the Sandinistas as it was to everyone else that the Soviet Union was becoming a spent power. It was not evident, however, that the Cold War was over, especially not in Third World flashpoints like Afghanistan, and in Nicaragua where the Contra War was raging. Amid the conflicting signals, the Sandinistas hedged their bets by signing on to the peace process, but they were not about to abandon the Soviet–Cuban world. In July 1987, 1 month before Daniel Ortega committed Nicaragua to the Esquipulas peace process, his brother Humberto concluded a 5-year military cooperation plan with the Soviet Union. Among other things, the Soviets committed to help enlarge the EPS to an improbable 600,000 men and to deliver the squadron of MIGs first promised in 1980 that had caused the Reagan Administration so much grief. Soviet aid to Nicaragua in 1988 totaled nearly $1 billion, including new petroleum guarantees and a 10 percent increase in military assistance over the previous year to around $575 million.[27] The Bush Administration, joined by Oscar Arias, denounced this continued Soviet military involvement in Central America as an obstacle to peace. Soviet officials were at the same time expounding the "new thinking" of Mikhail Gorbachev's kinder and gentler foreign policy, and the message that Assistant Secretary Aronson was receiving from his counterpart Yuri Pavlov was that the Soviets supported peace in Central America. Eager to transcend the limits of superpower competition and reduce the rancor, President Bush and Secretary Baker decided to make Central America a test case of what they considered "the biggest thorn" in U.S.–Soviet relations.[28] In a year of diplomatic exchanges, including at every face-to-face encounter between President Bush and Gorbachev, the Administration asserted that overall improvement in relations depended on Soviet willingness to reduce their aid to Nicaragua and to pressure Cuba and Nicaragua to abide by Central American peace agreements. Gorbachev called the U.S. bluff by stonewalling. He protested that he could do nothing to influence Castro and even lied inexplicably in a letter to President Bush that Moscow had stopped sending military aid to Nicaragua altogether in 1988. Gorbachev apparently had decided there was still advantage to be gained by troubling the United States in the region, most logically to offset to U.S. aid to the Mujahedin in Afghanistan and to demonstrate resolve to Fidel Castro, who was highly critical of *perestroika* and the new direction in the Soviet Union. National Security Advisor Brent Scowcroft concluded that Gorbachev was maintaining the "Brezhnev system with a humanitarian paint job,"[29] and desiring cooperation with Moscow on much more than Central America, the Bush Administration eventually dropped the linkage. The geostrategic fears about Soviet penetration into America's backyard that had preoccupied the Reagan Administration were no longer in effect. Moscow was to maintain a distinct passiveness once the peace process got underway. As Robert Kagan concludes, the most important thing the Soviet Union did to help end the wars in Central America was collapse.[30]

The Sandinista's decade-long gamble on the Soviets and the Cubans, sustained by ideological fatalism, had been their greatest strategic error from the beginning. Getting the Soviet strong arm on Central America after the Cold War entered its termination phase did not incline the United States to kindness toward the Sandinistas, who also continued playing their own double game up until the end. When Harry Shlaudeman, who had negotiated with them in Manzanillo and was now Ambassador to Managua, called on Minister of the Presidency Antonio Lacayo in December 1990, it was to demand that the Sandinista Army stop arming the Salvadoran FMLN with surface-to-air missiles. The United States had an abundance of evidence: guerrillas had recently brought down several Salvadoran aircraft with missiles; in November 1989, a small plane from Nicaragua had crashed in Eastern El Salvador carrying SAM-7s and Redeyes (that the CIA had originally supplied to the Contras); and in November 1990, the Salvadoran Armed Forces captured more advanced SAM-14s for the first time, and the Soviets had confirmed they had delivered them to Nicaragua in 1986.[31] By the end of 1990, detailed missile accounting and recovery had largely supplanted clandestine crossborder arms trafficking as a refined practice of the Central American peace process, overseen by the UN Mission to Nicaragua (ONUCA). Shlaudeman understandably dismissed as lacking in credibility Lacayo's protest that the EPS had stopped sending arms to the Salvadoran insurgents at the end of 1989 and was now leaning on them to negotiate with the Salvadoran Government. But Lacayo's explanation was apparently true. Several sympathetic EPS officers, acting independently, had "stolen" the latest shipment of missiles from Nicaraguan stocks and delivered them to the insurgents. From the U.S. perspective, it was distasteful enough to tolerate the Sandinistas who had lost an election and still controlled the Armed Forces, but some brow beating was in order when they appeared to persist in helping their FMLN compatriots now that the Salvadoran combatants had begun creeping with great repugnance into negotiations.

Chasing down the flow of armaments to the FMLN had been a frustrating enterprise ever since the Reagan Administration first published the El Salvador White Paper in early 1981. There had never been any doubt that Cuba and Nicaragua sustained the insurgency, but the smoking gun weapons hauls that did turn up never had much public impact. Worse, in over a decade of trying, the ESAF with U.S. intelligence support, never did achieve a significant interdiction, much less slow the FMLN's sophisticated and multifaceted arms smuggling operations.[32] More broadly, despite a quadrupling in size and the best in U.S. counterinsurgency assistance, advice, and firepower, the ESAF had proven incapable of offsetting, but not defeating what had become the best-organized, best-trained, and most dedicated guerrilla army ever seen in Latin America. For all of its strength, its wiliness, and its ability to strike anywhere in the country while controlling nearly a third of it, neither had the FMLN been able to improve its strategic position. Over 75,000 Salvadorans, nearly 1.5 percent of the entire population, had died while the country became locked in an endless and corrosive cycle of violence. The civil war seemed eternally cursed with the ugly drudge of stalemate.

The nature of the war had not changed much, but politics in El Salvador had. Even though the original intent of the U.S.–Salvadoran joint venture was victory not peace, the groundwork for negotiation and demilitarization began with the U.S. project to institute democracy. When he became President in 1984, Napoleon Duarte had vindicated the strategy of building the center, but he had proven too eager to negotiate with the left and had only awakened the desire for peace without achieving results. Now in 1989, dying of cancer and with his Christian Democratic Party having self-destructed in successive legislative and presidential elections, he handed power over to his other adversaries on the right. But the ARENA that came into office was not the implacable and reactionary party of Roberto D'Aubuisson, the "godfather of the politics of hate," as journalist James Lemoyne called him.[33] There were clear motives to seek resolution of the civil war even while holding to the notion of victory. President Cristiani and his more moderate associates who had taken control of the party had a conflict-fatigued electorate to respond to and business to get on with. They were as sick of the killing as most other Salvadorans and were seriously interested in intelligent reform. Above all they were businessmen, this war was terrible for the economy, and the protection racket state was no longer a reliable means for advancing these interests. This put ARENA in a much better positioned than the left-leaning PDC to speak of peace to the military, which had also become more discriminate now that they no longer felt they were fighting on death ground. Many officers were certain that they could rely on time and continued U.S. aid to prevail. However, in 1989, new Bush Administration officials who were weighing the consequences of the past decade found little appeal in the idea of remaining in El Salvador for a generation, as some thought it might take to defeat the rebels, especially now that the Cold War that had justified intervention in the first place was ending. As with Nicaragua, the change in attitude that accompanied the change in U.S. regime made a critical difference.

The regional environment had also shifted. Duarte signed the Central American Peace Accord at Esquipulas in 1987 for three reasons. First, as Oscar Arias recognized, Duarte was the most seriously motivated among the other leaders to end the war, even if it put him at crosspurposes with his U.S. ally. Second, the agreement unequivocally recognized the legitimacy of sovereign states, reinforced elections and democracy, and granted no formal status to insurgent organizations. Third, Daniel Ortega had looked him in the eye and given him a handshake on August 7 and told him that Nicaragua would comply with its terms.[34] Ortega's promise did not impress the Americans nor exactly seal the FMLN's fate, but Duarte took it seriously. The Arias plan did link the Sandinista's interest in ending the Contra insurgency to the Salvadoran Government's interest in ending the FMLN insurgency. As the regional dynamics of conflict resolution began to take effect in Nicaragua, even in the tentative phase when the participants were more concerned with obtaining tactical advantage, there was an inevitable impact on the Salvadoran conflict.

A FINAL FINAL OFFENSIVE

This did not mean that El Salvador became quiescent at the initial outbreak of peacemaking. Many in the government and the military were still confident that they were winning and insisted on demanding that the guerrillas lay down their arms if they wanted to talk. There were years of war-making yet to go, and it took a sudden tempest of violence to impel the contestants into the crossroads of negotiation. When the FMLN launched its second "Final Offensive" on November 11, 1989, the country went into shock, and its effects rippled through the region, waking up the international media, and shaking offices in Washington, DC. The offensive was in part a rerun of the 1981 Final Offensive, and it seemed for a moment as if the *Tiempos de Locura* had returned. There had been warnings. For several months, the pace of small-scale attacks and urban infiltration had picked up, and along with it selective terrorism, including bombings and assassinations, had increased the climate of fear and insecurity. The Army captured a document that revealed a distinct shift in FMLN strategy. Prolonged political–military warfare, adopted in 1984, had the objectives of wearing down the ESAF in the field, creating the impression that government could not govern, and weakening the wills of the population and the United States. Called *Plan Fuego* (Plan Fire), the new strategy aimed to accelerate these cumulative effects while building once again to a national insurrection. Developed in consultation with Cuba, and counting on close operational coordination with Nicaragua, the FMLN began planning in late-1988 and stockpiling arms and ammunition in mid-1989.[35] Arms shipments became almost brazen, and the ESAF began capturing AK-47s and other Soviet Bloc weapons for the first time. The introduction of shoulder fired antiaircraft missiles threatened to upset the strategic balance by neutralizing the Salvadoran Air Force, and when missiles were seized, Humberto Ortega did not deny that they had originated in Nicaragua.

The FMLN called the 1989 Final Offensive *Al Tope y Punto,* which roughly translates as "all at once to the max." After staging for weeks before the November 11 d-day, guerrillas from all five FMLN factions converged on San Salvador. Their minimum objective was to occupy the capital for 72 hours and ultimately to spark insurrection. Calling on the population to support them in the streets, the FMLN initially occupied much of the city from the poorest barrios to upper class neighborhoods. In the United States, El Salvador suddenly leaped from the back pages to breaking news for several days during a dramatic standoff between the guerrillas and a group of Special Forces trainers who barricaded themselves on a floor of the downtown Sheraton Hotel. Despite the intimations, the United States and the Salvadoran Government had let themselves be lulled by assumptions that they were winning the war, albeit slowly, and that the FMLN lacked the capacity for serious offensive action. As they had in 1981, the population declined to rise up, but the sudden seizure of the capital sent the new Cristiani Government reeling. Caught off guard, the ESAF found itself forced to recapture the city street-by-street in a grueling 3-week counteroffensive, in which they resorted to aerial bombing large sectors of the city. About 3,000 guerrillas were killed or wounded, along with hundreds of soldiers and several thousand civilians. The offensive ended when the remaining FMLN units withdrew overnight unopposed by the ESAF.

How and why the General Command of the five guerrilla factions agreed to shift gears from dedication to prolonged warfare and take such a risky course of action offers intriguing insight into the transformation of an insurgency from war to peace. The FMLN launched the 1989 Final Offensive proclaiming one goal, but it achieved something entirely different, although not necessarily unintended. Popular insurrection did not materialize, and like the 1968 Tet Offensive in Vietnam, government forces regained control after the initial shock and ultimately defeated the FMLN militarily. It would be natural to conclude that nearly a decade of isolation in the bush had led to a lack of perspective among the FMLN, and that their assessment of the political conditions for insurrection resulted from a lack of strategic vision, essentially the same blunder they had committed when the first call failed 9 years earlier. The FMLN was certainly mistaken in their belief that, in the words of ever-eloquent ERP comandante Joaquin Villalobos, the FMLN could be distinguished from a terrorist organization because its "revolutionary language of violence" legitimized "military practices [that] seek to win the support of society."[36] The contrary was true; most of the population had long-ago rejected violence and the FMLN along with it.

If the guerrilla fighters came down from the hills to fight in San Salvador because they really believed the people were on their side and the time was ripe for revolution, their commanders knew better.[37] There were several reasons. The violence and sterile Marxism–Leninism of their rhetoric belied an ideological pluralism that had always characterized relations among the five different groups, and their flexibility only increased with the advent of Gorbachev and *perestroika* in the Soviet Union. The implications were pragmatic. It was evident to the FMLN in a way it was not to their allies in Nicaragua and Cuba that, operating as they were on the far periphery of the USSR, that there was little security in aspiring to join the Eastern Bloc. In addition, the Sandinistas were already under pressure from a strengthening regional peace process that granted insurgent movements no status. More directly, prolonged warfare was taking too long. As LeoGrande put it, "Endless war was not a viable strategy."[38] Forced recruitment was an increasing resort as attrition harvested its inevitable toll and combatant numbers steadily declined from their peak of around 14,000 in the mid-1980s. The FMLN needed a way out. Even if they held out a residual hope of victory, the primary reason they launched a second Final Offensive in 1989 was to maximize military conditions for political negotiations.

There was nothing contradictory about the FMLN's approach. Pounding counter-insurgency combined with political evolution had compelled them into accepting the need to negotiate, but they were not about to simply lay down their arms and commit suicide by Death Squad. They remained entirely Clausewitzian insurgents. With *Plan Fuego,* the FMLN revised their aims, and acting in coordination with the Sandinistas, approached the onset of the peace process as an opportunity to advance their own tough political–military strategy. Accordingly, the Arias Peace Treaty,

> ...will continue to be a positive instrument of the revolution...so long as the revolutionary forces use it offensively to divide and break up, maintaining concessions in a game of symmetry. The Yankees cannot give anything and must ask everything. The Sandinista popular revolution has established the basis for its symmetrical game; we have our own.[39]

At the same time, the Salvadoran government and the FMLN faced symmetry of a different kind stemming from the widespread popular desire for peace, and sought maximum advantage by maneuvering to appear flexible. In consequence of the August 1987 Esquipulas summit, several of the FMLN commanders departed the field, and consulting in Managua and Havana, traveled to San Jose where they discussed regional peace with Arias. In January 1989, the FMLN made a peace proposal in which it said it was willing to participate in elections. The first discussions with political party leaders, including ARENA, followed the next month, but foundered on the FMLN demand to postpone the elections from March to June. Resolution of the Salvadoran civil war was quickly incorporated into the agenda of ongoing regional peace meetings under Esquipulas, and initial contact in the form of dialogue between the FMLN and the ARENA government took place in Mexico in September.

In this context, with peace seemingly about to break out, the Final Offensive had all the more forceful impact. Initially the reaction was all negative. Betrayed and infuriated, Salvadoran President Cristiani renounced further talks with the FMLN and angrily broke relations with Nicaragua. Daniel Ortega responded that he was proud to help to fight the murderous Salvadoran regime. Regional efforts to achieve peace took a step backwards, and it seemed the two sides had returned to permanent confrontation. However, as is so often the case in war, the Final Offensive had unintended consequences and these consequences ultimately turned into a catalyst for negotiations. Shocked at the near-loss of the capital city, the ESAF reverted to kind, and in addition to using air power against the civilian population, the Death Squads reappeared. One incident out stood in notoriety. Plucked from its accustomed rural counterinsurgency role and thrust suddenly into an urban counteroffensive, the ESAF's toughest and best-known U.S.-trained and equipped unit, the Atlacatl Rapid Reaction Battalion, once again became the center of controversy. Their area of operation included the Jesuit University of Central America, and, after consulting with the High Command, Atlacatl officers detained the university rector along with five fellow priests and had them and two witnesses executed. The priests were widely regarded as authors of the revolutionary movement, and from the perspective of the ESAF, they more than deserved elimination for the threat and the embarrassment to honor they had provoked. These Jesuits were not anonymous peasants, and some of them were internationally prominent Catholic intellectuals; their cold-blooded murders instantly reevoked the assassinations of Archbishop Romero and the American nuns, and seemed a reversion to the horror of the early 1980s.

The Administration initially put the best face on things, dismissing the FMLN offensive as an act of desperation while urgently rushing military supplies to El Salvador. The U.S. Ambassador even suggested there was credence in the official Armed Forces explanation that the Jesuit murders had been the work of the guerrillas. It quickly became apparent that this was not the case, and realization that victory over the FMLN was not in the cards eventually sank in.[40] Coming after 10 years of American counterinsurgency support, the success of the offensive and the brutal ESAF response seemed to signal failure to reform the character of the Salvadoran military and a limit to the transformative power of intervention. President Bush, under considerable pressure from an outraged and skeptical Congress, signed the Foreign Aid bill for Fiscal Year 1991 with military aid at one-half of the Administration request, and officials convincingly informed the Salvadorans that if they did not bring the killers to justice further U.S. aid would no longer be assured. This was exactly the opposite from the reaction to the atrocity committed in 1981 by the same Atlacatl Battalion, when Thomas Enders had dissembled in testimony to Congress about the El Mozote massacre rather than risk an aid cut off. If the Reagan Administration's reaction to El Mozote was a parable of the clash between interests and principles during the Cold War, the Bush Administration's reaction to the Jesuit murders demonstrated how new global circumstances had changed U.S. priorities, and along with them the terms of the joint venture with El Salvador.

The scales now tipped definitely toward resolving the civil war at the table. Within weeks of the offensive, the FMLN and the government separately contacted the UN to request help in negotiating a settlement. For another 2 years, El Salvador continued to oscillate between war and peace. However, once the process began to unfold it became an almost classic case of conflict resolution, much more formal and structured than the ad hoc negotiations that took place in Nicaragua. In March 1990, the two sides met in Geneva under UN mediation for the first time. Hostility and distrust between the "terrorist delinquents" of the FMLN and the "repressive puppets" of the government was enormous. Nevertheless both unilaterally announced partial cease fires and were able to agree on three guiding principles: 1) the basis of the conflict was political not ideological; 2) the goal was democratization of El Salvador;

and 3) negotiation would continue in earnest until their completion.[41] The talks continued through tense encounters and crises of confidence in several locations—Venezuela, Mexico, New York—until they achieved a permanent cease fire and final peace accord, signed in an emotional ceremony at Chapultepec, Mexico on January 16, 1992. Instead of power sharing, the FMLN laid down its arms in exchange for full participation in the political system, in which they were to average 20 percent of the vote in future elections and become the second political force in the country. They also won significant reforms of the military. These included a 50 percent reduction in size from its peak of 63,000, a purge of the officer corps secured only after great resistance, introduction of civilian oversight, and restriction of its mission to defending national sovereignty, along with demilitarization of the security forces and incorporation of FMLN members into a new National Civilian Police force. As a result, the involvement of the military in politics effectively ended. Other provisions of the peace agreement covering the justice system, economic recovery, and land reform had less definitive results. The National Assembly approved a general amnesty after a UN Truth Commission investigated 22,000 cases and concluded in its report *From Madness to Hope* that the government was responsible for the vast majority of human rights abuses committed during the civil war. A small UN observer mission in El Salvador (ONUSAL), arbitrated implementation of the peace accords until it substantially withdrew following national elections in March 1994. By then, the end of the conflict and the consolidation of democracy had proved enduring.[42]

Virtually all of the protagonists of the peace process agreed that the termination of the Salvadoran civil war and the transformation that accompanied it was evolutionary, and in some respects was a model of conflict resolution. In their 2001 assessment,[43] Mark Peceny and William Stanley conclude that the Salvadoran experience demonstrated how noncoercive international intervention can under certain circumstances substitute for security guarantees in helping to end internal conflicts. They suggest that "liberal social reconstruction"—in which the acceptance of democratic values and practices takes the place of armed conflict—occurs in a three-phase process. In the first phase, active combatants adopt liberal postures as a tactic to attract international legitimacy. In the second phase, internationally mediated negotiations create an environment in which adversaries can build trust and begin to agree on and follow rules. Once settlements are in place, the presence of international actors ensures that the commitment to liberal reform deepens and becomes self-reinforcing. Any peace agreement, whether it results from victory or negotiation, must sufficiently resolve fundamental political and security issues if it is going to prevent the conflict eventually from reoccurring. This the Salvadoran Peace Accords did, even though the war's end did not fundamentally transform the country's economic inequity or social injustice that could be considered as underlying causes. Clearly security was the first priority, and other factors had to align in order to guarantee the conditions under which internationally mediated negotiations could begin in the first place. Strategic stalemate and the onset of exhaustion created a shared realization among combatant leaders on the ground that continued warfare was futile. Geopolitical developments, including the end of the Cold War and the regional peace initiative, effectively transformed the international dimension into a source of pacification rather than confrontation. Accordingly, and most critically, the United States became an indispensable agent of peace.

This peacemaker role was not limited to U.S. diplomatic support for the peace process in the UN Security Council and pressure on the government. In December 1988, the FMLN sent a private letter to President-elect Bush indicating its readiness to enter into dialogue. The receptive but nonspecific response delivered by the State Department spokesman was the first-ever positive U.S. reply to a political initiative from the left, and it prompted great optimism in the General Command. In February 1990, Secretary Baker and Soviet Foreign Minister Shevardnadze announced support for a UN-mediated settlement in El Salvador. This joint position held throughout the peace process despite tension over the supply of antiaircraft missiles to the FMLN and tribulations over Nicaragua. Most importantly, although the conditions in El Salvador for international mediation and liberal social reconstruction were close to ideal, the presence of the United States as a backdrop security guarantor for both sides made it much more feasible for the UN to oversee the peace process without any form of peacekeeping arrangement. While maintaining pressure on the Salvadoran government and the Salvadoran Armed Forces throughout the negotiations, the United States did not abandon them. At the same time, the United States straddled the two sides by demonstrating to the FMLN that it was dedicated to achieving authentic resolution of the conflict. For example, it welcomed FMLN participation in the democratic process, and embraced its proposals for reform of the Armed Forces and creation of the civilian National Police. When Ambassador William Walker, accompanied by Congressman Joe Moakley and USAID official Richard McCall, visited the guerrilla camp at Santa Marta on the slopes of Guazapa volcano in July 1991, and followed up with a second visit the next month, FMLN Commanders regarded these as major confidence building events that redoubled the seriousness of their participation in the negotiations.[44]

The experience and consequences of intervention in El Salvador were decidedly mixed for three U.S. Administrations between 1979 and 1992. Even if containing the threat of a communist victory defined a clear national security line of decision and the exercise of U.S. power was sufficient to act as a governor on the overall situation most of the time, its direct impact was often a muddle. The United States acted as a revisionist power by sponsoring political and military reform, but it did so to maintain the geopolitical status quo, and then only out of necessity when descent into violent anarchy and radical revolution threatened. Support for democracy and counterinsurgency were integral to each other, and the result was reform with repression. The switch to supporting conflict resolution rather than victory in El Salvador came with a change in global circumstances, when national interests, most broadly defined, determined that there was relative advantage in doing so. Prior to that, even in the condition of military stalemate, the executive resisted congressional and international efforts to promote of conflict resolution. U.S. intervention unquestionably prolonged and increased the costs of the Salvadoran civil war. At the same time, the liberal transformation of El Salvador that culminated with the Peace Accords in

1992 is unlikely to have occurred without the prior decade of U.S. support. As for alternatives, there is the contingent question of how the United States might have responded had the Carter Administration chosen not to intervene in El Salvador when it did and as a result faced not one, but two revolutionary regimes supported by Cuba and the Soviet Union on its Southern flank.

There remains one other as yet unmentioned dimension of El Salvador's civil war and U.S. intervention. Fourteen Americans did give their lives in El Salvador, but it was overwhelmingly the Salvadorans who paid the price for U.S. actions, and ending intervention there was less painful than it otherwise would have been, because no American troops were involved and therefore much less was at stake. This could be viewed as a strategic benefit for the United States, but another benefit hidden within the tragedy of the civil war also accrued to the Salvadorans. Close to one-fifth of the entire nation removed itself from the line of fire and fled the country, most for the United States, and nearly all as illegal immigrants. Once established in Los Angeles, Chicago, Washington, DC, and thousands of other locales, they sent back to family members a portion of the incomes they never could have earned in El Salvador. This immigration was eventually acknowledged officially in the form of Voluntary Departure Status that allowed Salvadorans to remain temporarily in the United States. Remittances, which surpassed $2.5 billion in the closing years of the war and continue today, accounted for 15–20 percent of GDP and prevented the economy from going into terminal decline.[45] This largely informal flow of U.S. dollars blunted the FMLN's strategy of sabotaging the economy; offset largely negative fluctuations in prices for agroexports, especially coffee; injected hard currency directly into the economy; helped to equalize income distribution; and supplemented U.S. economic assistance, that was in any case largely dedicated to filling shortfalls in the government budget, 50 percent of which was going to war expenses in any case. Out-migration was a huge social escape valve and the flow of remittances an economic life preserver. It was another way out, perhaps a decisive one and without it, the entire proposition might not have survived. The spontaneous flow of Salvadorans to the United States was a crucial corollary to the joint venture, one that originated in the realms of chance and unintended consequence rather than in the intentional aims of strategy and policy.

Aftermath and Epilogue

Wars transform the future....

—Fred Iklé, *Every War Must End*

ISTHMUS WITHOUT JOY

The wars in Nicaragua and El Salvador that ended over a decade and a half ago are perhaps best forgotten, swept down the river of history. These were after all small wars, footnotes inconsequential among the course of great world events. Yet even in the forgetting, there is something worth remembering, and the concept of Central America as a bridge between the tragedy of Vietnam and the disaster of Iraq bears further reflection. If there are great differences in origin and circumstance among these three conflicts, there are at the same time fundamental and recurring similarities in the nature of United States involvement in them. Occurring within the span of a generation, each was an intervention of choice justified by portraying a threat to vital national security interests that brought a peripheral region to the center of attention. Each compelled a prolonged and open-ended entanglement in the intractable, inseparable, and inescapable political and military challenges of irregular warfare. None resulted in victory. In the end, domestic political controversy enveloped all the three interventions and ultimately made them much more costly than anticipated. The absence of U.S. combat forces in Central America is the outstanding difference and the one reason that intervention there did not become a quagmire on the scale of Vietnam or Iraq.

The recurring nature of these experiences suggests that competent policy and strategy matters when intervening in any war, no matter how small or irregular, not just the big ones. Certain other lessons seem elementary if not quite iron clad. Three areas for consideration emerge from the battlegrounds of Central America: What has come in the aftermath of the conflicts in Nicaragua and El Salvador, and in particular from the transformations that grew out of their terminations? How does the course of action the United States pursued stand up in terms of the purposes it served, its execution, and its outcome? And finally, what broader conclusions and applications emerge from the U.S. experience with irregular warfare and intervention in Central America, especially in light of just how difficult this period proved to be?

"The wars in Central America ended, but there is no peace." This commentary emerged from an unusual conference that took place in March 2006 in Toledo, Spain where former Presidents, military officers, guerrilla commanders, and other protagonists of the conflicts met to discuss the lessons of the Central American peace process.[1] Their judgment is widely shared in both El Salvador and Nicaragua. This seems an odd conclusion for two countries that went from sustained turmoil to definitive peace, and are now reasonably stable democracies, at peace with their neighbors, with positive, if modest rates of economic growth, and where life is certainly better than it was during the ordeals of civil war. Fear that revenge would be unleashed never materialized, except in a few isolated cases, and if anything the probability of renewed civil conflict among Nicaraguans and Salvadorans is less than the probability that the United States and Russia will restart the Cold War. But there is nevertheless, a ringing sense that somehow, all is not quite complete. In Nicaragua, dictatorship and revolution are equally dead. Democracy has revived the opera of politics, with the Sandinistas now solid members of the cast. Tourism is booming, but for most people life is much the same, a struggle for survival where progress is still a dream in slow motion. In El Salvador, economic growth is more evident (if still sustained by remittances), the FMLN left has become a semipermanent opposition that competes in elections against successive ARENA governments of the right, and former guerrillas and soldiers can reflect peacefully on their deadly cat and mouse struggle. But the country is still not free from preoccupation with violence. The gangs called "Maras" are a legacy of illegal immigrant life on the streets of cities such as Los Angeles and the traditional Salvadoran propensity to violence. They have created a newly corrosive mix that has left society pervaded with a sense of insecurity and defied all means to eliminate then.[2]

If as strategist Fred Iklé says, "Wars transform the future...and the most important transformations come in how they end,"[3] the aftermath of the civil wars in Nicaragua and El Salvador was unperfected. The advent of democracy at the point of bayonets did curtail armed ideological competition and supplanted the legitimacy of seeking political change through violence. Governance is no longer a sterile choice between revolution and military authoritarianism, while electoral politics has solved the problem of how power is disputed and achieved. Yet the task of state-building in both countries is far from complete. There remain basic problems with how groups perform once they achieve power, with checks and balances that tend to operate only on the margins, with sustained failure to address socioeconomic issues, and with corruption. Despite significant political evolution, by these criteria democracy in El Salvador and Nicaragua must be assessed generally as "low quality."[4] Looking back, it is true that war was transforming, but there are the further questions as to whether wars were necessary for these changes to take place or whether they were worth the cost. An answer would require a speculative stretch, but the questions do lead to another: Did anyone benefit from these prolonged conflicts?

WHO BENEFITED?

Both Nicaragua and El Salvador were broken and failing states that brought armed revolutions on themselves, and it seems reasonable to conclude that Central Americans are better off as a result of the transformations that occurred as the conflicts terminated. But what the combatants desired and intended when their civil wars began and where they ended up are two different issues. As for the Nicaraguans, when the betrayed dictator Somoza fled, his regime collapsed and he soon met his end, assassinated in Paraguayan exile. The Sandinistas had their moment of insurrectional triumph, but their revolution failed to endure and they lost power due to their own folly and relentless American opposition. The Contras helped bring their Sandinista enemies down, but they faded altogether once their role as shadow warriors ended. The Salvadoran government and Armed Forces emerged from a decade of civil war strengthened and much changed, but not victorious. The FMLN became the most proficient guerrilla army in Latin America, but unlike the Sandinistas, it won no taste of revolutionary power and had to settle for reform instead. Among the international sponsors, Fidel Castro briefly enjoyed the company of his Sandinista protégés, but the Cuban investment in Central American revolution, as in the rest of Latin America, came to nothing. The Soviets, far from the calculating evil empire and about to be overtaken by their own collapse, found that their haphazard subsidy of proxy war in Central America crystallized rather than distracted Washington's determination and brought no compensating benefit in the Third World or anywhere else. It was a meager harvest.

When the United States chose to intervene in the Central American maelstrom, it was with propriety born of the Cold War and the Monroe Doctrine, but without any idea what would come next or that it would last a dozen years through three Administrations. Jimmy Carter's policy was well-intended but misconceived, and its execution politically incompetent. Dedication to principles of human rights and a benign U.S. presence that denied the Cold War presumed too much. Ironically, the approach actually helped produce the revolution that overthrew Somoza. Carter's attempt to balance ideals with realism after the Soviet invasion of Afghanistan came too late, and the result was failure in Nicaragua and near failure in El Salvador. For Ronald Reagan, like Carter, ideology was a powerful animus that led to excess, but the President's "sunny patriotism" belied a more somber view of the threat. With enemies at the gate, his Administration chose Central America to draw a line against global communism by containing it in El Salvador and rolling it back in Nicaragua. There was as much symbolism as strategy in the crusade. Reagan and the pragmatists around him were prudent, even cautious, although the hardliners tended to be less so. By sticking to a strategy of indirect intervention and irregular warfare, the limited investment of U.S. blood and treasure matched the level of concrete interests.

As for outcomes, creating the Contra insurgency fed Bill Casey's fantasy of unraveling the USSR from the periphery, but Ronald Reagan's determination in Central America could hardly have had that much impact on the sclerotic Soviets. The effect on the United States itself was more significant if terribly contradicted; helping begin the long redemption from Vietnam, while fuelling war with Congress and stumbling into political disaster with Iran–Contra. The pragmatism of the Bush Administration relieved 8 years of partisan tension, fit the changed global circumstances, and was well suited to getting rid of "the sore of Central America" while overseeing the termination phase. The consequences of U.S. policy in Central America itself are measurable: the Sandinistas did say uncle, El Salvador did not fall, and both became democracies; regional stability has prevailed, security issues are now of a transnational second order—drug transshipment, gang crime—and the most important controversies revolve not around civil war, but support for the Central American Free Trade Area. As another reward, El Salvador joined that small group of unquestioning U.S. allies, and demonstrated it by being the only Latin American nation to contribute troops to Iraq in 2003. It would be incorrect to argue in summary judgment that the United States failed in Central America, even if the Contra war and the Death Squads place its legacy on the dark side of human nature. Strictly in terms of its stated goals, U.S. intervention was a success, although at high cost and without victory.

HOW DID THE UNITED STATES DO?

Sun Tzu's maxim, 'Know your enemy, know yourself and in 100 battles you will never be defeated,' expresses an elementary principle of strategic judgment. In irregular war, understanding how knowledge and self-knowledge apply not only to military matters, but equally and at all levels to the political dimension is an abiding and crucial challenge. By implication, understanding how capabilities and limits—both political and military—interact is a requirement for effective intervention in an irregular conflict. While all wars are unique, these broad principles characterize the unavoidable dilemmas of every intervention and the recurring problems of every irregular war. The consequences are avoidable only in a few exceptions, as noted, for brief invasions of small island nations or small covert actions in remote locations that manage to remain discreet. In this sense, the Cold War quagmires into which the United States blundered in Vietnam and skirted in Central America were not aberrations. Neither are the comparable challenges of strategy and policy the United States now confronts for a third time in far different circumstances with the interventions in Iraq, Afghanistan, and other so-called fronts in the so-called war against Islamic terrorism.

Capacity was not the problem in Central America where the United States possessed predominant power at the heart of its sphere of influence. As Ronald Reagan liked to say about drawing the line against the Soviet Union in the Cold War, "If not in Central America, then where?" It was limits, not capabilities that determined the nature of U.S. interventions in Nicaragua and El Salvador. When those limits were understood and respected implicitly or explicitly, strategy had a reasonable chance of serving policy. Whenever those limits were exceeded or ignored, difficulties arose. Reagan realized that however desirable it might have been to halt communist penetration in Central America, risking unwarranted escalation with the Soviets by going to the source against Cuba or violating the Vietnam syndrome by sending U.S. troops into combat lay outside the bounds of the politically acceptable and effectively excluded those courses of action. Public disquiet and opposition from a determined minority in Congress over the morality, legitimacy, and value of intervening against questionable threats in Nicaragua and El Salvador provoked further complications and constraints. Thus limited, indirect intervention proved a viable alternative strategy that, while it remained controversial, had the advantages of demonstrating the will to use U.S. power by drawing the line somewhere in the Third World, but in a place and manner that maximized the chances of success and minimized the costs and risks.

By limiting itself to supporting counterinsurgency and political reform in El Salvador, the great preponderance of American power was unavailable, but the advantages of a low footprint came to outweigh the disadvantages, especially once democracy began to take hold after the first elections in 1982. Democratic reform trumped guerrilla insurrection, but at the cost of complicity in a prolonged war of repression where the majority of casualties were victims and decisive force unachievable. The joint venture that the United States established with the Salvadoran government was a reasonably effective alliance model that helped to keep the essential triangle of relations between the government, army, and people in tact through a vicious civil war, and had an ultimately transforming effect. The major disadvantage was it took a decade and put the United States doubly into the commitment trap, unable unilaterally to set the terms or bring sufficient pressure to effect short-term behavior changes, especially in curtailing indiscriminate and counterproductive violence by the Armed Forces and the extreme right. Enlightened counterinsurgency of the winning hearts and minds variety was well beyond Salvadoran capabilities, and although the use of force became somewhat more discriminate, there never really was any such thing as a "clean counterinsurgency." As a further note, without venturing into detailed operational checklists and organizational recommendations, the U.S. success in El Salvador reinforces some commonplace, but often misplaced wisdom about the right way to support a counterinsurgency strategy. A first principle is that the military program is not a separate track, but must support the political effort. In consequence, implementation demands effective coordination of the instruments and resources of the U.S. government, above all of people from many agencies. Competent counterinsurgency is much more than a job for the U.S. military alone.[5] The final conclusion is that unity of effort, and preferably of command, is essential for success, and here the Country Teams in the U.S. Embassy in Salvador under Ambassadors such as Deane Hinton and Thomas Pickering during the 1980s serve well as models.

Nicaragua was a different puzzle. Here again, it was not a matter of capabilities, but of limits. Militarily, the United States was perfectly capable of deterring Sandinista crossborder aggression and intimidating them through permanent exercises in

Honduras, its presence in Panama, naval maneuvers in the Caribbean, and the implicit threat of invasion. Halting arms shipments from Cuba and the Eastern Bloc and cutting off clandestine support for the Salvadoran guerrillas proved trickier propositions. Direct intervention, although feasible and perhaps inevitably successful, was completely out of the question. Such bellicosity, while tolerable in the quick decisive invasions of Grenada in 1983 and Panama in 1989, toward Nicaragua would have met a firestorm of domestic political opposition, not to mention a fierce reversion to guerrilla resistance. The Weinberger Doctrine (subsequently refined into the Powell Doctrine) with its high barriers to employing U.S. troops was in public circulation with general approval from the Joint Chiefs. These circumstances made the lowball option of using the Contras to bleed the Sandinistas while remaining ambiguous about the real aim an attractive if second-best strategy. The Reagan Doctrine's notion of supporting insurgencies may have seemed unorthodox for the United States, but its strategic logic was clear: if weak states in the Third World were vulnerable to revolutionary overthrow, newly established revolutionary states were also weak and vulnerable.

If the Reagan Doctrine was at least conceptually defensible, there were major problems with its applications. According to Constantine Menges' original formulation, U.S.-backed anticommunist insurgents were supposed to be democratic, but neither the Contras themselves nor their CIA caretakers cared sincerely about their political program. The patron–client model had its operational advantages, but it was strategically inadequate. Rather than warriors for democracy the Contras were just warriors who satisfied their military purpose, and the absence of positive political aim could be considered a felony violation of the principles of irregular warfare. In the end, the Contras suffered only ignominy after their U.S. sponsorship ceased. This same lapse applied to the other beneficiaries of the Reagan Doctrine, who brought with them not democracy, but more serious and entirely unintended consequences. Power-hungry Jonas Savimbi and his National Union for the Total Independence of Angola (UNITA) carried on Angola's civil war for years, wrecking two major UN peacekeeping operations and destroying much of the country until the Army finally hunted him down and killed him in 2002. Then there are the Mujahedin who defeated the Soviet superpower, and metamorphosing into the Taliban and al Qaeda, decided they could do the same to the United States. Although the originators of the Reagan Doctrine cannot be blamed for lacking foreknowledge, the terrorist sequel to the Afghan Freedom Fighters is a matter of consequences. The cautionary lesson of paying insufficient attention to political matters while pursuing military expediency, then abandoning protégés when they have served their purpose, is tragically evident today.

THE WORLD AS IT SHOULD BE

A further accounting of two general problems with long and uneven pedigrees can be derived from the way that the United States went about intervening in Central America between 1979 and 1992. First, as in other times and places, when an imbalance between reality and idealism infected American ambitions, confusion resulted, and execution suffered. Second, although restraint ultimately prevailed, the tendency to resort to military force when faced with complex and daunting situations was a dubious recourse.[6]

In the world of decision and action, the line between ideology and *realpolitik* can be thin and rarely is as distinct as it might be. Because they can, great powers often enough attempt to extend their systems to others and thereby broaden their influence, a notion commonly attributed to Stalin, but with a more ancient precedent in Thucydides' assessment of democratic Athens.[7] As the first place where U.S. neoconservatism was fully exercised, Central America presents a mixed case. The political strategy of building the center and supporting elections worked in El Salvador, but it was the practical if enlightened product of necessity adopted in the midst of crisis, and it took effect through a full decade of extremely bloody civil war. In the case of Nicaragua, an excess of ideology produced poor results. The underlying source of Jimmy Carter's incompetence in trying to steer benignly between Somoza and the Sandinistas was his immoderate optimism that the power of the United States could dispense a benevolent world. Similarly, the hardliner's failing during the Reagan Administration was a Cold War exuberance that led them to exclude all possibility of rapprochement with the Sandinistas and miscast the Contras as moral equivalents of the Founding Fathers, thereby widening the political battlefront with Congress.

It was one thing to use democracy as part of a strategy to succeed in El Salvador; it was another to use it as an excuse to make war in Nicaragua. Democracy was a solution in and of itself in neither country, and it is entirely possible that U.S. involvement in Central America would have continued for a generation, as many had begun to imagine it would, or until exhaustion and discontent settled in. The road opened for democracy to take its full effect as the basis for resolving the conflict between the Salvadoran government and the FMLN and reforming the Sandinista regime only once circumstances intervened. Regional consensus grew around the Arias Peace Process and the Central Americans took control away from the United States, the Soviet Union imploded and removed the global rationale for containment, and regime change from Reagan to Bush replaced ideology with pragmatism.

When the time comes again to devise a strategy for intervening in an internal conflict, there is no reason to condemn out of hand the ideal of building democracy as a centerpiece of nation-building or to regard it merely as a rhetorical default option.[8] There is no inherent contradiction in promoting democracy while using force, although countervailing interests will be obstacles and some minimal preconditions must exist on the ground for a constructive transformation. It is also true that war and elections make for a double gamble that can produce a botch instead of success (viz Vietnam), for example, by increasing the risks of undesirable results and provoking uncontrollable turbulence during transition.[9] However, the advantages can clearly outweigh the disadvantages. Principles of democracy and its freedoms after all are the essence of America's origins as well as being sources of international legitimacy. As a cause, democracy can make insurgents or counterinsurgents more dedicated fighters by imparting their struggle with a positive aim. Liberal social reconstruction can provide an enduring basis for conflict termination, whether it occurs by military victory or political negotiation. Democracies, once consolidated, tend to be resilient, resist corrosion, and increase security both internally and externally among other democracies. George Shultz, a consummate pragmatist, recognized that supporting democracy in Central America was the key to building sufficient consensus in Congress and among the American people, without which there was not much hope of sustaining the policy. This was the purpose of the Kissinger Commission and its focus on political solutions in Central America, just as it was of the Iraq Study Group. What these observations suggest more broadly is that, while great powers generally have great margin for error, authentic investment in democracy guided by balanced pragmatism, if not a formula for success, can at least improve the chances avoiding folly.

One of the reasons that it was so difficult to comprehend the nature of the threat after the September 11 terrorist attacks and that the misconceived invasion of Iraq became a disaster—whatever its outcome—is not because America was overprepared to fight the last war, but because of a failure to absorb that war's lessons. The U.S. intervention in Vietnam and the one that followed in Central America were battles of the Cold War in the Third World that may seem entirely disconnected from the challenges of current conflicts. However, the larger study in their sequence is that being the most powerful is not the same as being all powerful and consequently that belief in the ability of U.S. military force to achieve any result is a hollow myth.[10] One of the reasons Central America worked out, more or less, and at least did not risk serious national disaster, was precisely because Vietnam was still a tragedy near enough in time that it served as an effective prohibition on sending in troops. As a result, when challenged with radical adversaries in El Salvador and Nicaragua allied to a global threat, U.S. leaders chose to adopt strategies of limited and indirect intervention, even though there was strong precedent for more forceful measures.

Big ideas carry with them the dragon's teeth of big problems, and in such situations it would seem that political competence depends on taking counsel of Clausewitz's observation that the greater the ambition the greater the risk.[11] The problem of senior leaders imbued with an excess of ideology and a gross overestimation of U.S. power was clearly evident in the blitheful attempt to export democracy to the Middle East by invading Iraq. This was a hypermagnification of what Frank Fukuyama calls hardened neoconservatism, which has its roots the first application 20 years earlier in Central America.[12] Richard Cheney himself said as much during the Vice Presidential debate, and although El Salvador is certainly a better model than the post-World War II occupation of Japan and Germany, he garbled the lesson (see chapter 1). Apparently, because the gradual redemption of the U.S. military from Vietnam— culminating with easy conventional success in the first Gulf War—was so successful, some of the same leaders who were compelled into restraint in Central America felt that caution over using U.S. military force no longer need apply. However, it is simply not possible to dream away the hard realities of intervention, especially when occupation confronts irregular warfare. Whether the enemy is labeled as guerrillas, subversives, or terrorists, insurgency provides a good general model,[13] and fighting one inevitably becomes dirty and takes time. That every war ends is a certain truth, but ending an irregular war is much more likely to involve a long slog to a less than ideal political outcome than a mission accomplished through a quick decisive victory. The cycle is turning for the third time in a generation, and the experience of Iraq will almost certainly inspire reticence rather than enthusiasm the next time the United States stands at a crossroads of intervention. Whether it is in our own backyard or some other obscure place on the periphery, remembering the lessons of strategy and policy from Central America should at least help diminish the chances of being condemned to repetition.

Notes

CHAPTER 1

1. The repetition of patterns and fundamental errors in war and the struggle for power is a commonplace of history and strategic theory. For two outstanding discussions of this problem with direct relevance to the themes of this book, see Donald Kagan's consideration of the underlying causes of the Peloponnesian War in *On the Origins of War*, 6–8, and Bernard Brodie's application of Clausewitz to the Vietnam War in *War and Politics*, 451–53.

2. PBS "Vice Presidential Candidates' Debate" (Case Western Reserve University, Cleveland, Ohio, October 5, 2004. Host: Gwen Ifill of PBS's "Washington Week"). Others remarking on the analogy between American promotion of democracy in Central America and the Middle East include, Greg Grandin, *Empire's Workshop*, 87–88 and Mark Engler, "El Salvador No Model for the Future of Iraq," *Newsday*, (December 1, 2004).

3. Elliot Abrams, Gary Bauer, William J. Bennett, Jeb Bush, Dick Cheney, Eliot A. Cohen, Midge Decter, et al., "Statement of Principles," Project for the New American Century (June 3, 1997): http://www.newamericancentury.org.

4. Carl Von Clausewitz, *On War*, Book 8: chap. 9, 627. All Clausewitz citations are from *On War*, edited and translated by Michael Howard and Peter Paret, Princeton, New Jersey: Princeton University Press, 1976.

5. See for example: Peter Maas, "The Salvadorization of Iraq?" *The New York Times Magazine* (May 1, 2005) and Christopher Dickey, "Death Squad Democracy," *Newsweek/MSNBC*, (January 11 and 14, 2005): http://www.msnbc.msn.com.

6. Joseph S. Nye, "The Freedom Crusade, Revisited," *The National Interest*, no. 82 (Winter 2005–06): 15–17.

7. Ronald Schaffer, "The Small Wars Manual and the 'Lessons of History'," *Military Affair* (April 1972): 7.

8. U.S. Marine Corps, *Small Wars Manual*, chap. I, sect. II, Strategy 1–7: 11; and chap. II, sect. I, Campaign and Operational Plans 2–9: 8.

9. See for example, Max Boot, *The Savage Wars of Peace*, on Woodrow Wilson and Mexico, 182–204; and Frank Hoffman, "Small Wars Revisited," *The Journal of Strategic Studies*, 913–34.

10. For detailed accounts of internal divisions concerning Central America in the Carter Administration see Robert Pastor, *Not Condemned to Repetition;* and for the Reagan Administration see Peter Rodman, *More Precious than Peace. Our Own Backyard* by William LeoGrande contains a thorough record of domestic political controversy over Central America.

11. President Ronald Reagan's first news conference January 29, 1981 began with the question "How do you intend to avoid having El Salvador become a another Vietnam for this country?" and Walter Conkrite's first interview with the new president on March 3 began with the question "Do you see any parallel in our committing military advisors and military assistance to El Salvador and the early stages of our involvement in Vietnam?" Cited in Rodman, *More Precious than Peace,* 235.

12. George Shultz, *Turmoil and Triumph,* 312.

13. Excerpts from the Iran–Contra Congressional investigation minority report drafted primarily by Cheney's then-legislative aid David S. Addington. House Select Committee to Investigate Covert Arms Transactions with Iran and Senate Select Committee on Secret Military Assistance to Iran and the Nicaraguan Opposition, *Iran–Contra Affair,* November 13, 1987, 100th Cong., 1st Sess. See also, "Cheney in His own Words," PBS *Frontline* (2004) http://www.pbs.org/wgbh/pages/frontline/darkside/themes/ownwords.html.

14. Discussion of the Iran–Contra scandal in connection with the Administration of President George W. Bush, and specifically Vice President Cheney, are contained, for example, in John Nichols, *Rise of the Vulcans: The History of Bush's War Cabinet* (New York: Viking), 151–56; and John Nichols, *The Rise and Rise of Richard B. Cheney* (New York: The New Press), 95–100.

15. The focus of U.S. intervention in Central America was on Nicaragua and El Salvador, and these are the primary subjects of this book, although related conflicts were also taking place in Guatemala and Honduras during the period under consideration. Nascent efforts at revolutionary organizing in Honduras were effectively suppressed. In Guatemala, ethnic divisions between Mayan Indians and Ladinos figured in a way it did not in El Salvador or Nicaragua, and the United States remained largely silent while the Guatemalan military conducted a fierce and sustained counterinsurgency campaign directed largely against the Indian population. As for U.S. policy toward El Salvador's and Nicaragua's neighbors, "We left Guatemala alone to its bloody fight, did what we could with Honduras, and pressured Costa Rica less than we might have." Fred Iklé, former Undersecretary of Defense for Policy, in discussion with the author October 11, 2006.

16. Nicholas Sambanis, "It's Official: There is Now a Civil War in Iraq," Op-Ed, *New York Times* (July 23, 2006).

17. LeoGrande, *In Our Own Backyard,* 580.

18. Among the two most comprehensive histories of the Central American conflicts are LeoGrande, *In Our Own Backyard;* and Robert Kagan, *A Twilight Struggle,* which focuses on Nicaragua.

19. *The U.S. Army/Marine Corps Counterinsurgency Field Manual,* general publication edition by the University of Chicago Press (2007).

20. Among the irregular warfare classics are David Galula, *Counterinsurgency Warfare* (1964); Robert Thompson, *Defeating Communist Insurgency: Experiences from Malaya and Vietnam* (1966); Bernard Fall, *Street without Joy* (1964); and T.E. Lawrence, *The Seven Pillars of Wisdom,* (1926). The revival of interest in irregular warfare, and especially counterinsurgency

is exemplified by recent books such as *Resisting Rebellion* by James Joes, *The Sling and the Stone* by Thomas X. Hammes, *Insurgency and Counterinsurgency in Iraq* by Ahmed Hashim, and *Learning to Eat Soup with a Knife* by John A. Nagl. Nagl, an active duty Army officer with experience in Iraq and an Oxford PhD, makes the historical linkage explicit by taking the title of his study of counterinsurgency in Malaya and Vietnam from Lawrence's *Seven Pillars of Wisdom.*

21. Former Sandinista Vice President Sergio Ramirez ruefully shares this conclusion with former CIA Latin America Division chief Dewey Clarridge. See Ramírez, *Adiós Muchachos,* 272; and Clarridge, *A Spy for All Seasons,* 294.

22. Merriam Webster Unabridged Dictionary, s.v. Intervention (http://unabridged. merriam-webster.com/cgi-bin/unabridged?va=intervention).

23. These elemental factors of a decision to intervene follow the formulation outlined in Graham Allison, Ernest May, and Adam Yarmolinsky, "Limits to Intervention," *Foreign Affairs* 48, no. 2 (January 1970): 245–61.

24. Brodie, *War & Politics,* 8, 452; LeoGrande, *Our Own Backyard,* 5–8.

25. Chaim Kaufman, "Intervention in Ethnic and Ideological Civil Wars," *Security Studies* 6, no. 1 (Autumn 1996): 80.

26. Anthony James Joes, *Resisting Rebellion,* 8.

27. The term "fourth generation war" originated in a short article that appeared in the October 1989 *Marine Corps Gazette,* "The Changing Face of War: Into the Fourth Generation," 22–26, by William S. Lind, Col. Keith Nightengale (USA), Capt. John F. Schmitt (USMC), Col. Joseph W. Sutton (USA), and LtCol. Gary I Wilson (USMCR). Martín van Crevald expanded the concept in his book, *The Transformation of War,* (New York: The Free Press, 1991), and it has since achieved wide acceptance. For a more skeptical assessment see Frank Hoffman's review of irregular warfare literature, "Small Wars Revisited," cited in note 9.

28. See Frank Hoffman, "Small Wars Revisited." David Kilcullen argues effectively that counterinsurgency provides the best model for grasping the strategic problems of the struggle against terrorism. See, for example, David Kilcullen, "Countering Global Insurgency: A Strategy for the War on Terrorism," http://www.smallwars.quantico.usmc.mil/search/Articles/CounteringGlobalInsurgency.pdf (accessed July 2007.)

29. Clausewitz, *On War,* 6: 26, 479–83.

30. Ibid., 8: 6, 605.

31. Michael Handel, *Masters of War,* 98.

32. David Galula, *Counterinsurgency Warfare,* 9.

33. Rafael Menjívar Ochoa, *Tiempos de Locura,* 100; LeoGrande, *Our Own Backyard,* 59–60.

34. Clausewitz, *On War,* 1: 7, 119–20.

35. Kagan, *Origins of War,* 444–45; Thomas Nichols, "Athens vs. Sparta" (Strategy and Policy course lecture, U.S. Naval War College, Newport, RI, November 20, 2004.)

36. Thucydides, Book 3.82, 199. All Thucydides citations are from *The Landmark Thucydides: A Comprehensive Guide to the Peloponnesian War,* edited by Robert Strassler (New York: Touchstone, 1998).

37. Theoretical writings, underpinned with case studies, that emphasize the critical relationship between security, violence, and state competence can be found in Hedley Bull, *The Anarchical Society: A Study of Order in World Politics* (New York: Columbia University Press, 1977); Jeff Goodwin, *No Other Way Out: States and Revolutionary Movements* (Cambridge, UK: Cambridge University Press, 2001); and Samuel Huntington, *Political Order in Changing Societies* (New Haven, CT: Yale University Press, 1968).

38. The phrase is taken from Mark Peceny's *Democracy at the Point of Bayonets,* an analysis of 93 American military interventions between 1898 and 1996, including six detailed case studies, El Salvador among them, in which the United States used coercion to promote democracy. Other valuable explorations among the expanding body of literature concerning efforts to install liberal institutions in conflict situations are Larry Diamond, *Developing Democracy: Toward Consolidation,* Baltimore, MD: Johns Hopkins University Press, 1999; Larry Diamond and Marc F. Plattner (eds.), *Civil–Military Relations and Democracy* (Baltimore, MD: Johns Hopkins University Press, 1996); Francis Fukuyama, *State-Building: Governance and World Order in the 21st Century* (Ithaca, NY: Cornell University Press, 2004); and Francis Fukuyama (ed.), *Nation Building: Beyond Afghanistan and Iraq* (Baltimore, MD: Johns Hopkins University Press, 2006).

CHAPTER 2

1. Clausewitz, *On War,* 8: 3, 586; 8: 6, 606.

2. National Security Council. "National Security Decision Directive on Cuba and Central America," (NSC-NSDD-37), May 28, 1982, (Federation of American Scientists: http://www.fas.org/irp/offdocs/nsdd/nsdd-037.htm, accessed September 3, 2006.)

3. *The Report of the President's National Bipartisan Commission on Central America.* (The Kissinger Commission Report), January 1984, 1991–92.

4. Lt. Gen. Gordon Sumner (USA, retired). Interview with the author, March 15, 2007. Draft copy of the first Report of the Committee of Santa Fe provided courtesy of General Sumner.

5. Michael Desch, *When the Third World Matters* (Baltimore, MD: Johns Hopkins University Press, 1993).

6. Ibid., 10.

7. Ibid., 116. Two contemporary assessments that draw similar conclusions are Robert Leiken, "Eastern Winds in Latin America," *Foreign Policy,* no. 42 (Spring 1981): 94–113; and Howard Wiarda, "Updating U.S. Strategic Policy: Containment in the Caribbean Basin," *Air University Review* xxxvii, no. 5 (July–August 1986.): 26–38.

8. Christopher Andrew and Vasili Mitrokhin, *The World Was Going Our Way: The KGB and the Battle for the Third World,* 53.

9. Desch, *When the Third World Matters,* 116.

10. John Lewis Gaddis, *We Now Know: Rethinking Cold War History* (New York: Council on Foreign Relations/Oxford University Press, 1997): 278–79.

11. Maj. W.A. Warner, USMC, "Defense of the Western Hemisphere," (unpublished paper, U.S. Naval War College, Command and Staff College, 1988).

12. Patrick Haney, "Soccer Fields and Submarines in Cuba," *Naval War College Review,* L, no. 4 (Autumn 1997); Strobe Talbot, *Deadly Gambits,* (New York: Knopf, 1984): 158–59.

13. White House Office of Media Relations and Planning, "The Strategic and Economic Importance of Caribbean Sea Lanes" (Washington, DC, White House Digest April 14, 1984).

14. George Baer, *One Hundred Years of Sea Power: The U.S. Navy 1890–1990* (Palo Alto, CA: Stanford University Press, 1996): 194–200.

15. Desch, *When the Third World Matters,* 120.

16. Ibid., 198 (n. 23 citing CINCLANT Adm. Lee Baggett.)

17. Baer, *One Hundred Years of Sea Power,* 412.

18. In addition to official threat assessments, see Desch, *When the Third World Matters,* 118–36; Leiken, "Eastern Winds in Latin America"; and Alberto Coll, "Soviet Arms and Central American Turmoil," *World Affairs* 148, no. 1, (Summer 1985): 7–17.

19. Leiken, "Eastern Winds in Latin America," 95.

20. Colin Gray, *The Leverage of Sea Power: The Strategic Advantage of Navies in War* (New York: The Free Press, 1992): 47.

21. Baer, *One Hundred Years of Sea Power,* 412.

22. Andrew and Mitrokhin, *The World Was Going Our Way,* 125.

23. Desch, *When the Third World Matters,* 117.

24. Brodie, *Politics and War,* 343.

25. Ibid., 342.

26. Osgood, *Limited War Revisited,* 104.

27. Haig *Caveat,* 123.

28. Jeanne Kirkpatrick, (speech to the National Press Club, Washington, DC, May 30, 1985.)

29. Ronald Reagan (speech to the Joint Session of Congress, April 27, 1983.)

30. LeoGrande, *Our Own Backyard,* 81.

31. Michael S. Sherry, *In the Shadow of War: The United States Since the 1930's* (New Haven, CT: Yale University Press, 1995): 393.

32. Personal observation by the author.

33. Howard Wiarda, "Updating U.S. Strategic Policy: Containment in the Caribbean Basin," *Air University Review,* July–August 1986.

CHAPTER 3

1. Osgood, *Limited War Revisited,* 3.

2. Rodman, *More Precious than Peace,* 112.

3. Kagan, *Twilight Struggle,* 270.

4. John D. Waghelstein, "What's Wrong in Iraq: Ruminations of a Pachyderm," *Military Review* (January–February 2006): 112.

5. John D. Waghelstein, "Military-to-Military Contacts: The El Salvador Case" *Low Intensity Conflict and Law Enforcement* 10, no. 2 (Summer 2003): 32.

6. Osgood, *Limited War Revisited,* 3–7.

7. Rodman, *More Precious than Peace,* 137.

8. Fred Iklé, *Every War Must End,* 38–41. In this classic study of war termination, Iklé makes a critical distinction between the two dimensions of escalation. In irregular warfare, standard doctrine holds it is the insurgent side that generally benefits from prolonging the struggle. The Central America case demonstrates that this is not necessarily true, but that prolonging a conflict rather than escalating, for example, by extending it to additional territory, adversaries, weapons, or level of force, results from imposed limits rather than choice.

9. Raymond Aron, *Peace and War* (New York: Doubleday, 1966): 536. Aron expresses this essence of the Cold War: "The idea that the two great powers of the international system are brothers at the same time as being enemies should be accepted as banal rather than paradoxical. By definition each would reign alone if the other did not exist...and both fear total war more than the limited advances of their rival."

10. Osgood, *Limited War Revisited,* 94. Here is a clear statement of the principal assumption underlying containment.

11. See for example, Nicola Miller, *Soviet Relations with Latin America,* 194; and Zbignew Brzezinski, "Afghanistan and Nicaragua," *The National Interest,* no. 1 (fall 1985): 48–51.

12. Andrew and Mitrokhin, *The World Was Going Our Way,* 40–50.

13. Ibid., 122.

14. Coordinator of Public Diplomacy for Latin America and the Caribbean, "The 72-hour document: The Sandinista blueprint for constructing communism in Nicaragua" (U.S. Dept. of State Washington, DC, 1986).

15. Andrew and Mitrokhin, *The World Was Going Our Way,* 131.

16. Uri Pavlov, interviewed by National Security Archive, CNN.com/Cold War, Episode 18—Backyard (February 21, 1999).

17. "Kennedy–Khrushchev Exchanges," *Foreign Relations of the United States 1961–1963* (U.S. Department of State, Washington, DC, VI, 1996): 169–90.

18. Walter LaFeber, *Inevitable Revolutions: The United States in Central America* (New York: W.W. Norton, 1991): 200; Miller, *Soviet Relations with Latin America,* 114–15; and Andrew and Mitrokhin, *The World Was Going Our Way,* 47.

19. Miller, *Soviet Relations with Latin America,* 120.

20. Andrew and Mitrokhin, *The World Was Going Our Way,* 127.

CHAPTER 4

1. Quoted in William Meara, *Contra Cross,* 11.

2. Three of the several excellent and largely consistent accounts of the Sandinistas and the success of their 1979 insurrection can be found in Kagan, *Twilight Struggle,* and memoirs by two FSLN leaders, Sergio Ramírez, *Adiós Muchachos* and Humberto Ortega, *La Epopeya del La Insurreción.*

3. Jon Lee Anderson, *Ché Guevara,* 396

4. Ortega, *Epopeya,* 143. There was no exact hour, date, agenda, or program for the founding of the FSLN, rather it emerged–was "baptized"–through the inclusion of Sandino's name to the FLN (National Liberation Front). On the Soviet role, Fonseca's relationship with the KGB was well-established; its exact role is subject to debate, but some details appear in the Mitrokhin archives. *The World Was Going Our Way,* 41–44.

5. *Trinchera,* no. 35, November 1963, cited in Ortega, *Epopeya,* 145–46.

6. Ramírez, *Adiós Muchachos,* 46

7. Arturo Cruz, Jr., *Memoirs of a Counter-Revolutionary,* 60.

8. Dept. of State Coordinator of Public Diplomacy, "The 72-hour Document."

9. Shirley Christian, *Nicaragua: Revolution in the Family,* 43.

10. The term originates with Max Weber. Jeff Goodwin, *No Other Way Out,* 13 and 143–44.

11. Anastasio Somoza, *Nicaragua Betrayed,* 23–26.

12. Ramírez, *Adiós Muchachos,* 118.

13. Castro's advice to the Sandinistas is much cited. See Ramírez, *Adiós Muchachos,* 116–17; Leogrande, *Our own Backyard,* 28; Walter LaFeber, *Inevitable Revolutions,* 231–38; and Richard Gott, *Cuba: A New History* (New Haven, CT: Yale University Press), 269–70.

14. Ortega, *Epopeya,* 394; Kagan, *Twilight Struggle,* 80.

15. Ibid., 391–92.

16. Kagan, *Twilight Struggle,* 81.

17. Alfred Stepan, "The U.S. and Latin America: Vital Interests and the Instruments of Power," *Foreign Affairs,* America and the World (1979): 682. Stepan provides an excellent

summary of the international dynamics and consequences of the Sandinista victory and its immediate aftermath.

18. Sergio Ramírez, *Adiós Muchachos*, 74.

19. The basic version of events is well documented in various sources, but Ortega provides a detailed account of the FSLN final offensive in *Epopeya*, 388–99

20. Ortega, *Epopeya*, 398.

21. Kagan, *Twilight Struggle*, 82–83; Ortega, *Epopeya*, 406.

22. Ibid., 85–86; Somoza, *Nicaragua Betrayed*, 239, 257–260.

23. Cruz, *Memoirs of a Counterrevolutionary*, 77.

24. Robert Pastor, *Not Condemned to Repetition*, 141.

25. Pastor, *Not Condemned to Repetition*, 139.

26. Ibid., 129.

27. Ortega,*Epopeya*, 420.

28. Ramírez, Kagan, and Ortega all provide narrative accounts of the FSLN final offensive and collapse of the Nicaraguan National Guard. A more analytical perspective on the insurrection can be found in Goodwin, *No Other Way Out*, 186–95.

29. Goodwin, *No Other Way Out*, 186.

30. Galula, *Counterinsurgency Warfare*, 9.

31. In outlining the "strategic patterns" of insurgencies and the factors that contribute to their success or failure, Galula focuses on orthodox prolonged guerrilla war and notes that the terrorism can be a revolutionary accelerator. In the Nicaraguan case, the short cut was popular insurrection. *Counterinsurgency Warfare*, 43–62.

32. Robert W. Tucker and David C. Hendrickson, "The Sources of American Legitimacy," *Foreign Affairs*, 83, no. 6 (November/December 2004): http://www.foreignaffairs.org/2004/6.html.

33. Chaim Kaufman, "Intervention in Ethnic and Ideological Civil Wars," *Security Studies*, 6, no. 1, (1996): 62–103.

34. Clausewitz, *On War*, 1: 1, 89.

35. Handel, *Masters of War*, 104.

36. Kagan, *Twilight Struggle*, 32.

37. Ibid., 51.

38. See for example, George Crile, *Charlie Wilson's War* (New York: Grove Press, 2004); and Steve Coll, *Ghost Wars* (New York: Penguin, 2004).

39. Pastor, *Not Condemned to Repetition*, 117–8.

40. Ibid., 98.

41. Quoted in Lafeber, p. 232

42. Pastor, *Not Condemned to Repetition*, 71–74.

43. Brzezinski recorded this warning to Carter in his diary. From Pastor, *Not Condemned to Repetition*, 120 and 148.

44. Ibid., 70.

45. Somoza, *Nicaragua Betrayed*, 327–29.

46. Robert Tucker, *The Purposes of American Power*, 146.

47. The Carter Administration's failure to learn, anticipate, and adapt to the challenges of revolution in Nicaragua echoes Eliot Cohen and John Gooch's framework for analyzing military failures. Their exploration is itself a subset of the larger issue of why competent organizations fail, that in the case of the U.S. contribution to Sandinista victory in Nicaragua, reinforces the criticality of politics and of demonstrating political competence in irregular

warfare. Eliot A. Cohen and John Gooch, *Military Misfortunes* (New York: Free Press, 1990).

48. Jeane Kirkpatrick, "Dictatorships and Double Standards," *Commentary* (November 1979): 34–45.

49. Pastor, *Not Condemned to Repetition,* 138.

CHAPTER 5

1. See for example, Mo Hume, *Armed Violence and Poverty in El Salvador* (Center for International Violence and Security, Liverpool: University of Bradford, November 2004).

2. The definitive account is Thomas P. Anderson, *Matanza* (University of Nebraska, 1971). The issue of how many died remains and will likely remain unresolved, but it is less important than the impact of the massacre which is not in dispute.

3. William Stanley, *The Protection Racket State,* 6–7.

4. Andrew J. Bacevich, James D. Hallums, Richard H. White, and Thomas F. Young, *American Military Policy in Small Wars: The Case of El Salvador,* 26.

5. The phrase is taken from Rafael Menjívar Ochoa, ed., *Tiempos de Locura: El Salvador 1979–1981* (SanSalvador, El Salvador: FLACSO, 2006).

6. For detailed accounts of the Death Squads see the series of articles "Salvadoran Rightists: The Deadly Patriots," by Craig Pyes and Laurie Becklund that ran in the *Albuquerque Journal* from December 18–22, 1983 (reprint); *From Madness to Hope: the 12-year war in El Salvador: Report of the Commission on the Truth for El Salvador,* 1993 (www.usip.org/library/tc/doc/reports/el_salvador/tc_es_03151993_toc.html); and *Los Escuadrones de la Muerte en El Salvador* (San Salvador, El Salvador: Editorial Jaraguá, 2004).

7. The bibliography regarding the significance of Archbishop Romero and his assassination is extensive. Among the more authoritative sources are: Marquez Ochoa, *Martirologio de Mons. Romero* (San Salvador, El Salvador: Comunidades Eclesiales de Base de El Salvador, 2005); the *Report of the Commission on the Truth for El Salvador;* and *Proceedings in the Case of Doe v. Alvaro Rafael Saravia for Extrajudicial Killings and Crimes Against Humanity,* U.S. District Court, District of Eastern California, 2004 (www.cja.org/cases/romero.shtml).

8. Thucydides, 3.82, 199.

9. Clausewitz, *On War,* 1: 7, 119–21.

10. Benjamin Schwartz, *American Counterinsurgency Doctrine and El Salvador,* 67.

11. Interview with Luigi Einaudi, former Director of Policy Planning, Bureau of Latin American Affairs, U.S. Department of State, October 2006.

12. There has been some speculative debate over the degree of U.S. involvement in the 1979 coup in El Salvador. See for example, Stanley, *Protection Racket State,* 144–5.

13. LeoGrande, *Our Own Backyard,* 43–44.

14. Hilton Root, "Walking with the Devil: The Commitment Trap in U.S. Foreign Policy," *National Interest,* no. 88 (March/April 2007): 42–45.

15. Stanley, *Protection Racket State,* 214–15.

16. Ibid., 180.

17. The concept originated with El Salvador's former Vice Foreign Minister and Ambassador to the UN Ricardo Castaneda.

18. LeoGrande,*Our Own Backyard,* 70.

19. Cynthia McClintock, *Revolutionary Movements in Latin America,* 254.

20. Elisabeth Jean Wood, *Insurgent Collective Action and Civil War in El Salvador,* 119–20.

21. LeoGrande, *Our Own Backyard,* 38.

22. Joaquin Villalobos, "A Democratic Revolution for El Salvador," *Foreign Policy,* no. 74 (Spring 1989): 107.

23. Figures on insurgent strength are naturally subject to different estimates among various sources, but are consistent by order of magnitude. See, for example, José Angel Bracamonte and David Spencer, *Strategy and Tactics of the Salvadoran FMLN Guerrillas,* 5; and Wood; *Insurgent Collective Action,* 10–11.

24. Eduardo Colindres,*Fundamentos Económicos de la Burguesía Salvadoreña* (San Salvador, El Salvador: ECA, 1977).

25. Stanley, *Protection Racket State,* 187.

26. Substantiation has largely replaced the denials, obfuscation, and propaganda that all parties engaged in regarding political orientation and external support for the Salvadoran guerrillas during the war. In a notable example, the February 1981 Department of State publication known as the *El Salvador White Paper* was intended to present convincing evidence of Eastern Bloc arms shipments to the FMLN, but it inadvertently became notorious for its anti-communist rhetoric and the inclusion of a few interpretive ellipses. Drafted by senior Foreign Service Officer Jon Glassman, the author participated in the collection and assessment of FMLN documents recovered during security force operations and used for the *White Paper;* there was little doubt about their authenticity. Multiple sources, including testimony from direct participants, subsequently verified the version presented in this section. Interviews conducted in February and March 2006 with former Sandinista Army Chief of Staff Joaquín Cuadra and former ERP Comandante Joaquín Villalobos covered operational collaboration among the Cubans, Nicaraguans, and Salvadorans in extensive detail. For a published description of the FMLN logistics network, see Bracamonte and Spencer, *Strategy and Tactics of the Salvadoran FMLN,* 175–86. On the Soviet–Cuban–Nicaraguan role, see Coll, "Soviet Arms and Central American Turmoil"; and LeoGrande, *Our Own Backyard,* 68–69 and 85–89.

27. Facundo Guardado, interview with author January 13, 2006. On the general effectiveness of repression there is little disagreement. See for example, the very insightful article about the inner workings of the FMLN first published in the Mexican monthly *Vuelta,* by Gabriel Zaid, "Enemy Colleagues," *Dissent* (February 1982): 13–40.

28. LeoGrande, *Our Own Backyard,* 68.

29. Zaid, "Enemy Colleagues," 34.

30. Ignacio Martin-Baro, "La Guerra Civil en El Salvador," *Estudios Centroamericanos* (ECA) 387/388 (January/February 1981).

31. Menjívar, *Tiempos de Locura,* 205.

32. Zaid, "Enemy Colleagues," 34.

33. McClintock, *Revolutionary Movements in Latin America,* 53–55.

34. LeoGrande, *Our Own Backyard,* 58.

35. Ibid., 63–64, 100.

36. Hugh Byrne, *El Salvador's Civil War: A Study of Revolution,* 108.

37. Bacevich and others, *American Military Policy in Small Wars: The Case of El Salvador,* 4–5.

38. Byrne, *El Salvador's Civil War,* 158–61.

39. Joaquín Villalobos, "El Estado Actual de la Guerra y Sus Perspectivas," *Estudios Centroamericanos* 449 (March 1986): 37.

40. Ignacio Ellacuría, "Visión de Conjunto de las Elecciones de 1984," *Estudios Centroamericanos* 426/427 (April/May 1984): 16; "Editorial: 1988, Un Año de Transición para

El Salvador," *Estudios Centroamericanos* 471/472 (January/February 1988): 315; "Editorial: Recrudiciamiento de la Violencia,"*Estudios Centroamericanos* 480 (October 1988): 874.

41. For the most detailed account of Executive-Congress deliberations on El Salvador, Nicaragua, and other Central American see Cynthia Aronson, *Crossroads: Congress, the President, and Central America.*

42. Fred C. Iklé, "U.S. Policy for Central America—Can We Succeed?" (Speech to the Baltimore Council on Foreign Relations, Baltimore, Maryland, September 12, 1983.)

43. Author was present for this speech and witnessed the immediate reaction of the audience to it. See also, LeoGrande, *Our Own Backyard,* 174–80.

44. A heavily redacted version of the "Report of the El Salvador Military Strategy Assistance Team" is available at: http://www.gwu.edu/~nsarchiv/nsa/DOCUMENT/930325.htm.

45. James D. Marchio, "The Evolution and Relevance of Joint Intelligence Centers," *Studies in Intelligence* 49, no. 1 (2005): https://www.cia.gov/library/center-for-the-study-of-intelligence/csi-publications/csi-studies/studies/vol49no1/html_files/the_evolution_6.html (accessed July 2006.)

46. Bacevich and others, *American Military Policy in Small Wars;* and Schwartz, *American Counterinsurgency Doctrine and El Salvador.*

47. Bacevich and others, *American Military Policy in Small Wars,* Executive Summary, italics in the original.

48. A team of Argentine forensic anthropologists that conducted on-site excavations in 1992 for the UN Truth Commission at the end of the war documented a total of 767 victims and left no doubt that it was an Army massacre.

49. According to fellow ESAF officer and close friend, then-Col. Juan OrlandoZepeda, Monterrosa said this shortly before he died in October 1984, when the helicopter he was riding in exploded after the ERP detonated a disguised bomb the Army had unwittingly placed on board. This Trojan horse ruse was a major FMLN triumph. See Mark Danner, *The Massacre at El Mozote,* 150–54; and for the guerrilla version, José López Vigil, *Las Mil y Una Historias de Radio Venceremos,* 316–38.

50. Mark Danner's *Massacre at El Mozote* is a definitive account of this incident. The author investigated the massacre as a U.S. Embassy officer in early 1982.

51. Bacevich and others, *American Military Policy in Small Wars,* 46.

52. Schwartz, *American Counterinsurgency Doctrine and El Salvador,* 55

53. Bacevich and others, *American Military Policy in Small Wars,* 43–45; and Manwaring and Prisk, eds., *El Salvador at War,* 222–27 and 472–73.

54. Former MILGROUP Commander Col. John Waghelstein provides a detailed and well-considered assessment of the National Campaign Plan in "Military-to-Military Contacts: The El Salvador Case," *Low Intensity Conflict and Law Enforcement* (Summer 2003).

55. Benjamin Schwarz, "Dirty Hands," *The Atlantic Monthly* (December 1998).

56. Gen. Paul Gorman (USA ret.), roundtable discussion, Johns Hopkins SAIS, October 20, 2005.

57. Peceny, *Democracy at the Point of Bayonets,* 115–47. In the section on El Salvador, Peceny traces the evolution of the Reagan Administration from outright support of extreme rightists in early 1981 to a thorough commitment to liberal democracy that helped center-left PDC candidate Napoleon Duarte win the presidential elections in 1984. He attributes the primary motive for this change to fear of a Congressional aid cut off, and this negative role of Congress in influencing policy on El Salvador is undeniable. As Peceny concludes, the outcome can be judged a reasonable success and marked a strong contrast with the concurrent

acrimony that persisted on Nicaragua. The point of emphasis here is that, whatever its impetus, building the democratic center in El Salvador had its own strategic logic which constituted the political object of support to counterinsurgency.

58. *Small Wars Manual,* Chapter XIV, 1–35.

59. Guevara, Ché, *Guerrilla Warfare,* 8. Guevara later abandoned the view that guerrillas had little chance against an elected government, but the El Salvador case validates his original wisdom. Social science theorists such as Theda Skocpol and Samuel Huntington, along with Jeff Goodwin and Cynthia McClintock cited in this work, all focus on the same point, but it takes on special significance coming from an insurgent icon like Ché.

60. For an authoritative series of investigative reports on the Salvadoran Right and the Death Squads see Craig Pyes and Laurie Becklund, "Salvadoran Rightists: The Deadly Patriots," *Albuquerque Journal* (December 18–22, 1983).

61. A comprehensive if sympathetic account of D'Aubuisson and his politics is contained in Geovani Galeas, "Mayor Roberto D'Aubuisson: El Rostro Más Allá Del Mito," *La Prensa Gráfica,* Special Edition, San Salvador, El Salvador (November 2004).

62. The author reported on many of the events surrounding this election and other political developments, including attitudes of ARENA backers and the Salvadoran military. Supplemental sources include interviews and correspondence with former Minister of Defense Gen. Eugenio Vides Casanova, former National Police Commander and Deputy Public Security Minister Reynaldo Lopez Nuila, and Hugo Barrera, an independent businessman and D'Aubuisson running mate who continued to serve as an ARENA leader.

63. LeoGrande, *In Our Backyard,* 261.

64. Manwaring and Prisk, eds., *El Salvador at War,* 453.

CHAPTER 6

1. Kagan, *Twilight Struggle.* See also, for example, Cynthia Aronson, *Crossroads: Congress, the President, and Central America, 1976–1993;* LeoGrande, *In Our Own Backyard;* and Holly Sklar, *Washington's War on Nicaragua* (Cambridge, MA: Southend Press, 1988). For memoirs of U.S. policy and politics regarding Nicaragua see George Shultz's *Turmoil and Triumph,* and Peter Rodman's *More Precious than Peace.*

2. See Clarabel Alegria and Darwin Flakoll, *Death of Somoza* (Willmantic, CT: Curbstone Press, 1996).

3. Robert W. Tucker, "American in Decline: The Foreign Policy of 'Maturity,'" *Foreign Affairs* (1979). Carter was responding to the Soviet invasion of Afghanistan, but hope lingered longer with the Sandinistas.

4. LeoGrande, *In Our Own Backyard,* 29

5. Dewey Clarridge, *A Spy for All Seasons,* 196–97; Kagan, *Twilight Struggle,* 150–51.

6. Pastor, *Not Condemned to Repetition,* 192–93; Kagan *Twilight Struggle,* 190–94; and U.S. State Department, *Revolution beyond Our Borders,* 21–23.

7. Kagan, *Twilight Struggle,* 348.

8. Government of Nicaragua Memorandum of Conversation, "Case Concerning Military and Paramilitary Activities in and against Nicaragua," *International Court of Justice Judgment,* 1986.

9. Kagan, *Twilight Struggle,* 196.

10. LeoGrande, *In Our Own Backyard,* 28.

11. Sergio Ramírez, *Adiós Muchachos,* 158–59; Kagan, *Twilight Struggle,* 94–95.

12. U.S. Department of State, *El Salvador White Paper,* 4.

13. Joaquín Cuadra, former Chief of Staff of the Sandinista Peoples' Army, interview with author, January 24, 2006.

14. Miller, *Soviet Relations with Latin America,* 202–03.

15. Glenn E. Curtis, ed., *Russia: A Country Study* (Washington, DC: GPO for the Library of Congress, 1996): 89.

16. Ramírez, *Adiós Muchachos,* 114

17. Clarridge, *A Spy for All Seasons,* 220–21.

18. Joaquín Cuadra and Arturo Cruz, Jr., interviews with author January 24 and 25, 2006.

19. Alexander Haig, *Caveat,* 131.

20. Kagan, *Twilight Struggle,* 272.

21. Peter Rodman, *More Precious than Peace,* 262; James Scott, *Deciding to Intervene,* 22–24; Menges, Constantine, *Democratic Revolutionary Insurgency as an Alternative Strategy;* and Fred Iklé, interview with author, October 2006.

22. Rodman, *More Precious than Peace,* 239.

23. Clarridge, *A Spy for All Seasons,* 197.

24. Scott, *Deciding to Intervene,* 58; and Rodman, *More Precious than Peace,* 414.

25. Kagan, *Twilight Struggle,* 297.

26. Rodman, *More Precious than Peace,* 413–14; and Kagan *Twilight Struggle,* 599.

27. Arturo Cruz, Jr., *Memoirs of a Counter-Revolutionary,* 229.

28. Clarridge, *A Spy for All Seasons,* 290–93, Kagan, *Twilight Struggle,* 341.

29. LeoGrande, *In Our Own Backyard,* 212–13; 311–25; and George Shultz, *Turmoil and Triumph,* 310–11.

30. Ibid., 320.

31. Kagan, *Twilight Struggle,* 392.

32. Scott, *Deciding to Intervene,* 168–71; and Clarridge, *A Spy for All Seasons.*

33. Kagan, *Twilight Struggle,* 340.

34. For a thorough account of the various schemes Administration officials conceived to "maneuver around the shoals of congressional hostility" see LeoGrande, *In Our Own Backyard,* 381–87.

35. Kagan, *Twilight Struggle,* 466.

36. Ibid., 295.

37. Nicola Miller, *Soviet Relations with Latin America,* 209–16; and Rodman, *More Precious than Peace,* 415.

38. Scott, *Deciding to Intervene,* 39.

39. Psychiatrist turned conservative columnist Charles Krauthammer coined the phrase "Reagan Doctrine" in a famous April 1, 1985 *Time* magazine column that enthusiastically promoted U.S. support for the Contras and other noncommunist insurgents who were combating Soviets around the world.

40. National Security Decision Document 75, 1982, 1; and Scott, *Deciding to Intervene,* 21.

41. Peter Schweizer, *Victory: The Reagan Administration's Secret Strategy That Hastened the Collapse of the Soviet Union* (New York: Atlantic Monthly Press, 1994): 25.

42. Rodman, *More Precious than Peace,* 284

43. Fred C. Iklé, "U.S. Policy for Central America—Can We Succeed?" (Speech to the Baltimore Council on Foreign Relations, Baltimore, Maryland, September 12, 1983).

44. Rodman, *More Precious than Peace,* 411–12.

45. Steve Coll, *Ghost Wars,* 91; and George Crile, *Charlie Wilson's War,* 263–66.

46. See for example, Robert Tucker, *Intervention and the Reagan Doctrine,* 13; and Rodman, *More Precious than Peace,* 283–84.

47. Zbigniew Brzezinski, "Afghanistan and Nicaragua," *National Interest,* no. 1 (Fall 1985): 48–51.

48. Shultz, *Turmoil and Triumph,* 266.

49. Rodman, *More Precious than Peace,* 277. As assistant to the Special Envoy for Central America between 1983 and 1985, the author participated in negotiations with the Sandinista leadership as well as talks with the Salvadoran FMLN–FDR, was involved in multiple trips to consult with regional governments, and witnessed the intense politics within the USG that surrounded the Central American diplomatic track.

50. Secretary of state George Shultz, "Speech to the Commonwealth Club of San Francisco" (February 22, 1985). Drafted by Robert Kagan and Luigi Einaudi.

CHAPTER 7

1. Fred Iklé, *Every War Must End.* Iklé's point is that the way a war ends has decisive and lasting impact, but those who go to war tend to dedicate a great deal more attention to fighting them than to terminating them. As a result, wars often end haphazardly without achieving clear objectives and with mixed consequences for all of the participants. This essentially Clausewitizian insight (*On War,* 8: 2, 579) is equally true of wars large and small, regular and irregular, as the Central America case amply demonstrates.

2. Haig, *Caveat,* 122.

3. For a summary assessment of the Contadora regional peace process see LeoGrande, *In Our Own Backyard,* 349–52.

4. Shultz, *Turmoil and Triumph,* 409–28.

5. LeoGrande, *In Our Own Backyard,* 352.

6. Rodman, *More Precious than Peace,* 255, applies this point to the Sandinistas, but it applied equally to both sides.

7. Kagan, *Twilight Struggle,* 237.

8. Comisión Político Diplomática FMLN/FDR, "El Conflicto Armado en El Salvador y la Posición del FMLN/FDR para Alcanzar una Solución Justa," (The Armed conflict in El Salvador and the Position of the FMLN/FDR to Reach a Just Solution), insurgent negotiating proposal presented in August 1981.

9. LeoGrande, *In Our Own Backyard,* 262.

10. Frances Hagopian and Scott Mainwaring, eds., *The Third Wave of Democratization in Latin America,* 5. Between 1978 and 1990, all of the countries of Latin America with the exception of Cuba became democracies, and the 2001 OAS Inter-American Democratic established democracy as the political norm of the region. In the introduction to *Third Wave,* the editors argue that the advent of elected governments in Central America during the civil wars of the 1980s clearly demonstrated the possibly of installing democracy "during hard times and in inauspicious places."

11. For a blow-by-blow account of the diplomacy surrounding the Arias Peace Plan see Kagan, *Twilight Struggle,* 497–515 and 531–55.

12. LeoGrande, *In Our Own Backyard,* 509–10.

13. Arturo Cruz, Jr. and Vincente Cerezo, former President of Guatemala. Statements made to the Conference on Lessons Learned on Regional Peace-Building: The Experience of the Central American Peace Process (Toledo, Spain, March 1–3, 2006).

14. Kagan, *Twilight Struggle,* 540

15. Shultz, *Turmoil and Triumph,* 961.

16. Rodman, *More Precious than Peace,* 430.

17. Kagan, *Twilight Struggle,* 574.

18. Ibid., 591.

19. LeoGrande, *In Our Own Backyard,* 554.

20. Kagan, *Twilight Struggle,* 620.

21. Ibid., 720.

22. LeoGrande, *In Our Own Backyard,* 562.

23. Kagan, *Twilight Struggle,* 692.

24. Arturo Cruz, Jr. and Joaquín Cuadra, interviews with the author, January 24, 2006; and Sergio Ramírez, *Adiós Muchachos,* 284.

25. Antonio Lacayo's memoir, *La Difícil Transición Nicaraguense,* offers a lucid and eloquent record of these dramatic events.

26. Antonio Lacayo, interview with the author, January 23, 2006.

27. Kagan, *Twilight Struggle,* 679

28. *World Transformed,* 134

29. Ibid., 155

30. Kagan, *Twilight Struggle,* 687.

31. Joaquín Cuadra and Joaquín Villalobos, joint interview with the author March 2, 2006; Lacayo, *La Difícil Transición Nicaraguense,* 223; and Child, *The Central American Peace Process,* 128.

32. Byrne, *El Salvador's Civil War,* 151–52.

33. James Lemoyne, "El Salvador's Forgotten War," *Foreign Affairs,* (Summer 1989): 108.

34. Kagan, *Twilight Struggle,* 541.

35. Cuadra and Villalobos interview, March 2, 2006; and Byrne, *El Salvador's Civil War,* 152.

36. Joaquín Villalobos, "A Democratic Revolution for El Salvador," *Foreign Policy,* no. 74 (Spring 1989): 107.

37. This assessment of the transformation of the FMLN is derived from the author's discussions with three of the five FMLN senior commanders, interviewed in San Salvador and Toledo, Spain during January and March 2006: Facundo Guardado, FPL; Eduardo Sancho (Ferman Cienfuegos), FARN; and Joaquín Villalobos, ERP. Berne Ayala's *Al Tope y Más Allá* is a poignant memoir of a guerrilla combatant's journey from faith to deception to relief between the 1989 Final Offensive and the 1992 Peace Accords.

38. LeoGrande, *In Our Own Backyard,* 568.

39. FMLN, "Strategic Appraisal," captured by the Salvadoran Army and published in *Análisis,* journal of the Instituto de Investigación Cientifica de la Universidad Nueva San Salvador, 1989.

40. LeoGrande, *In Our Own Backyard,* 570–73.

41. Fen Osler Hampson, "The Pursuit of Human Rights: The United Nations in El Salvador", in William Durch, ed., *UN Peacekeeping, American Policy, and the Uncivil Wars of the 1990's,* 73.

42. Salvador Samayoa, was a member of the FMLN negotiating commission. His *El Salvador: La Reforma Pactada* is a thorough and objective account of the Salvadoran peace process and its aftermath.

43. Mark Peceny and William Stanley, "Liberal Social Reconstruction and the Resolution of Civil Wars in Central America," 149–82.

44. Richard McCall, former Salvadoran Deputy Minister of Defense and Public Security Col. Reynaldo Lopez Nuila , and former FARN Comandante Eduardo Sancho, interviews with the author in San Salvador and Toledo, Spain during January and March 2006; Samayoa, *La Reforma Pactada,* 149.

45. See, for example, the World Bank El Salvador Country Brief: http://web.worldbank.org /WBSITE/EXTERNAL/COUNTRIES/LACEXT/ELSALVADOREXTN/0,,menuPK: 295253~pagePK:141132~piPK:141107~theSitePK:295244,00.html.

CHAPTER 8

1. Conference on Lessons Learned on Regional Peace-Building: The Experience of the Central American Peace Process (Toledo, Spain, March 1–3, 2006). See also, chap. 7, note 13.

2. On Central American street gangs, and El Salvador in particular where the problem is most acute, see Ana Arana, "How the Street Gangs Took Central America," *Foreign Affairs,* (May/June 2005): 98–110.

3. Iklé, *Every War Must End,* 1.

4. Larry Diamond and Leonardo Morlino, eds., *Assessing the Quality of Democracy,* xi–xiii; and Guillermo O'Donnell, Jorge Vargas Cullell, and Osvaldo M. Iazzetta, eds., *The Quality of Democracy,* 135–36.

5. The discussion regarding counterinsurgency capabilities, roles, and missions of USG agencies has taken on urgency in light of interventions in Iraq and Afghanistan. See, for example, Nadia Schadlow, "Root's Rules," *The American Interest,* (January–February 2007). In El Salvador, the U.S. Embassy Country Team led by the ambassador ensured relatively effective unity of effort, even when competition and political controversy dominated in Washington. Agreement on policy goals, strategy , and lines of authority between Ambassador Deane Hinton and SOUTHCOM Gen. Paul Gorman in 1981 was critical to establishing a relatively harmony.

6. The themes of the imbalance between idealism and reality and the use of military force to address complex conflicts are frequently reprised staples of U.S. interventions. For historical precedent, see for example, Brian Linn, *The Philippine War 1899–1902,* and Robert Tucker, *Woodrow Wilson and the Great War;* for more recent experience, see Andrew Bacevich, *The New American Militarism,* and Chester Crocker, "A Dubious Basis for Policy," *Survival* (Winter 2005).

7. Joseph Stalin, "Everyone imposes his own system as far as his army can reach." April, 1945, quoted in *Conversations with Stalin* (1963) by Milovan Djilas. Thucydides, "...the strong do what they can and the weak suffer what they must;" Book 5.89, 352 (The Melian Dialogue). Interventions in internal conflicts were a regular feature of the Peloponnesian War. When possible, the democratic Athenians would intervene on the side of pro-democratic factions, but they would not hesitate to support oligarchic factions when it was in their interest.

8. For a systematic assessment of the recurrent challenges and lessons of the U.S. experience with nation-building see Francis Fukuyama, ed., *Nation-Building: Beyond Afghanistan and Iraq.*

9. See, for example, comparison of U.S. attempts to install democracy in the Philippines, Vietnam, El Salvador, Haiti, and Bosnia in Peceny, *Democracy at the Point of Bayonets.*

10. This is the core premise of Andrew Bacevich's *The New American Militarism.*

11. The relationship of ambition to risk is elemental to Clausewitz's strategic theory. See especially his discussion in Book Eight on limited war and the relationship of political objective to the scale of military effort, *On War,* 8: 3, 585–94.

12. Francis Fukuyama, *America at the Crossroads,* 40–44.

13. David Kilcullen, "Counter-insurgency Redux," *Survival* 48 (Winter 2006–07).

Selected Readings

Allison, Graham, Ernest May, and Adam Yarmolinsky. "Limits to Intervention." *Foreign Affairs* 48, no. 2 (January 1970): 245–61.

Anderson, Thomas P. *Matanza*. Lincoln, NB: University of Nebraska Press, 1971.

Andrew, Christopher, and Vasili Mitrokhin. *The World Was Going Our Way: The KGB and the Battle for the Third World*. New York: Basic Books, 2005.

Aronson, Cynthia J., ed. *Comparative Peace Processes in Latin America*. Washington, DC: Woodrow Wilson Center Press; Stanford, CA: Stanford University Press, 1999.

Aronson, Cynthia J. *Crossroads: Congress, the President, and Central America, 1976–1993*. University Park, PA: Pennsylvania State University Press, 1993.

Ayala, Berne. *Al Tope y Mas Allá: Testimonio de la Guerrilla Salvadoreña desde la Ofensiva de 1989 a los Acuerdos de Paz*. San Salvador, El Salvador: Cipitio Editores, 1996.

Bacevich, Andrew J. *The New American Militarism: How Americans Are Seduced by War*. New York: Oxford University Press, 2005.

Bacevich, A.J., James D. Hallums, Richard H. White, and Thomas F. Young. *American Military Policy in Small Wars: The Case of El Salvador*. Institute for Foreign Policy Analysis. New York: Pergamon-Brassey's, 1988.

Bonner, Raymond. *Weakness and Deceit: U.S. Policy and El Salvador*. New York: Times Books, 1984.

Boot, Max. *The Savage Wars of Peace: Small Wars and the Rise of American Power*. New York: Basic Books, 2002.

Bracamonte, José Angel, and David Spencer. *Strategy and Tactics of the Salvadoran FMLN Guerrillas*. Westport, CT: Praeger, 1995.

Brodie, Bernard. *War and Politics*. New York: Macmillan Publishing Co., 1973.

Bull, Hedley. *The Anarchical Society: A Study of Order in World Politics*. New York: Columbia University Press, 1977.

Byrne, Hugh. *El Salvador's Civil War: A Study of Revolution.* Boulder, CO: Lynne Rienner Publishers, 1996.

Child, Jack. *The Central American Peace Process, 1983–1991.* Boulder, CO: Lynne Reinner Publishers, 1992.

Christian, Shirley. *Nicaragua: Revolution in the Family.* New York: Vintage Books, 1986.

Cienfuegos, Ferman (Eduardo Sancho). *Crónicas Entre los Espejos.* San Salvador, El Salvador: Editorial Universidad Francisco Gavidia, 2002.

Clarridge, Duane R. *A Spy for All Seasons.* With Digby Diehl. New York: Scribner, 1997.

Clausewitz, Carl von. *On War,* edited and translated by Michael Howard and Peter Paret. Princeton, NJ: Princeton University Press, 1976.

Cohen, Eliot A. and John Gooch. *Military Misfortunes: The Anatomy of Failure in War.* New York: Free Press, 1990.

Colindres, Eduardo. *Fundamentos Económicos de la Burguesía Salvadoreña.* San Salvador: ECA, 1977.

Coll, Alberto. "Soviet Arms and Central American Turmoil." *World Affairs* 148, no. 1, (Summer 1985): 7–17.

Coll, Steve. *Ghost Wars: The Secret History of the CIA, Afghanistan, and Bin Laden, from the Soviet Invasion to September 10, 2001.* London: Penguin Books, 2004.

Crile, George. *Charlie Wilson's War: The Extraordinary Story of How the Wildest Man in Congress and a Rogue CIA Agent Changed the History of Our Times.* New York: Grove Press, 2004.

Crocker, Chester A. "A Dubious Template for US Foreign Policy." *Survival* 47, no. 1, (Spring 2005): 51–70.

Crocker, Chester A., Fen Osler Hampson, and Pamela Aall, eds. *Taming Intractable Conflicts.* Washington, DC: United States Institute of Peace Press, 2004.

Cruz, Arturo, Jr. *Memoirs of a Counter-Revolutionary.* New York: Doubleday, 1989.

Desch, Michael C. *When the Third World Matters.* Baltimore, MD: Johns Hopkins University Press, 1993.

Diamond, Larry and Leonardo Morlino, eds. *Assessing the Quality of Democracy.* Baltimore, MD: Johns Hopkins University Press, 2005.

Dickey, Christopher. *With the Contras.* New York: Simon and Schuster, 1985.

Dillon, Sam. *Comandos: The CIA and Nicaragua's Contra Rebels.* New York: Henry Holt and Company, 1991.

Durch, William J., ed. *UN Peacekeeping, American Policy, and the Uncivil Civil Wars of the 1990's.* Henry L. Stimson Center. New York: St. Martin's Press, 1996.

Editorial Jaraguá. *Los Escuadrones de La Muerte en El Salvador.* San Salvador, ES: Editorial Jaraguá, 2004.

Fall, Bernard B. *Street without Joy.* New York: Schocken Books, 1972.

Fukuyama, Francis. *America at the Crossroads: Democracy, Power, and the Neoconservative Legacy.* New Haven, CT: Yale University Press, 2006.

———. *State-Building: Governance and World Order in the 21st Century.* Ithaca, NY: Cornell University Press, 2004.

Galula, David. *Counterinsurgency Warfare: Theory and Practice.* New York: Frederick A. Praeger, 1964. Reprinted 2005.

Goodwin, Jeff. *No Other Way Out: States and Revolutionary Movements, 1945–1991.* Cambridge, UK: Cambridge University Press, 2001.

Grandin, Greg. *Empire's Workshop: Latin America, the United States, and the Rise of the New Imperialism.* New York: Metropolitan Books, 2006.

Guevara, Ernesto "Ché." *Guerrilla Warfare.* Lincoln, NB: University of Nebraska Press, 1985. Introduction by Marc Becker. Originally published in Spanish in 1960.

Hagopian, Frances and Scott P. Mainwaring, eds. *The Third Wave of Democratization in Latin America: Advances and Setbacks.* New York: Cambridge University Press, 2005.

Haig, Alexander M. *Caveat: Realism, Reagan, and Foreign Policy.* New York: Macmillan, 1984.

Hammes, Thomas X. *The Sling and the Stone: On War in the 21st Century.* St. Paul, MN: Zenith Press, 2004.

Handel, Michael I. *Masters of War: Classical Strategic Thought.* 3rd ed. London: Routledge, 2005.

Hashim, Ahmed. *Insurgency and Counterinsurgency in Iraq.* Ithaca, NY: Cornell University Press, 2006.

Hoffman, Frank G. "Neo-Classical Counterinsurgency?" *Parameters* (Summer 2007): 71–87.

———. "Small Wars Revisited: The United States and Nontraditional Wars." *The Journal of Strategic Studies* 28, no. 6 (December 2005): 913–40.

Huntington, Samuel P. *Political Order in Changing Societies.* New Haven, CT: Yale University Press, 1968.

Iklé, Fred Charles. *Every War Must End.* New York: Columbia University Press, 1991.

Joes, Anthony James. *Resisting Rebellion: The History and Politics of Counterinsurgency.* Lexington, KY: The University Press of Kentucky, 2004.

———. *America and Guerrilla Warfare.* Lexington, KY: The University Press of Kentucky, 2000.

Kagan, Donald. *On the Origins of War and the Preservation of Peace.* New York: Doubleday, 1995.

Kagan, Robert. *A Twilight Struggle: American Power and Nicaragua 1997–1990.* New York: The Free Press, 1996.

Kapuscinski, Ryszard. *The Soccer War.* New York: Alfred A. Knopf, 1990.

Kaufman, Chaim. "Intervention in Ethnic and Ideological Civil Wars." *Security Studies* 6, no. 1 (Autumn 1996): 62–100.

Kilcullen, David. "Counter-Insurgency *Redux.*" *Survival,* 48 (Winter 2006–07).

Kinzer, Stephen. *Blood of Brothers: Life and War in Nicaragua.* New York: Putnam, 1991.

Kirkpatrick, Jeane. "Dictatorships and Double Standards." *Commentary* (November 1979): 34–45.

Lacayo Oyanguren, Antonio. *La D ifícil Transición Nicaraguense: En El Gobierno con Doña Violeta.* Colección Cultural de Centro América, Serie Ciencias Humanas no. 12. Managua, Nicaragua: Fundación UNO, 2005.

Lawrence, T.E. (Thomas Edward). *Seven Pillars of Wisdom: A Triumph.* New York: Anchor Books, 1991.

Leiken, Robert. "Eastern Winds in Latin America." *Foreign Policy,* no. 42 (Spring 1981): 94–113.

Lemoyne, James. "El Salvador's Forgotten War." *Foreign Affairs* (Summer 1989).

LeoGrande, William M. *Our Own Backyard: The United States in Central America, 1977–1992.* Chapel Hill, NC: The University of North Carolina Press, 1998.

Linn, Brian McAllister. *The Philippine War 1899–1902*. Lawrence, KS: University of Kansas Press, 2000.

Long, Austin. *On "Other War": Lessons from Five Decades of RAND Counterinsurgency Research*. Santa Monica, CA: RAND Corporation, 2006.

López Vigil, José Igancio. *Las Mil y Una Historias de Radio Venceremos*. San Salvador, El Salvador: UCA Editores, 2005.

Manwaring, Max G. and Court Prisk, eds. *El Salvador at War: An Oral History*. Washington, DC: National Defense University Press, 1988.

Mao Tse-Tung and Ché Guevara. *Guerrilla Warfare*. London: Cassell, 1965.

McClintock, Cynthia. *Revolutionary Movements in Latin America: El Salvador's FMLN and Peru's Shining Path*. Washington, DC: United States Institute of Peace, 1998.

Meara, William R. *Contra Cross: Insurgency and Tyranny in Central America, 1979–1989*. Annapolis, MD: Naval Institute Press, 2006.

Menges, Constantine. *Democratic Revolutionary Insurgency as an Alternative Strategy*. Santa Monica, CA: RAND, 1968.

Menjívar Ochoa, Rafael. *Tiempos de Locura: El Salvador 1979–1981*. San Salvador: FLACSO, 2006.

Miller, Nicola. *Soviet Relations with Latin America*. New York: Cambridge University Press, 1989.

Montobbio, Manuel. *La Metamorfosis del Pulgarcito: Transición Política y Proceso de Paz en El Salvador*. Barcelona, Spain: Icaria-FLACSO (Antrazyt Colleción no. 130), 1999.

Nagl, John A. *Learning to Eat Soup with a Knife: Counterinsurgency Lessons from Malaya and Vietnam*. Chicago: The University of Chicago Press, 2005.

National Security Archive. "El Salvador: The Making of U.S. Policy, 1977–84." The George Washington University. http://www.gwu.edu/~nsarchiv/nsa/publications/elsalvador/elsalvador.html.

———. "El Salvador: War, Peace, and Human Rights, 1980–1994." George Washington University. http://www.gwu.edu/~nsarchiv/nsa/publications/elsalvador2/index.html.

———. "Nicaragua: The Making of U.S. Policy, 1978–1990." George Washington University. http://www.gwu.edu/~nsarchiv/nsa/publications/nicaragua/nicaragua.html.

———. "The Iran–Contra Affair: The Making of a Scandal, 1983–1988." George Washington University. http://www.gwu.edu/~nsarchiv/nsa/publications/irancontra/irancon.html.

O'Donnell, Guillermo, Jorge Vargas Cullell, and Osvaldo M. Iazzetta, eds. *The Quality of Democracy: Theory and Applications*. Notre Dame, IN: Notre Dame University Press, 2004.

Ortega Saavadera, Humberto. *La Epopeya del La Insurrección*. Managua, Nicaragua: LEA Grupo Editorial, 2004.

Osgood, Robert E. *Limited War Revisited*. Boulder, CO: Westview Press, 1979.

Pastor, Robert. *Not Condemned to Repetition: The United States and Nicaragua*. Boulder, CO: Westview Press, 2002.

Peceny, Mark. *Democracy at the Point of Bayonets*. University Park, PN: Pennsylvania University Press, 1999.

Peceny, Mark, and William Stanley. "Liberal Social Reconstruction and the Resolution of Civil Wars in Central America." *International Organization*, 55, (Winter 2001): 149–82.

Pyes, Craig, and Laurie Becklund. "Salvadoran Rightists: The Deadly Patriots." *Albuquerque Journal*, December 18–22, 1983.

Ramírez, Sergio. *Adiós Muchachos: Una Memoria de la Revolución Sandinista.* San José, Costa Rica: Santillana SA, 1999.

The Report of the President's National Bipartisan Commission on Central America. (The Kissinger Commission Report.) New York: Macmillan, 1984.

Rodman, Peter W. *More Precious than Peace: The Cold War and the Struggle for the Third World.* New York: Charles Scribner's Sons, 1994.

Samayoa, Salvador. *El Salvador: La Reforma Pactada.* San Salvador, El Salvador: UCA Editores, 2005.

Schadlow, Nadia. "Root's Rules: Lessons from America's Colonial Office." *The American Interest,* 2, no. 3 (January–February 2007).

Schwartz, Benjamin. *American Counterinsurgency Doctrine and El Salvador: The Frustrations of Reform and the Illusions of Nation Building.* Santa Monica, CA: RAND, 1991.

Scott, James M. *Deciding to Intervene: The Reagan Doctrine and American Foreign Policy.* Durham, NC: Duke University Press, 1996.

Shultz, George P. *Turmoil and Triumph: My Years as Secretary of State.* New York: Charles Scribner's Sons, 1993.

Somoza, Anastasio. *Nicaragua Betrayed.* As told to Jack Cox. Belmont, MA: Western Islands, 1980.

Stanley, William. *The Protection Racket State.* Philadelphia: Temple University Press, 1996.

Thompson, Robert. *Defeating Communist Insurgency: Experiences from Malaya and Vietnam.* New York: Frederick A. Praeger, 1966.

Thucydides. *The Landmark Thucydides: A Comprehensive Guide to the Peloponnesian War,* edited by Robert B. Strassler. New York: Touchstone Books, 1998.

Tucker, Robert W. "American in Decline: The Foreign Policy of 'Maturity.'" *Foreign Affairs, America and the World 1979,* 58, no. 3, (1979): 449–84.

———. *The Purposes of American Power.* New York: Praeger, 1981.

———. *Intervention and the Reagan Doctrine.* New York: The Council on Religion and International Affairs, 1985.

———. *Woodrow Wilson and the Great War.* Charlottesville, VA: University of Virginia Press, 2007.

Tucker, Robert W. and David C. Hendrickson. "The Sources of American Legitimacy." *Foreign Affairs,* 83, no. 6 (November/December 2004): http://www.foreignaffairs.org/ 2004/6.html.

U.S. Army and Marine Corps. *The U.S. Army/Marine Corps Counterinsurgency Field Manual.* With forewords by General Peter Petraeus, LtCol. John A. Nagl, and James F. Amos, and an introduction by Sarah Sewell. Chicago: University of Chicago Press, 2007.

U.S. Department of State. *Communist Interference in El Salvador.* (The White Paper.) Special Report no. 80, February 23, 1981.

———. *Revolution Beyond Our Borders: Sandinista Intervention in Central America.* Special Report no. 132, September 1985.

U.S. Institute of Peace. *From Madness to Hope: the 12-year war in El Salvador: Report of the Commission on the Truth for El Salvador.* Washington, DC: USIP 1993. www.usip.org/ library/tc/doc/reports/el_salvador/tc_es_03151993_toc.html.

U.S. Marine Corps. *Small Wars Manual.* Washington, DC: U.S. Government Printing Office, 1940 (declassified 1972.) With an introduction by Ronald Schaffer. Manhattan, Kansas: Sunflower University Press (n.d.).

Villalobos, Joaquín. "A Democratic Revolution for El Salvador." *Foreign Policy,* no. 4, (Spring 1989): 103–122.

Waghelstein, John D. "Post-Vietnam Counterinsurgency Doctrine." *Military Review* (January 1985): 42–29.

———. "Military-to-Military Contacts: The El Salvador Case." *Low Intensity Conflict and Law Enforcement,* 10, no. 2 (Summer 2003.)

Waghelstein, John D. (USA, ret.) "What's Wrong in Iraq: Ruminations of a Pachyderm." *Military Review* (January–February 2006): 112–17.

Wood, Elisabeth Jean. *Insurgent Collective Action and Civil War in El Salvador.* Cambridge, UK: Cambridge University Press, 1998.

Zaid, Gabriel. "Enemy Colleagues." *Dissent* (February 1982): 13–40.

Index

ABOUT THE AUTHOR

TODD GREENTREE is a Visiting Scholar at the Johns Hopkins University School of International Studies. He teaches national security and international politics at the University of New Mexico, and is a former professor of Strategy and Policy at the U.S. Naval War College. Serving as a Foreign Service Officer for 25 years, his personal experience with the political and military dimensions of irregular conflict extends from Central America to Angola.